Sermons On The First Readings

Series III

Cycle B

Richard Gribble, CSC
Ken Lentz
William J. Carl III
Donna E. Schaper
Robert A. Hausman

CSS Publishing Company, Inc., Lima, Ohio

SERMONS ON THE FIRST READINGS, SERIES III, CYCLE B

For more information about CSS Publishing Company resources, visit our website at www.csspub.com or email us at csr@csspub.com or call (800) 241-4056.

Cover design by Barbara Spencer

ISSN: 1937-1446

ISBN-13: 978-0-7880-2542-6
ISBN-10: 0-7880-2542-2

PRINTED IN USA

Table Of Contents

Sermons For Sundays
In Advent, Christmas, And Epiphany
Hope And Renewal In Christ
by Richard Gribble, CSC

Sermons For Sundays
After Pentecost (First Third)
Dancing In Holy Places
by William J. Carl III

Sermons For Sundays
After Pentecost (Middle Third)
Being Two People At Once
by Donna E. Schaper

Sermons For Sundays
After Pentecost (Last Third)
From Emptiness To Fullness
by Robert A. Hausman

Sermons On The First Readings

For Sundays In Advent, Christmas, And Epiphany

Hope And Renewal In Christ

Richard Gribble, CSC

Hope and renewal are virtues and ideals that people of faith seek to find and foster in their lives. Without hope in the present and the future, we would live in a perpetual state of mere existence with no prospect for advancement. With hope, however, we can seek and secure the renewal that is endemic to the Christian journey to God. Throughout my life, those who have most strongly and consistently helped me to find hope and secure renewal are my immediate family. Thus, it is appropriate that this book be dedicated to them: to Judy, Barbara, John, Sarah, David, and Erin.

Preface

Through the wisdom of the church and the cycle of life, opportunities abound for us to search for and grasp hope and renewal in our lives. The church provides liturgical seasons that ask us to center our prayer and reflection on particular aspects of our Christian lives. Advent, the first liturgical season, is a time of waiting, but we do not wait in a passive way, but rather actively in hope for the future. Advent asks us to wait in hope for two very important events — the coming of the Lord at the end of time and the coming of Christ in the incarnation. While few people spend much time reflecting on the future return of Christ, it is a basic Christian teaching. Jesus said he would come again (John 14:1-3) and Saint Paul (1 Thessalonians 4:13-18) amplified the Lord's words into a theology of the *parousia.* Advent provides us with an opportunity to think about this future reality to which all of human history must ultimately point. More pointedly, we wait in great hope for the coming of Christ in history, his birth in time. While the *parousia* is indeterminate, the incarnation is celebrated at a particular time each calendar year. Preparations for both, however, must be made.

We need to wait for Christ's incarnation and look forward to his second coming. We do so as people of hope. We wait in hope for the peace of Jerusalem, the peace which only Jesus, the Prince of Peace, can bring. Hope must be central to our belief that ultimately the light that Jesus brings will always overcome the darkness of our oftentimes problematic world. The gospel of John (1:5) reminds us, "The light shines in the darkness, and the darkness did not overcome it." Yes, hope is essential and central to our Advent season of patient waiting.

The Advent season is followed by the hope of Christmas and the new year that follows. Many people make New Year's resolutions that are centered in hope and renewal. We have hope for a good year ahead and for renewal in all aspects of our lives. We seek renewal in our personal lives — physically, intellectually, and most assuredly spiritually. We seek renewal in our family, making it more like the holy family of Nazareth. We seek renewal in our neighborhoods, our places of work, and certainly our communities of faith. The gospel calls us to be renewed in faith; the new year provides an excellent opportunity to manifest this in our lives.

The sermons in this book challenge us to find hope and seek renewal. Jesus allows us to find hope in so many ways. He provides new life when destruction and death encircle us. He rescues us from problems and is always willing to lead us home. Jesus is ever faithful to us. As the "Hound of Heaven" he will never miss an opportunity to reach out and assist us, even when we choose not to accept his guidance, strength, and help. God's message of hope for us continues in the realization that we are in good hands with the Lord and that he accepts us, regardless of problems, sinfulness, or our estrangement from him.

The hope of the Advent season and the new year challenges us to find renewal in our lives. We need to recognize and attach ourselves to Christ. We must respond freely to God's overtures to us. The Lord will never come where he is not invited or welcomed. It is necessary to accept the challenge of reconciliation, both to be forgiven and to forgive others. Lastly, we must accept our commissions as Christians in the world: to go forth and proclaim Jesus' message of love and peace to all people. God is counting on us. A little story helps us to understand our responsibility. Legend says that when Jesus returned to heaven, the angel Gabriel asked him if all people knew of his love for them. "Oh, no!" said Jesus, "only a handful do." Gabriel was shocked and asked, "How will the rest learn?" Jesus said, "The handful will tell them." "But," said Gabriel, "What if they let you down? What if they meet opposition? What if they become discouraged? Don't you have a backup plan?" "No," said Jesus, "I'm counting on them not to let me down." Yes, my friends, Jesus is counting on us to continue his work in this world. May he never be disappointed in our efforts. Let us in hope and through renewal build God's kingdom this day!

Richard Gribble, CSC

Advent 1
Isaiah 64:1-9

Jesus Brings New Life

The end of World War II and the onset of the Cold War, which saw the super powers of the United States and the Soviet Union at odds, brought a dark night to eastern Europe, which almost overnight seemed to come under the control of the Soviets and their ideology of Communism. The Iron Curtain, as it came to be known, seemed impenetrable. In 1980, however, at the Lenin Shipyard in Gdansk, Poland, some brave workers, seeking rights and freedom, provided the catalyst to bring this dark night to an end.

The Independent Self-Governing Trade Union — or, as it was better known, "Solidarity" — formed in the summer of 1980. Initially organized to protest the government's raising of meat prices, the union, under the leadership of Lech Walesa, quickly became a broad anti-Communist movement and was a sign and symbol for workers and oppressed people throughout eastern Europe. Under Walesa's direction, members of Solidarity boldly and fearlessly participated in numerous strikes, marches, and other nonviolent resistance actions seeking justice. The government attempted to destroy the union when it was clear that national and international sympathy for the movement was increasing. In December 1981, General Wojciech Jaruzelski, First Secretary of the Communist Party in Poland, ordered a massive military operation and imposed martial law. Solidarity leaders were arrested and the organization was driven underground where it remained until 1989. Yet, the indomitable spirit of Walesa, his lieutenants, and thousands of workers could not be broken.

Eventually, the Polish government, weakened by its inability to crush the union, was forced to initiate a series of round-table discussions with Walesa and his people. By the end of August 1989, a Solidarity-led government was formed and in December Walesa was elected president.

The Solidarity movement in Poland ended the dark night of Communism in one nation, but it initiated a more regional movement that culminated in the dissolution of the Iron Curtain and the end of Communist rule in the Soviet Union. Solidarity's example was in various ways repeated by opposition groups throughout eastern Europe. Men and women of great faith and courage, inspired by what they observed from Solidarity, pushed for human liberty in their own nations. The map of eastern Europe, as we view it today, reflects the victory of liberty and human justice over totalitarianism and human oppression. It was a new day for eastern Europe; it was necessary to rejoice.

The Solidarity movement and the consequent end of Communist oppression in eastern Europe provide an important example of how darkness is defeated and a new day of liberty arises. It also demonstrates clearly how the timeless nature of scripture, as we hear today, continues to echo and be relevant in our lives. As a Christian community throughout the world begins a new year through the celebration of the season of Advent, we need to understand and believe in the possibility of new beginnings for all, confident that God will assist us in our everyday efforts to build his kingdom in our world.

The season of Advent, which inaugurates a new liturgical year in our church, encourages us to prepare for the coming of Christ in two different ways. While the world, especially the secular world, concentrates on the coming of Jesus in time, namely the incarnation, the church also asks us to reflect upon the return of Christ at the end of time. On this first Sunday of Advent, it is this latter theme that is emphasized. The second coming or *parousia* is not an event that most people think about in their daily lives. Tucked neatly in the back of our brains, the knowledge that Jesus will come once again to our world is an idea that is distant at best or distasteful at worst. Who wants to contemplate the end of the world and the coming of Christ to reclaim all for God? Yet, as Isaiah reminds us in our first lesson today, the second coming will provide a new beginning for the world, both collectively and individually. It is a time when all will be made new in Christ. It is not a time from which to run, but an event that we should seek and embrace.

Today's reading from the prophet Isaiah comes from the latter third of this longest book in the Bible. Isaiah prophesied to the Hebrews before, during, and after the infamous Babylonian exile, that fifty-year period when the majority of the Jews were away from their homeland and, in their minds possibly, forgotten by God. Having returned to their homeland, the prophet encourages the people to reflect upon the new beginnings God has provided them by reminding them of the past and instructing them of what the future will hold.

Probably somewhat bewildered from the series of events in the life of the Hebrew community, Isaiah speaks of the future and God's return to the world. He writes to the people, "O that you [God] would tear open the heavens and come down, so that the mountains would quake at your presence — as when fire kindles brushwood and the fire causes water to boil" (Isaiah 64:1-2a). He continues by asserting that God will make his name known to all adversaries so that nations will tremble at his presence. The prophet is suggesting that, as the Hebrews now experience a new existence in their life after the exile, so in the future God will return to create a new world that will be obedient to him. Isaiah indicates that the future will be somewhat like the past when God did awesome deeds to assist his people Israel.

Certainly the people hearing Isaiah's message remembered, as do we, the escape of the Israelites through the Red Sea and how God crushed the Egyptians in their wake. Additionally, the people remembered how God fought on the side of Israel, eliminating all their enemies when, after their long sojourn in the desert, they finally reached the promised land. God then raised up judges, kings, and prophets to aid the people and gave them direction in life. God did so much for the people, all of which was unexpected, to demonstrate his loyalty to the covenant and his love for his chosen people. Certainly no one could imagine all that God had done for the nation of Israel. Isaiah makes his point very clear: "From ages past no one has heard, no ear has perceived, no eye has seen any God besides you, who works for those who wait for him" (Isaiah 64:4). Saint Paul understood this same idea writing to the Corinthians many generations later: "What no eye has seen, nor ear heard, nor the human heart conceived, what God has prepared for those who love him" (1 Corinthians 2:9).

It was crystal clear to the people to whom Isaiah spoke that God firmly and consistently stood on the side of Israel. Truly God was the refuge and strength of the nation, a helper close at hand at all times. Possibly Isaiah and his listeners remembered the words of the psalmist: "Blessed be the Lord, for he has heard the sound of my pleadings. The Lord is my strength and my shield; in him my heart trusts; so I am helped, and my heart exults, and with my song I give thanks to him" (Psalm 28:6-7). Israel knew and proclaimed that God was on its side. Again, the psalmist wrote: "My help comes from the Lord, who made heaven and earth" (Psalm 121:2). Since God had chosen Israel and manifest many times over his love and care for the nation, there should be no fear of his return.

Still, the prophet does remind the people of the nation's failures so they may better understand the goodness of God demonstrated toward them in their return from exile. For many generations, Israel sinned and transgressed God's laws and, after numerous warnings, God removed his protection. As the prophet says, God hid himself from Israel, a situation that led directly to the Babylonian exile. Still, Isaiah says, it is a new day. God will come again to rescue Israel to make the world new. As he suggests God is the potter and we are the clay in his hands.

Isaiah's words that recall past events and future possibilities must echo in our daily lives as followers of Christ. Through its wisdom, the church provides us with this season of grace, Advent, a four-week period of preparation where we wait in patient expectation for new beginnings and new possibilities in our life. As Isaiah foresaw the coming of God into the life of the Hebrew people, so we await with great anticipation the return of Jesus Christ, the new Adam, to our world. The Solidarity movement in Poland in the 1980s, a contemporary event that manifest the same action of God found in the return of the Hebrews from exile, inaugurated a new day for eastern Europe. Similarly, during this Advent season we must seek to refocus on that which is most important in our lives. It is a season of grace that we must not pass by; we must engage its opportunities and possibilities.

New beginnings, such as a new liturgical year that we begin today or a new calendar year that will come in one month, provide the opportunity to reflect upon the past and look to the future. Our review must see both the good things we have done and accomplished and those things for which we are not proud, both our sinfulness and our failures. However, as Isaiah wrote and the psalmist promises in numerous places, we must always see God as our help and our shield. God will never abandon us nor let us down.

Our reflection upon the future coming of Christ to our world should begin with the recognition of our need for God. Contemporary society suggests we should seek other priorities, other answers to our problems and difficulties. We are constantly bombarded with secular answers to the problems that often vex our personal and communal lives. For want of any easy or fast fix to whatever troubles us, we too often fall into a pattern that exalts the world and what it offers to the detriment of the power and presence of God in our lives. But, as the dark night of Communism was dispelled to the courage and hard work of Solidarity and similar movements in eastern Europe, as God brought a new day to the Hebrews through their return from exile, God will bring a new day to our lives, as well. We can be confident that if we give ourselves to God, all will be fine. Years ago, a popular television commercial stated, "You're in good hands with Allstate." We must know and have complete confidence and conviction that we are in much better hands with God.

Sin in its many manifestations creates deadness in us that, knowingly or unknowingly, is palpable and visible to most, especially those who know us well. The deadness we find inside is apathy, problems with addictions and other aberrant behavior, or our penchant for the new and the finest when the ordinary will satisfy. These are all manifestations of the darkness in our lives. As we began this season of grace, this Advent period of patient expectation, when we wait for the coming of Christ both at the end of time and in time, the incarnation, let us be open to the power and presence of Jesus in our lives. As we await the newborn king of the Jews, let us see our need for transformation. Made in the image and likeness of God, let us follow Christ who came to save the world and bring eternal life to all who believe. Amen.

Advent 2
Isaiah 40:1-11

Jesus Will Lead Us Home

The voyage of Sir Ernest Shackleton and his 28 men aboard the *Endurance* bound for Antarctica, which began in 1914, is a story too few know but all should hear. The Imperial Trans-Atlantic Expedition, under Shackleton's command, was the first British Antarctic expedition after Norwegian Ronald Amundsen became the first man to reach the South Pole in December 1911. Inspired by this feat, and his own earlier efforts to reach the pole, Shackleton proposed an expedition that would traverse the Antarctic continent from the Waddell Sea on the Atlantic to the Ross Sea on the Pacific, transiting via the pole. It was to be a journey of discovery, but one fraught with much danger.

On August 9, 1914, Shackleton and his crew left Plymouth, England, bound for Antarctica. The *Endurance* stopped briefly in Buenos Aires and South Georgia Island before proceeding further south. Some days the ship was unimpeded in its progress, but other days ice was a significant hazard to navigation. By mid-January, the ship had made its furthest southern point as it became encased in ice. Initially, Shackleton was not worried, knowing that similar events that happened with other ships in the past without significant problems. However, as time continued and the *Endurance* drifted in its ice prison further north and, thereby, away from land, Shackleton realized that his dream to traverse the continent would not be possible on this trip. The situation, over time, only grew worse. On October 24, 1915, the hull of the *Endurance* was crushed; water began to pour into the ship forcing Shackleton on October

27 to abandon the vessel and move onto the ice. By late November, the ship had sunk completely beneath the water and ice.

Since the objective of the expedition had been compromised, Shackleton turned his complete attention to getting his crew back home. The severe conditions, including temperatures often well-below-zero Fahrenheit, shortage of supplies of all types, and the difficulty in keeping morale high among the men, made Shackleton's task that much more difficult. With no means to communicate, Shackleton realized their only option was to move the crew to a place where rescue was possible. While several options existed, the conditions told Shackleton that he must try for Elephant Island to await rescue. This goal was achieved, but the island's barren terrain was very inhospitable, although there was sufficient food from seals and penguins. Almost immediately, however, Shackleton realized that his only option was to return to South Georgia Island, inform people of their status, and bring help. Thus, on April 24, 1916, Shackleton and a few of his men set out on the *James Caird*, a vessel no bigger than a lifeboat, to make the 800-mile journey to South Georgia Island.

The voyage of the *James Caird* is certainly one of the most remarkable maritime crossings ever undertaken. With winds often 45 mph and waves measuring at times sixty feet, the small boat proceeded through the Drake Passage. After fourteen days, the crew was in sight of the island. The boat landed on the unpopulated southern coast of the island. Thus, it was necessary to cross overland to Stomness, where personnel and ships were present for a possible rescue. In late August 1916, on his fourth attempt, he was able to return to Elephant Island and found all 22 men still alive. He took them aboard the Chilean vessel he had obtained and the expeditionary party returned to South Georgia and then eventually to England.

Ernest Shackleton was an adventurer, and pioneer explorer, but his heroism and leadership were inspirational and certainly contributed to the ultimate survival of his entire crew, a fact that is remarkable in many ways. Shackleton led his men home, earning their admiration and that of his countrymen. The crew possessed complete faith in Shackleton and his ability; he would do what was necessary to get them home.

The story of Ernest Shackleton and his heroic efforts in leading his men home to safety provides an excellent illustration of the second principle theme of advent, which today the church encourages us to engage. Last week we concentrated on the second coming of Christ, or as it is often referred to, the *parousia*, but as Isaiah tells us in our first lesson today we must build a highway for the coming of the Lord into our lives. We are to make preparations for Jesus' arrival through his incarnation.

Today's first lesson is from the second third of the prophet Isaiah. Chapters 40 to 55 were proclaimed to the Hebrews during their exile in Babylon. The people had transgressed God's law; they had ignored the warnings of the prophets whom God had sent one after the other to warn the people and help them to return to the proper road. However, their failure to heed the numerous warnings resulted in their exile. Despite the situation, however, God would never abandon his chosen people and, thus, Isaiah was sent to proclaim the message of peace and new life. We hear, "Comfort, O comfort my people, says your God. Speak tenderly to Jerusalem, and cry to her that she has served her term, that her penalty is paid, that she has received from the Lord's hand double for all her sins" (Isaiah 40:1-2). It will be a new day for Israel; God has forgiven the transgressions of the people. Their term of exile will soon end.

Having told the people that God will give them a new day, the prophet then begins to explain about the journey home. He predicts the voice of one speaking from the wilderness of the need to prepare the way for the Lord. Yet, at the same time, he speaks of what is necessary for the Hebrew people to return home. They are to build a highway that is straight and level. All valleys must be filled in and all mountains made low; the uneven ground is to be made level and the rough places smooth. From our twenty-first-century perspective, Isaiah is telling the people to build a superhighway that will allow them to return home quickly and safely. This, of course, is not a physical road but nonetheless a very important thoroughfare of the mind. The physical movement cannot be accomplished until the people understand and are able to create a straight path between themselves and God. In the past, many hurdles, obstacles, and detours, all of which were human-generated, were placed between the people and God. Now, with a new day approaching, it is necessary to build this superhighway, without curves, varied elevations, or obstacles so that the relationship between God and his chosen people will once again be whole.

The superhighway that the Hebrews construct will allow the power of God once again to be manifest. As in the past, when God fought on the side of Israel, Isaiah again says that the Lord will feed his people. Like a shepherd he will gather Israel, gently leading them home. The people will once again occupy their land; the darkest night of ancient Israel will be ended.

What Isaiah prophesied became reality. God rescued Israel and the people did return home. We can read in the books of Ezra and Nehemiah the great work of the Hebrews in rebuilding their society and their temple. With her honor restored and their sacred spaces rebuilt, Israel could now await the promised Messiah, the one, from the Jewish perspective, who would rescue Israel and restore the greatness of the Davidic kingdom in their land.

Jesus, of course, is the fulfillment of the Old Testament prophecies. He is the one who came to share his life, to teach his message, and ultimately, to lead us home. The Advent season, when we prepare for the coming of Christ in time, and by extension into our lives, is an opportunity to prepare ourselves by building our own superhighway to God. As Isaiah suggests, we must fill in the valleys and level off the mountains of our lives. Too often, knowingly or unknowingly, we place significant barriers between God and ourselves. Many times, as well, we become disheartened thinking that God is distant, uncaring at best, and not present at worst. But as clearly as the heroic efforts of Ernest Shackleton allowed him to save his crew, so Jesus stands ready to assist us and bring us home. Shackleton did what was necessary to bring his people home. So too Isaiah exhorts the people of his day as did John the Baptist prior to Jesus. All in different ways prepared superhighways that allowed their people to return home. In ways particular to our situations, we must build a straight, level, and obstacle-free highway to God.

Advent provides the best opportunity for us to reevaluate our lives and to admit that detours, barriers, and obstacles exist that keep us from the fullness of our relationship from God; they keep us from being the people God wants us to be. We often take a circuitous route to God; the straight path, the one of least resistance and shortest distance, for various reasons does not seem attractive. We must have sufficient faith to realize that Jesus is not one to be avoided. On the contrary, he is the source of our life, he is the one who leads us home.

Still, the Lord gives us free will and will never enter where he is not welcome. No, we must welcome the Lord into our hearts; we must open the door. A famous painting by Hans Holbein that hangs in the British National Gallery in London illustrates this reality. The painting depicts what the Lord says in the book of Revelation: "Listen! I am standing at the door, knocking; if you hear my voice and open the door, I will come into you and eat with you, and you with me" (Revelation 3:20). Yes, Jesus invites us, but as Holbein's painting depicts a door without a knob, so it is clear from Revelation that we must open the door from the inside. The Lord will not violate our personal freedom, but is ever ready to assist us. Saint Paul's letter to his traveling companion, Timothy, makes this clear: "If we have died with him, we will also live with him; if we endure, we will also reign with him; if we deny him, he will also deny us; if we are faithless, he remains faithful — for he cannot deny himself" (2 Timothy 2:11-13).

This Advent season we wait for Jesus to come to our world. He came to die and set us free; he came to lead his home. Let us demonstrate faith and courage as did Ernest Shackleton and his brave crew, who trusted each other so as to build a highway that would lead them home. Let us build our highway to God — to make a straight and level road to God. When Jesus arrives on Christmas Day, will our road be complete or not? Only you can answer! Amen.

Advent 3
Isaiah 61:1-4, 8-11

Jesus Rescues Us

Oskar Schindler, immortalized in Steven Spielberg's 1993 prize-winning film, *Schindler's List*, was a man who rescued the oppressed and brought them new life. He was born on April 28, 1908, in Moravia, Austria-Hungary, now the Czech Republic. After completing his education, he worked as a commercial salesman, changing jobs many times during the 1930s. He tried other businesses, but soon went bankrupt due to the Great Depression, which gripped Europe at the time. Though a citizen of Czechoslovakia, Schindler started to work for the German military intelligence service, eventually joining the Nazi Party in 1939.

As an opportunistic businessman, he sought to profit economically from the German invasion of Poland in 1939. He gained ownership of a factory in Krakow that manufactured enamelware. Schindler was given 1,000 Jews to work in his factory under almost slave-like conditions. Initially, it seems, Schindler was motivated by money in his business dealings, but after he witnessed a raid on the Krakow Ghetto in 1942, where soldiers rounded up the Jewish residents for shipment to concentration death camps, he began to change. A persuasive man and with many skills, he began to overtly protect his workers, referred to as *Schindlerjuden* (Schindler's Jews). Often Schindler called upon his charm and ingratiating manner to help his workers get out of difficult situations. On many occasions, he bribed the local German commandant to look the other way. He spent his whole life savings obtaining food and other necessities for his workers. Although arrested by the Gestapo on two occasions, he was able to affect his release so he could continue his work at the factory and, thereby, protect his Jewish employees.

In October 1944, with the Russian army bearing down on Poland, Schindler was able to move his 1,000-person workforce to another factory in Brunnitz, in occupied Czechoslovakia. This plant manufactured anti-aircraft munitions for the German Wehrmacht. In May 1945, the Russians moved into Brunnitz. As a member of the Nazi Party, Schindler was a marked man and, thus, he gathered his employees together for an emotional leave-taking ceremony. He told the people, "My children, you are saved. Germany has lost the war." Oskar Schindler had saved over 1,000 Jews. He rescued them from the darkness and brought them into the light.

Oskar Schindler used his money, influence, and position to answer his Christian call to rescue over 1,000 Jews from probable death at the hands of the Nazis during World War II. His efforts clearly illustrate the basic theme from Isaiah in today's first lesson. It also properly shows how we must respond to God's Son, Jesus, who came to rescue us from fear, problems, and death. As we await his coming in time at Christmas, we must ponder how we will respond to the call to assist others that comes from the newborn king of the Jews.

This scripture reading for the third Sunday of Advent returns to the third section of the prophecy of Isaiah, proclaimed to the Jewish people after they returned from exile. Through the prophet, God speaks of a new day for Israel, but more importantly how he will rescue Israel from its earlier cruel fate. The Lord comes to give good news to the oppressed, namely the nation of Israel, which has been subjugated at the hands of the Babylonians for the past fifty years. God comes to bind up the brokenhearted, the Hebrew community that possibly had lost faith in itself and in God. The Lord comes to proclaim liberty to captives and release to prisoners; God comes, in other words, to release the Hebrews from their bondage of exile. Having been captives and prisoners of the Babylonians for two generations, God will now proclaim a year of favor. God will comfort those who mourn; no longer will sadness prevail. Instead of ashes, God will provide a garland of flowers. Instead of a faint spirit, God will provide a mantle of praise.

God's rescue of the Hebrews will continue upon their arrival in their home country. God will build up the ancient ruins; the cities and the nation, in general, will be restored. The devastation of the land will be transformed and once again the pride of people in their land will be restored.

God will make an everlasting covenant with the people. God's faithfulness to the people will be complete and manifest in many ways. As a community is restored, the descendents of the Hebrews will be known among all the nations in the region. These lands will see that the Lord has blessed his people. The people will cause righteousness and praise to spring up before all the nations; God will be ever present to Israel.

God's rescue of the people will bring them rejoicing. God will clothe the people with new garments of salvation; God will favor Israel as a bridegroom and bride are adorned. Yes, it will be a new day for Israel, a time for the people to renew their spirits and their relationship to God. God will rescue his people from all their troubles.

The prophecy of Isaiah was fulfilled in many ways. A new day did come to Israel. The temple was rebuilt and the people once again felt a sense of community as they lived in the presence of God. God did not abandon Israel to its own senses, however, but rather continued to shower upon his chosen people more and more blessings. He continued to rescue them over the centuries. Ultimately, God sent Jesus to rescue the people from their slavery to sin and the law, but the people never recognized him, his message, or his mission. Because the Jews failed to recognize the presence of God in Jesus and the message that he brought, his great promise was passed on to us. Saint Paul put it very beautifully: "In former generations this mystery was not made known to humankind, as it has now been revealed to his holy apostles and prophets by the Spirit: that is, the Gentiles have become fellow heirs, members of the same body, and sharers in the promise in Christ Jesus through the gospel" (Ephesians 3:5-6).

Jesus came to rescue us from many things. He came to rescue us from fear. People are instinctively afraid of the unknown and the future; uncertainty is always filled with fear. People are also fearful of many present-day realities and day-to-day worries. Jesus is the solution to the fears and worries that many times plague our lives, weighing us down and not allowing us to move forward. But, as Jesus released Lazarus from death saying, "Unbind him, and let him go" (John 11:44c) so he will release us. But we must believe; we must know in our hearts that Jesus can act on our behalf. Jesus puts the challenge in this way: "Do not fear. Only believe ..." (Luke 8:50b).

Jesus came to rescue us from ourselves. Too often harmful practices, addictions, laziness, apathy, and indifference enter our lives causing a sense of malaise or possible darkness that obscures the light. Many times we think that we can defeat these manifest forms of evil by our own merits or efforts. But, as all twelve-step programs suggest, we must give our lives over to God, realizing that we cannot solve these problems alone. Apathy and indifference are major problems in our world. How often have we heard or even said ourselves, "I don't want to get involved. It is not my responsibility." Too often, as well, we hear people say that there are no differences in our options; that all things in the created world are equally good. But a moment's reflection tells us that such ideas simply are not true. We can convince ourselves at times, but in the end reality hits us between the eyes and we must admit that God's ways alone are proper.

Jesus came to rescue us from sin. During his three-year public life traveling about his native land of Israel, he clearly showed the people of his day, and all of us by extension, the proper road to take. It is generally not the easy path, but it is the only path that leads to life. Jesus told us, "Enter through the narrow gate; for the gate is wide and the road is easy that leads to destruction, and there are many who take it. For the gate is narrow and the road is hard that leads to life, and there are few who find it" (Matthew 7:13-14). Through his example, teachings, and charismatic personality, Jesus gave us a formula for life today and the path that will lead to eternal life tomorrow. Jesus died to set us free. The apostle Peter wrote, "For Christ also suffered for sins once for all, the righteous for the unrighteous, in order to bring you to God. He was put to death in the flesh, but made alive in the spirit" (1 Peter 3:18).

As God rescued the Jews from exile in Babylon and Jesus rescues us from fear, sin, and ourselves, we have the obligation to do what we can to rescue others from their many difficulties. We have the responsibility to rescue people from problematic situations. Tough love may be required, but it is our responsibility to rescue people from addictions, absorption by the world, or loneliness. We assist people by our presence; we must provide alternative answers and solutions, ones that have more attraction than the destructive behavior we seek to eliminate in others. We have a responsibility, as well, to rescue our world. We cannot change the world overnight; we may never be able to bring about systemic change, but we must do as the expression says: "Think globally, but act locally." We must combine our individual efforts with those of our sisters and brothers in Christ to bring about change in our world. We must rescue the world from discrimination, racism, poverty, and ignorance. Social sin, those problems in which we all participate, knowingly or unknowingly, must be the objective of our rescue mission. We cannot sit idly by and presume that others are responsible and we are not. On the contrary, we should take the lead and provide the proper example, so that others will follow in our footsteps. We should be proud to have such opportunities and responsibilities in our life.

Oskar Schindler was a great hero, earning the distinction "Righteous Among Nations," the highest award the state of Israel can confer on a Gentile, for his rescue of over 1,000 Jews during World War II. He saved his workers and gave them new life when death was all around them. In a similar way, God rescued and gave new life to the Hebrews in exile in Babylon. Jesus came centuries later to rescue us from the many ways we are prisoners. He died to set us free. As we continue to walk this Advent journey, as we await the coming of Jesus into our lives, let us emulate his actions and die to self so others may live. Let us rescue others and through our actions find eternal life, God's promise to all who believe. Amen.

Advent 4
2 Samuel 7:1-11, 16

The Faithfulness Of God

Mrs. Dowson stood in the doorway of Arthur's room and buttoned the cuff on the sleeve of her pink blouse. There had been a button missing but Marie had replaced it despite all the work she had to do: the cooking, cleaning, and all the other housework. Marie was a treasure — that is how Mrs. Dowson's mother would have described her. Mrs. Dowson crossed Arthur's room to the mantel where the Seth Thomas clock was located. She tried to set the time; the clock had stopped at two o'clock, but it was a lost effort; the brass key that had been under the clock was missing.

"I hope you slept well, Arthur," Mrs. Dowson said. "Toward morning I put on the light blanket and turned on the radio to listen to some music. It was an hour before I got back to sleep. The days are longer," she told him. "You know how I like to get up with the sun in the morning. How lovely it is to hear the first bird sing. Don't you think there are more birds this year? They say that since people stopped using all those insecticides that the birds are coming back. There were some new birds at the birdbath yesterday. I should look them up in your bird book. There were some gulls as well. Remember how the gulls used to fly off to meet the fishing boats returning to harbor? They seemed to know which boats were gutting fish and which were not.

"I used to wish you were not such an avid fisherman, Arthur. I was often lonely. Some days the ladies would josh with me and say they were golf widows but that I was a fishing widow." Mrs. Dowson began to weep, the tears running down her cheeks. "I saw you even less at home those days. It wasn't just the fishing, Arthur. It was anything that attracted you, anything at all.

"No more tears, Arthur," she said finally. "You don't like tears and I've never tried to annoy you. But how long will I have to wait? You are being cruel, though you are not a cruel man. Men do what they please and get away with it. But once when I was lonely," Mrs. Dowson said, "I fell. He meant nothing to me except that he was gentle and noticed my hair and touched my face. He was there Arthur, but God knows where you were, for days at a time.

"I atoned and God has forgiven me because God is good, but you never forgave me. It hurt your pride. I was one of your possessions that someone else had used. I guess I don't blame you, but Arthur, how long will you make me wait for a word — one word?"

Mrs. Dowson dabbed her eyes once more and then put on her gray coat. Henry was waiting with the blue Lincoln. They drove through the pylons of Auburn Cemetery. They passed many graves and Mrs. Dowson knew all the names — Longfellow, Francis Parkman, Edwin Booth, Winslow Homer. On Orchid Path, Henry stopped the car at a small mausoleum. The brass door opened easily to the key and disclosed a small space with a marble angel and a Latin phrase from Saint Paul. The chauffeur took yesterday's roses from the shelf and replaced them with a sheaf of yellow azaleas. Mrs. Dowson seated herself in the metal armchair, took off her gloves, and folded her hands in her lap. "Good morning, Arthur," she said, "I am here."

Mrs. Dowson was faithful to the end and without regard to the past. Her commitment to her husband was total and without reservation. This touching little story provides an excellent illustration of the message in today's first lesson on this fourth Sunday of Advent, namely that God is ever faithful to us and will be so to the end.

Today's second lesson from the second book of Samuel presents us with an image of King David toward the end of his life. The Lord, speaking through the prophet Nathan, reviews how God has been present and faithful to David throughout his life. When God rejected Saul, it was David, at the time a youth and very unkinglike in his appearance, who was chosen, to the surprise of his father, Jesse, as well as the great prophet Samuel. God was the one who gave David triumph over Goliath and the Philistines and then eventually brought him to his role as king. God gave David victory over all of his enemies, allowing Israel to become a great nation, one to which all other nations in the region looked with admiration. But not only was God faithful to David in his triumphs and greatness, he was also faithful in his great failures. Punishment was brought, but God forgave David his greatest transgression when he ordered the death of Uriah, the husband of Bathsheba with whom David had a relationship. Clearly, God was with David every step of the way; his faithfulness could never be questioned.

Now as David reflects back on his life, realizing all that God has done for him, he wants to "return the favor," and build a house for God. David realizes that the Ark of the Covenant, that sacred vessel that carried the law from Mount Sinai, had for many generations been housed in a tent. Feeling a deep inconsistency between his own luxury and the simplicity of God's "house," David seeks to rectify the situation. He wants to demonstrate his faithfulness to God. However, God through Nathan the prophet answers that it is not David's role to build a special house for the Lord. On the contrary, God wishes to demonstrate his continual faithfulness to the great king. God speaks of peace and security that will come to Israel; the greatness of Israel under David will continue in his line. More importantly, the Lord promises to David that he will build a house, a kingdom, in the line of David that shall live forever. In short, God is promising Israel a Messiah, one who will continue the greatness of the Davidic kingdom and permanently establish God's place in the world.

God's promise to David, as delivered by the prophet Nathan, is fulfilled quite obviously in the life, message, and mission of Jesus Christ. The lack of fidelity on the part of Israel notwithstanding, God could never forget his people and thus always maintained fidelity. As had been demonstrated throughout salvation history, God was ever faithful to his chosen people, providing precisely what he promised. The Jews did not recognize Jesus as the promised Messiah. To them, Jesus was not a manifestation of God's faithfulness.

They looked for a different type of Messiah; they failed to understand the fullness of the prophecies of the Torah.

Even after God's faithfulness reached its apex through the incarnation, which we await, God did not stop being present to his people. God's faithfulness is manifest in the word that we read, share, and apply to our daily lives. Faithfulness is present in many men and women over the centuries, holy people who have shown us the face of God and the proper path to life eternal. God's faithfulness is also present, while it might seem odd, in challenges that force us to reflect upon the goodness of God. Despite our many lapses in judgment, work, and action, God remains faithful. It is the only way God can be. The Pauline author puts it very powerfully: "If we have died with him, we will also live with him; if we endure, we will also reign with him; if we deny him, he will also deny us; if we are faithless, he remains faithful — for he cannot deny himself" (2 Timothy 2:11-13).

As God has been ever faithful to us, so must we be ever faithful to God and God's people. Our Advent journey has almost ended. We must review and evaluate how effective our journey has been. Have we taken seriously the opportunities that come our way? Have the resolutions we made at the outset of the season been kept? What more must we do to prepare ourselves for the coming of Christ into our world? We don't have much time so we must today recommit ourselves to a greater faithfulness to the God who first loved us!

Faithfulness certainly begins with our family. We must not only be faithful to the members of the family, but to the traditions and other practices that hold our family together. We must be faithful to the tasks given to us by God. We have been given that talent, time, and opportunity to productively work to better our world. Our commitment to such a task is a commitment to God, who provided the opportunity in the first place. We must also be committed to the community in which we live and what it might ask of us. We must avoid the tendency to "not get involved" but always put our best foot forward to move our society in a positive direction toward God. We must also be faithful to ourselves. We must never compromise who we are or what we believe and profess simply to get ahead. We must never be cowed by contemporary wisdom; we must avoid the tendency to be lazy and apathetic. We must raise a red flag against indifferentism in our attitude.

Ultimately, we must be faithful to God. We must be faithful in prayer, making certain that God is given top priority each and every day. We must manifest our prayer in some active way and stop making excuses for our failures. Faithfulness to God also requires service. The Greeks considered *agape* or service the highest form of love. Similarly, the service we render to our brothers and sisters is a direct manifestation of our faithfulness to God. Lastly, we must participate in the community of faith. Being integrally involved in our faith community is not for a few select people; participation in full is the call of all Christians.

Mrs. Dowson was faithful to her husband, Arthur, keeping his memory alive and speaking to and visiting him on a daily basis. She did so even when she knew he had not been present and could never forgive her. She maintained her faithfulness to the end. Similarly, God was ever faithful to the Hebrews. They were the chosen people; God made a covenant that would never be annulled or abandoned. The high point of God's faithfulness was the promise of a Messiah and to make a permanent house for David in the world. God's promise to the Hebrew king was fulfilled in Jesus. Despite all failures, lack of faithfulness, and at times utter disregard for God, the Lord remained faithful to the end.

God remains faithful to us despite our many transgressions and failures. Advent is the time for us to renew our commitment and faithfulness to God. We must be faithful to others and ourselves and thereby demonstrate our faithfulness to the Lord. As our Advent season concludes, let us continue our preparation, so that Jesus will find us ready, open, and faithful, now and to life eternal. Amen.

[illegible] avoid the tendency to be lazy and [illegible] ... [illegible] in our attitude.

[illegible] we must be faithful [illegible] ... making certain that [illegible] ... [illegible] making excuses for our [illegible] ... The Great [illegible] ... of love. [illegible] ... brothers and sisters [illegible] ... [illegible] of all [illegible].

[illegible]

Christmas Eve/Christmas Day
Isaiah 9:2-7

The Christmas Message Of Hope

The wife of a poor merchant died, leaving him with five children, ranging from age six to fifteen. The older children assumed many of the household chores — cooking, cleaning, and helping the younger children. When the merchant came home at night, he always brought a bag of groceries, food for the next day. After he set the bag on the table, he hugged each child. Before they ate, the father read from the scriptures and the family prayed. Many nights, before bed, the children begged their father to sing with them. He frequently played his guitar and sang quiet folk tunes.

The first Christmas after his wife died, the merchant said to his children, "This year there is insufficient money to buy presents in the store. Instead, we will all draw names, and you will make a present for one of your brothers or sisters. My gift to you will be a fine Christmas meal and a special song that I am writing. We will learn it in the weeks before Christmas and sing it in church on Christmas Eve." True to his word, the father wrote a beautiful song of joy for the children, and began to teach it to them three weeks before the Nativity. The children loved the song so much they sang it with great gusto and volume.

It so happened that a rich man who hated Christmas and hated music even more, lived above the family. Night after night he listened to the children singing the new Christmas song. It irritated him so much that he developed a plan to silence the singing. Several days before Christmas, he knocked on the door: "I have come to make you an offer," he said to the father who listened carefully with his children standing behind him. "I'll give you 100 gold coins if you promise not to sing for three months." The father looked at his children. He said, "That is more money than I can make in two years. We will be able to buy presents for everyone in the entire family." The children cheered as the father accepted the bag of money and the rich man's terms.

That night they began to plan silently how they would spend the money. Over the next few evenings, they ate, then sat quietly, reading and thinking. On the fourth night, however, one of the children said, "I would rather have music than any stupid present. This silence isn't worth it." One by one the children agreed. So the father walked into the bedroom, retrieved the sack of money, and climbed the flight of stairs to return the bag to its owner. He told the man, "We have discovered that there is something more important than money. I am sorry that our singing irritates you, but it fills us with joy. Our family cannot imagine Christmas, or life itself, without music. When singing, we celebrate the best news that is ever been given poor people, that God so loved the world that he became one of us, living as a human being."

When the merchant rejoined his children, he said, "We will learn to sing with greater feeling and less volume. In our joy, we don't want to irritate our neighbor. What do you say to that?" The oldest child spoke for all, saying, "We say, 'Let the music begin.' "

The merchant and his children did not have much in a material sense, but they had music, which was all they needed. In essence, they had hope. Today, our Advent journey has reached its goal; we celebrate the incarnation, God becoming human in Jesus Christ. It is a day of great festival joy for Jesus' arrival in our world provides a sense of hope that something greater and more permanent is possible. Jesus, the light of the world, has come to dispel the darkness, in our personal lives and that of our world.

The hopefulness of the merchant and Jesus is expressed clearly in the prophecy of Isaiah as we heard proclaimed in our first lesson today. Isaiah was sent to the people of God in the southern kingdom of Judah because God was displeased with them. The Hebrew rulers had chosen the world over God; they opted for darkness over light. This situation had led to many problems. Many felt oppressed by rulers and even circumstance. The prophet clearly states that the days of oppression and war are over. The light has dispelled the darkness. As Isaiah states, a people who live in darkness have now seen a great light. The darkness of sin and ignorance, which had pervaded the lives of the Hebrews, was now to be transformed by God. Thus, it is time for the people to rejoice as at the harvest.

Isaiah then proclaims an important prophecy. God will send a person who will be rich in authority. This authority will grow continually, and will lead to lasting peace. His name will be called Wonderful Counselor, Mighty God, Everlasting Father, Prince of Peace. This special manifestation of God's faithfulness to Israel will bring about the establishment of a new kingdom where justice and righteousness will reign. God will protect and provide for his people; he will never abandon them.

Jesus is, of course, the fulfillment of Isaiah's prophecy. Christ the light is the one of whom Isaiah wrote, the one to dispel the darkness of the world. People avoid the darkness for it is foreboding, cold, and unwelcoming. People seek the light because it provides safety, warmth, and bids us welcome. As the winter solstice passes here in the northern hemisphere and with it the dark night ends, so the light gradually returns. In a similar way Jesus, the light of the world, comes to bring the light of faith. He comes to bring hope. The Christmas message of peace is a missive of hope as well. Jesus' birth in Bethlehem brings hope to all who in any way feel the darkness, those who feel removed from the light.

In this story, the widower and his children preferred the music; they opted for hope over the promise of riches. They came to understand that wealth was fleeting and provided only a temporary sense of satisfaction; it could never sustain them. Riches were as empty as the silence created when the music stopped. Thus, the family members made their choice for hope and were happy to profess their joy through a chorus of music on Christmas morning. Is this the same hope that Jesus brings to the world through his incarnation? The reality that God would choose to become human and share our lot completely, save sin, demonstrates not only God's love for us, but the hope that comes from such unconditional love.

Yes, our Advent journey has ended. After four weeks in which we have patiently waited for the Lord, it is now time for us to rejoice. As Isaiah tells the Hebrews in today's lesson that they must cast off darkness and walk anew in the light, so must we cast off the darkness that pervades our life. All of us are victims of the darkness of ignorance. Ignorance in this sense is not so much lack of knowledge, but rather an unwillingness to be informed or to see other possibilities in our life. Too often we form attitudes and opinions and possess the conviction that these are the only possibilities that exist. Sometimes these attitudes say that certain people are acceptable and others are not. We shut out others and thereby miss the opportunity that many people bring. Ignorance is also found in accepting one way of doing things without the possibility of other solutions. Again, we miss the opportunities that come our way with such an attitude. Lastly, ignorance is found in being exclusive. Jesus was ever present to all people, but most especially to those who lived on the margins of Jewish society. He reached out to lepers, sinners, and foreigners. Jesus never asked anyone to pass a litmus test to be his follower; on the contrary, all that was necessary was openness to his message. Ignorance will not allow us to grow; it causes us to stagnate in our own little world. But Jesus came to open the eyes of the blind and the ears of the deaf, not only physically but, more importantly, spiritually. Spiritual blindness is our own ignorance, but Jesus came to bring light to those who live in darkness.

Jesus also came to dispel the darkness of sin. While we are made in the image and likeness of God, still we are broken and incomplete people. We need the healing power of the light in our lives. Habitual actions and words, which are destructive to others and ourselves, cause us to sin, to estrange ourselves from God. We need the grace and hopefulness brought by the light, the newborn King of the Jews, to transform us and mold us more into the image of Christ.

Christmas Day celebrates the birth of Christ in human history. In our society, people who celebrate birthdays are feted with parties and presents. The widower and his children were happy to be able to present their music as a special present to Christ and to each other. We need to ask what will we give to the newborn king of the Jews; what will be our birthday present to Jesus? The one and only thing that Jesus wants and asks of us is possibly the most difficult thing to give — the best possible person we can be. We owe Jesus at least this much. We can move toward the light of hope because God can be trusted. God came to fulfill the covenant with the Jews. He never wavered; he never gave up on his chosen people. Yes, God sent Jesus, his Son, into our world to fulfill the promise to send a Messiah. We must, therefore, respond to the God who first loved us by considering what is necessary in our lives to be the person God wants us to be. The gift we bring to the Lord will cost us nothing in a monetary sense, but it may cost us much in a spiritual sense. However, the one and only thing that Jesus desires is our hearts. Let us not disappoint him.

On Christmas Day, when we welcome the light and hope it brings, we must be bearers of hope to others in our troubled world. Let's take up the challenge, dispel the darkness, and welcome the light. May the Christmas mystery of the incarnation change us forever. Amen.

[illegible] as [illegible] [illegible]

Christmas 1
Isaiah 61:10—62:3

God Makes All Things New

It was just a small, white envelope that stuck out among the branches of our Christmas tree. There was no name, no identification, and no inscription. It peeked out from the branches of our tree for the past ten years or so. Its story, however, speaks of how God makes all things new.

It all began with Mike, a man who hated Christmas. Oh, he did not hate the true meaning of Christmas, but he did very much dislike the commercial aspects of it — overspending, the frantic running around at the last minute to get a present for this person or another, the idea of buying something in desperation simply because you could think of nothing else. Knowing Mike felt this way, I decided one year to bypass the usual gifts of a shirt, sweater, tie, or even the gift certificate. I wanted something special just for Mike but the inspiration came in an unusual way.

That year at school, Kevin, Mike's youngest son, was active on the wrestling team. Before Christmas, there was a non-league match against a team sponsored by an inner-city church. The youngsters on that team were dressed in sneakers so ragged that the shoestrings seemed to be the only thing holding them together. This presented a sharp contrast to Kevin's team in their spiffy blue and gold uniforms and spanking new wrestling shoes. As the match began, I was alarmed to see the other team was wrestling without headgear, those white helmets designed to protect wrestlers' ears. It was a luxury the ragtag team obviously could not afford.

At the end of the match, Kevin's team had won an overwhelming victory, taking every weight class. The boys on the defeated team still possessed a certain false bravado, a kind of street pride that could not be stifled through defeat. Mike, who attended his son's match, shook his head sadly. "I wish just one of them could have won," he said. "They have lots of potential, but losing like this could take the heart right out of them." Mike loved children — all children. He spent much time with them having coached Little League, Pop Warner football, and lacrosse.

That's when the idea for Mike's present came to me. That afternoon, I went to a local sporting goods store and bought an assortment of wrestling headgear and shoes and sent them anonymously to the inner-city church. On Christmas Eve, I placed an envelope on the tree with a note inside telling Mike what I had done and that this was his gift from me. His smile was the brightest thing about Christmas that year and in succeeding years. For each Christmas we followed the same tradition, one year sending a group of mentally challenged children to a hockey game, another year sending a check to a pair of elderly brothers whose home had burned to the ground one week before Christmas.

The envelope became the highlight of our Christmas. It was always the last thing opened on Christmas morning and our children, ignoring their new toys, would stand with wide-eyed anticipation as their dad lifted the envelope in the tree to reveal its contents. As the children grew, the toys gave way to more practical presents, but the envelope never lost its allure.

The story doesn't end here, however. You see, Mike died last year, a victim of cancer. When Christmas rolled around, I was so wrapped up in grief that I barely had energy to put up the tree, but on Christmas Eve, I placed the envelope on the tree and in the morning it was joined by three more. Each of our children, unbeknownst to the others, had placed an envelope on the tree for their dad. The tradition has grown and today it extends to our grandchildren who stand around the tree wide-eyed with anticipation watching as their fathers take down the envelope. We have all learned, that even in the midst of pain and suffering, God will renew us with whatever it is that we need.

The Christmas envelope brought a fresh and new sense of life to the family's holiday celebration. No longer was the celebration all about individuals; the family could take a new look, refocus its thinking and discover new ways to celebrate. The Christmas season that we continue to celebrate in our churches is a time to refocus our thoughts and actions and make them more like Christ Jesus, the newborn king of the Jews who brings a new beginning to our world. Jesus came to make all things new. As we now celebrate a new year and with the new life of the Christmas season, we can cast out the old and be renewed as Christ would have us do. It is an opportunity we must not pass by.

In today's first lesson, we hear from the latter third of the book of the prophet Isaiah, proclaimed to the Hebrew people after their return from exile in Babylon. The prophet speaks of a new day for the people. The transgressions of the past, those that led to the exile, will be forgotten; God will not concentrate on what happened before, but will look to the future. In the past, as the prophets Amos, Hosea, and even Isaiah (in earlier chapters) had dramatically described, God was disappointed with the Hebrews. As we hear today in our lesson, it is a new day. God says to the prophet that he will clothe the community with "the garments of salvation ... a robe of righteousness." God will care for Israel as a bride and groom care for each other on their wedding day. The nation will be adorned with flowers and jewels as if preparing to marry the Lord.

Isaiah speaks in metaphorical language that God will cause righteousness and peace to spring up as a garden refreshed by rain yields new growth. God, the one who has been ever faithful to the Hebrew people, will bring a new day. Additionally, he says Jerusalem — not only the city, but the entire nation — will be delivered from the past as the dawn indicates a new day. For God, the dark night of Israel has passed, but the new day of possibility is present. Salvation will be like a burning torch and the favor of the Lord will come upon the people.

The prophet continues by saying that the surrounding nations will see how God has favored Israel. They will see how the hand of their God can vindicate a nation. Rulers of other nations will observe this and see the glory in Israel. God will give Israel a new name, a name that will be pronounced by the mouth of the Lord. Israel shall be a crown of beauty, a royal diadem in the hand of the

Lord. God will once again favor Israel as a bride favors her jewels. As in the past, God will never give up on his chosen people. The covenant of God is fixed; it can never be broken.

The message proclaimed by Isaiah in today's first lesson is one of the key missives of the postexilic prophets. God will continue to be faithful; the past will be forgotten. Now it is time for Israel to make all things new; it is time to rebuild the lives of the people, both figuratively and literally. It is the opportunity to once again place Yahweh as the chief reason for the community's existence. History has proven that without Yahweh the community will die, but with Yahweh the community flourishes. Thus, while a choice remains before the people, the decision to follow God is readily obvious.

As God made all things new for the Hebrews, so the Lord will make all things new in our lives, as well. Many things, people, and events estrange us from God and one another. The Christian message of new beginnings that Isaiah proclaims must be our incentive to refocus our lives and make them conform more clearly and closely to the message and mission of Jesus. As Christians, this is our task, our common vocation to holiness. We can never be holy people if we live and speak in ways that are contrary to the Christian faith proclaimed through our baptism.

The vicissitudes, those hurdles of life that we must all endure, often throw us off stride. We take many detours from the correct path. Jesus is the one who makes all things new; he is the one who can get us back on track, right our sinking or wayward ship and guide us in the proper direction. We, however, must first be open to Jesus' message; we must see its relevance in our lives and believe in its efficacy.

Once we are open to Christ's message, then we need to seek new beginnings, confident that God will make all things new for us. Some of us need to mend or renew relationships that have been strained, damaged, or broken. Such new beginnings will not happen without our effort and, even with our best effort, are often not easy. Great things are possible with God's help. Some of us need a change of venue — either our work, physical environment, or life situation. Sometimes we feel stifled; we feel like a prisoner to our place of work, geographic location, or circumstance. To voluntarily change is frightening because we must move out from our zone of comfort and enter the realm of uncertainty that always comes with new things. Some of us need to change our habits. We realize there are things we do or words we use, almost continually, that are bothersome or possibly even hurtful to others as well as ourselves. We must have the courage to change, confident again that God's power and grace will help us be the people the Lord wants us to be.

Our new beginnings reach out in other areas as well. Some of us need to transform our attitudes toward others, whether individuals or groups. We need to make things new and to realize how much we have lost by our exclusive thinking. We must realize all the new opportunities that will be ours, if we will allow ourselves to be open to what others say and do and how they think.

Undoubtedly, for all of us the most important renewal in our lives must be our relationship with God. This was precisely what Isaiah was saying to the Hebrews. The exile forced the people to rethink their previous ideas and actions. We may feel exiled from God, but this is not because God has abandoned us. On the contrary, it is because we have abandoned God. God gave Israel a second, a third, and a hundredth chance. So, too, the Lord grants us numerous opportunities to draw near. The Christmas celebration and season, this period of new birth, and the advent of the new year cause us to rethink our lives and once again situate ourselves on the proper road that leads to God and life eternal.

The new custom of the Christmas envelope, which allowed one family to serve others, brought renewal in that family, as well. The family was transformed from an emphasis on the individual to the belief that in reality life is about community. Let us renew our commitment to Christ by rethinking and refocusing our lives. The road will not always be easy, it will often be cluttered, but if we are faithful, God will always remain faithful to us. Then one day we will hear as all the saints of past have heard, "Come, you that are blessed by my Father, inherit the kingdom prepared for you from the foundation of the world" (Matthew 25:34b). Amen.

Christmas 2
Jeremiah 31:7-14

God Is The Hound Of Heaven

Students of American history have always been fascinated by the life and career of the sixteenth president of the United States, Abraham Lincoln. Honest Abe, as his Kentucky and Illinois peers knew him, is the subject of history lessons from primary school through graduate school education. Lincoln was the stereotypical backwoodsman who felt the call to public service on local, state, and national levels. He became well known for his anti-slavery political and moral stance and saw his goal as president to preserve the Union. Few have ever looked carefully at the method he used to fulfill his call and meet his goal.

The historian and Pulitzer Prize winning author, Doris Kearns Goodwin, has in a recently published book, *Team of Rivals: The Political Genius of Abraham Lincoln,*[1] demonstrated the path Lincoln used to preserve the Union, a path that could not have been easy, but the only course to best guarantee his goal of national unity, which for Lincoln was absolute. As the book clearly demonstrates, Lincoln would do anything that was possible or necessary to achieve his goals, even if it might seem odd, unlikely to succeed, or even self-deprecating.

Professor Goodwin demonstrates how Lincoln brought together for his cabinet a team that on one level was the most unlikely combination, but on a second was absolutely the perfect team for the task at hand. In the 1860 Republican presidential nomination race, Lincoln was clearly the dark horse candidate. His rivals were all better known and possessed more experience. The chief rival was the well-known senator and former governor of New York, William H. Seward. Ohio Governor Salmon P. Chase was at the forefront of the nascent Republican Party and clearly better qualified, at least on paper, than Lincoln. The distinguished elder statesman from Missouri, Edward Bates, had served his state and nation in many avenues and seemed poised for higher office. All three had studied law, were great orators, and opposed slavery. Historians, therefore, attribute Lincoln's nomination to chance and good political maneuvering at the Chicago convention.

What is most interesting about the story, however, is who Lincoln chose to be his cabinet, those who would assist him daily on his vital task of keeping national unity. Ironically, it seems, he chose his most ardent rivals, for the top spots in his cabinet: Seward was made Secretary of State, Chase was made Secretary of the Treasury, and Bates was appointed Attorney General. For the remaining top posts, Lincoln chose men from the other side of the political aisle, the Democratic camp: Gideon Welles was made Secretary of the Navy, Montgomery Blair was appointed Postmaster General, and Edwin Stanton, a man who on more than one occasion publicly repudiated Lincoln, calling him unqualified to be president of the United States, but later at his funeral referred to him as "A man for the ages," was made Secretary of War. Thus, Lincoln weaved together a team of rivals for his cabinet, all of whom were better known, better educated, and more experienced in public life. Because the goal, namely the preservation of the Union, was so critical, and completely consistent with his call, Abraham Lincoln chose the rough road, but the only one that he believed could achieve his purpose. He was willing to do whatever was necessary to get the job done, even if that meant working with a "Team of Rivals."

Abraham Lincoln's "Team of Rivals" seemed on paper to be the least likely group to serve the new president and the country well, but actually it was the only possible group to get the job done. Lincoln was not above personal pride or doing what seemed to be ridiculous, or political suicide, including discarding past political differences that might interfere in his quest to maintain national unity.

This political tale, unknown to most, is a good image of how God will do whatever is necessary to help his people. It was true for the Jews, the chosen people, and it is true for us as well. Our first lesson from the prophet Jeremiah, proclaimed to the Jews just prior to the infamous Babylonian exile, shows how God will do whatever is necessary to save his people.

The care God has shown to the Jews is related in salvation history. The story, as we recall, begins with the call of Abram, whom we call Abraham, and the covenant God made with him and his people. Abram and his descendents, who would be as numerous as the stars in the sky and would occupy the land from the great river Euphrates to the wadi of Egypt, would be God's chosen people. God would care for them; they in turn were to be loyal to God alone. The story continued in the land of Egypt when the Israelites, who had been placed in bondage by Pharaoh, called out to God seeking deliverance. Thus, God raised Moses who was charged to lead the people from slavery in Egypt back to the land promised to Abraham many generations earlier.

After the land was settled, God continue to be present to the Hebrews, sending first judges, then kings and prophets to lead the people and to help them understand and maintain the covenant that defined the relationship between God and his people. While the people broke the covenant often and wandered far, nonetheless God remained faithful; the Lord was ever present to his people. God sent Amos and Hosea to warn the people that the Lord was dissatisfied with their rulers. Even after the northern kingdom of Israel was destroyed by the Assyrians, God continued to send more prophets, such as Isaiah and, as we heard in today's first lesson, Jeremiah, to the southern kingdom of Judah with the hope that their fate would be better than their neighbors to the north.

Scripture scholars often refer to the message Jeremiah proclaims in today's first lesson as the "New Exodus." While the north had been lost to history over a hundred years earlier, nonetheless a remnant of the people remained, a remnant that sought to be purified. These people, as we hear in the reading, call out to God asking the Lord to save them. God, the ever-present one, and the one who would do anything for his people, hears their cries and answers. God says through Jeremiah that the blind and the lame, all the remnant of the northern kingdom, will be returned to Israel. God will lead the people back; the Lord will not allow his people to stumble. Like a shepherd who gathers his flock, so God will gather the people. God will ransom Jacob and will redeem Israel. In other words, God will do what is necessary to be present and to aid his people, even if that might mean, as it did for Abraham Lincoln, creating a "Team of Rivals" to get the job done.

Once God has done what is necessary to rescue the people and bring them home, then, as Jeremiah says, the glory of Israel will once again appear. God will restore the land to its great production. The lands will once again become like a watered garden; the grain, the wine, and the oil will be produced in abundance. Prosperity will return to the land and thus the people will rejoice. Young men and women, as well as the old, will be made merry for God will comfort his people. The Lord will replace sorrow with gladness; the people will be satisfied at what God has done.

Salvation history's message of the active presence of God is both a consolation and a challenge. Certainly the Jews must have taken great consolation in the fact that no matter what they did, no matter how many times they broke the covenant, God was always present to them, lending a hand, and searching diligently for them. Similarly, we in our increasingly busier and more complex society must take great consolation in the fact that God is ever present to us. We are all too busy and, therefore, do not take sufficient time to be present to God as the Lord is present to us. Nevertheless, even though the partnership, the contemporary covenant, is not a 50-50 proposition, God continues to be faithful. God will always go out of his way, do whatever is necessary, to save us.

Francis Thompson, the famous British poet, in his epic work, "The Hound of Heaven," has it right. Thompson speaks of a God who searches for us relentlessly, without rest, leaving no stone unturned in a diligent search for our souls. God will look high and low, near and far for us as he searched out the remnant of Israel and made every effort to return the people to the land. He shepherded them and so will he do for all of us.

Besides consolation, we must take serious our responsibility to do to others as God has done for us. The Christmas season is one of giving. On Christmas Day, we gave presents to members of our family, good friends, and coworkers as a gesture to show our care and love for them. Many people at this time give of their time, talent, and treasure to those who are less fortunate, especially the marginalized of our society. This "Christmas spirit" should be part of our everyday lives and not something that is put away, such as our house decorations, when the holiday season ends. Thus, our great challenge is to do for others as God does for us. We must leave no stone unturned in a diligent search to help others, especially those for whom we have responsibility in this world. Parents must seek out their children, especially those who may have gone astray or been problematic. God never gave up on us and thus we cannot give up on others. Siblings must seek each other as well. Rivalries in families and past hurts often place people in estranged positions. We must do whatever is necessary to find the brother or sister whom we have lost. Old friends as well must seek each other. We must drop the attitude that says it's not my responsibility to seek reconciliation. We need to take the initiative, to do what is necessary, to bring our relationships and friendships back to the level we want and need.

Our outreach must go beyond those we know. Those with more resources must do what they can to seek out the poor and those who have less in society. The goods of the earth are not simply for those who have the material resources to possess them. The world is for all peoples and thus all peoples must share. We must break down barriers of discrimination or hostility that keep us apart and build bridges that will bring us closer together. Yes, we must do what is necessary to be present to others.

One of the great hurdles that we must negotiate in understanding God's presence among us is to let go of the past and see today and the future as our goals. God certainly did not remember the mistakes and misdeeds of the Jews, but constantly sought ways to reach out and be present to them. The attitude of God is illustrated well in a story. There once was a parish in which a very holy woman lived. Everyone knew she was very close to God and they admired her. One day, the woman announced to her fellow parishioners that she was receiving visions from the Lord Jesus. Word of this woman's stunning revelation spread rapidly and eventually reached the ears of the local bishop. The bishop went to the holy woman and said, "I understand you are receiving visions from the Lord Jesus." The holy woman replied, "Yes, bishop, I regularly converse with the Lord." The bishop was skeptical and thus to test the authenticity of the woman's revelations, he told her, "The next time you speak with the Lord, ask him this question: 'What was the bishop's great sin before he became bishop?' " A few weeks later, the bishop encountered the holy woman and asked, "Well, have you recently spoken with your friend the Lord Jesus?" "Yes," she replied. "What is the answer to my question? What was my great sin before I became bishop?" The woman replied, "I asked the Lord Jesus that question directly, but his response to me was, 'I don't remember.' "

The story illustrates an important point. The Lord is ready and open to be present to us at any moment, to forgive our sins and allow us to join him in building the kingdom of God in our world. Yes, God is ever present to us and God does not remember our transgressions. This certainly must be our great consolation.

If there should be any shred of doubt in anyone's mind that God is ever present to his people, just waiting for us to return, a poignant image describes God's faithfulness. It is a hot and beautiful summer day and a little girl stands on the edge of a large swimming pool. She looks out at the shimmering water and her eyes well up with tears. She is afraid, for she does not know how to swim. Then she raises her eyes, looks out and sees her mom, with her arms outstretched. Mom says, "Go ahead, jump in, there is nothing to fear; I will hold you up." In a similar way, my friends, Jesus has his arms outstretched on the cross and he says to all of us, "Go ahead, take a chance, I will hold you up; I will bring you to eternal life." Amen.

---

1. Doris Kearns Goodwin, *Team of Rivals: The Political Genius of Abraham Lincoln* (New York: Simon and Schuster, 2006).

The Epiphany Of Our Lord
Isaiah 60:1-6

Recognizing The Lord

In 1950, sportswriters selected him as the greatest athlete of the first half of the twentieth century. He was a star in the National Football League, perfecting the dropkick as an effective scoring weapon, and played professional baseball for seven years. He was a star in basketball, track and field, swimming, and lacrosse. Jim Thorpe, a true All-American athlete, was the best there was. His recognition for a lifetime achievement in sports did not come, however, without help.

Thorpe was born in 1886 in the Indian territory, now the state of Oklahoma. He lived with his family in relative obscurity. No one cared about him, his family, or his people. He was a Native American, an Indian; by this fact alone he was labeled as one who would not produce anything good. Through some good fortune, however, Jim was chosen to attend Carlisle Industrial School in Pennsylvania, a special college for American Indians. At Carlisle, Jim Thorpe would receive the recognition that his talent deserved.

In the early years of this century, Carlisle was a recognized school in major college athletics. Glenn "Pop" Warner, Carlisle's famous football coach, noticed Jim Thorpe's athletic ability. Jim had never seen a football, let alone played the game. Yet, he was a natural. Carlisle played the eastern football powerhouses of the day: Army, Penn, and Princeton; Carlisle beat them all. Led by Jim Thorpe, Carlisle amassed one of the best records in the country. Thorpe was recognized as an All-American in 1911 and 1912. Jim was a natural athlete; he excelled in everything.

In the summer of 1912, before his final year at Carlisle, Jim represented the United States in the summer Olympic games, held that year in Stockholm, Sweden. He entered and won both the heptathlon (seven events) and decathlon (ten events) in track and field. He is the only person in Olympic history to accomplish such a feat. The king of Sweden told Jim, "Sir, you are truly the world's greatest athlete."

Jim Thorpe was a great athlete, an All-American, maybe the best that has ever lived. As they say, he was one who could do it all. Yet, he lived in obscurity until fortune allowed him to be discovered through his presence at Carlisle, and his association with the legendary coach, Pop Warner.

Jim Thorpe's recognition as a star athlete presents a good illustration to the principal theme we celebrate in our churches today, the Epiphany of our Lord. Jesus was born in an obscure town in a stable and placed initially after his birth in a manger, a feeding trough for animals. He, like Jim Thorpe, was unknown. Yet, through the appearance of the star and its ability to guide others to his location, the three magi recognized Jesus as Lord and king.

Today's first lesson from the prophet Isaiah speaks of how Israel will once again be recognized by God. This recognition will be complemented by acknowledgment from people outside the Jewish nation. Not only were Isaiah's words prophetic for the people of this day and for the time of Jesus, they speak to us today of our need to recognize the power and presence of God in others.

Isaiah's message, proclaimed to those who had returned from exile, speaks of how God recognizes Israel once again. The prophet speaks of a new day when he says that people should arise and shine for the light has come. Although darkness will continue to cover much of the earth, the darkness of ignorance to God's message, the glory of God will shine upon Israel. God will favor Israel, as the Lord has been present to his chosen people from the beginning. God recognizes Israel for who they are — a community that is special to the Lord.

God's recognition of Israel is bolstered by the nation's recognition by outsiders. The prophet says that those who observe the light as it comes to Israel will come to this nation. Kings and rulers will be drawn by the brightness of the dawn, the new light that Israel possesses. They will come from many lands; they will come together to celebrate something great in Israel. Sons and daughters of the ancient Israelites will come from many locations. They and those who have returned from the exile will be radiant. Those who return will bring with them the wealth of nations as a gesture to demonstrate the importance of God's presence in Israel. They will come from many nations, such as Midian and Ephah, and will bear with them special gifts of gold and frankincense. As they come they will proclaim the praises of the Lord.

While the presence of God will be in Israel, the prophet clearly says that those who fail to recognize the Lord will come away empty-handed. Recognition of God's presence lies in the hands of people. The prophet suggests all that is necessary for this recognition is one's attention, but the individual must choose to find God.

Today's celebration of the Epiphany of our Lord speaks of how God was recognized by people outside the confines of Israel. When the magi arrived in Bethlehem, they brought with them special gifts that indicated how they understood the significance of the newborn king of the Jews. Their gift of gold recognizes that Jesus was a king; the gift of frankincense demonstrates their understanding that he was Lord. Finally, the gift of myrrh demonstrates how they understood, far in advance, the need for Jesus to die for his people.

The recognition of Jesus as Lord and king, from the outset, presents a central message that will be communicated by Christ throughout his public ministry, namely that Jesus' life and work were oriented outward to others. As the gospels relate, while King Herod sought Jesus' destruction, the three magi, all foreigners, and illustrative of those outside the purview of Israel, sought to honor him. As Jesus was recognized by outsiders, so the Lord consistently and intentionally sought out the marginalized of Jewish society without losing contact with his own people. He taught in the synagogues, telling the Jews who he was and the nature of his mission. As he instructed his apostles, "Go nowhere among the Gentiles, and enter no town of the Samaritans, but go rather to the lost sheep of the house of Israel" (Matthew 10:5-6).

Jesus' mission to his own people was clear, but he also reached out to many different people, discovering in them things equally special and important that he found in his own Jewish people. Jesus' long conversation with a Samaritan woman (John 4:1-42), his encounter with the Syro-Phoenician woman (Mark 7:24-30), and his numerous encounters with lepers (Matthew 8:1-4; Mark 1:40-45; Luke 17:11-19) demonstrated his desire to reach out to others but especially those on the margins of society. Jesus took his message outside Israel as well, to the regions of Tyre and Sidon, and numerous times to the eastern shore of the Sea of Galilee. Clearly, Jesus made every effort to reach out to all peoples; his message was universal. That is why Saint Paul could proclaim: "In former generations this mystery was not made known to humankind, as it has now been revealed to his holy apostles and prophets by the Spirit: that is, the Gentiles have become fellow heirs, members of the same body, and sharers in the promise in Christ Jesus through the gospel" (Ephesians 3:5-6).

The fact that God has recognized us mandates that we, in turn, recognize the presence of God in others. We would all agree it is relatively easy to recognize the presence of God in and associate with those whom we like — members of our family, friends, and trusted coworkers. Few of us have any problems when our associations are advantageous to us, whether that is in business, politics, education, or many other fields. We must recognize, however, that Jesus did not play people to his advantage, but rather was completely open to all who were willing to listen to his message and transform their lives. The gospels also clearly show that he had a preferential option for those who stood on the margins. Thus, as people who bear the Lord's name, we must do likewise.

Our Christian call necessitates that we seek out the lost and forsaken in our society. We must search for those who have no voice and those who are despised; we must reach out to those whom society has forgotten. We might refer to all of these people as contemporary lepers. Our challenge is to find God in the aged and those, who in the minds of some, no longer contribute positively to our society. We are to find God in the immigrant, who simply seeks justice, to earn a living, and to live freely without the fear of persecution or possible death in his native land. We have the challenge to find God in criminals and victims of AIDS. Our task, in short, is to not dwell on what might be problematic in people but, like Jesus, to seek the good that each human being possesses.

Certainly, finding God in the "lost" of society, those who are problematic and possibly those we do not like, is not an easy road, but the Christian life should not be easy. We should not expect anything less than the master whom we seek to follow and serve experienced in his life. The difficulty of the road should not be the criterion by which we judge our entry, but rather where the road leads. Jesus is quite clear in the Sermon on the Mount: "Enter through the narrow gate; for the gate is wide and the road is easy that leads to destruction, and there are many who take it. For the gate is narrow and the road is hard that leads to life, and there are few who find it" (Matthew 7:13-14).

Jim Thorpe was an unknown, living in obscurity in the Oklahoma territory until he received the privilege of attending Carlisle and was recognized for his athletic prowess. In a similar way, Jesus of Nazareth was born in obscurity, but from the outset was recognized as Lord and king, as prophesied by Isaiah many generations earlier. Jesus, in turn, recognized the presence of God in others. Now, we must do as our master and find the Christ in others. The road will be hard and detours will happen, but the goal is worth every ounce of our effort — life eternal. Amen.

The Baptism Of Our Lord
Epiphany 1
Ordinary Time 1
Genesis 1:1-5

Baptism: The Light Shatters The Darkness

Winston Churchill, the famous British statesman who led England as prime minister through the horrors of World War II, was a man who prepared the people for future joy. He was born in 1874 to a British Lord and an American heiress. His heroics during the infamous Boer War in the last days of the nineteenth century made him a national hero and greatly aided his election to Parliament in 1900. In only four years he renounced his aristocratic background and joined the Liberal Party. During World War I and the interwar years, Churchill's political career was almost ruined due to his controversial positions on many issues, including his denunciation of Prime Minister Neville Chamberlain's appeasement policy, "Peace in Our Time," signed with Adolf Hitler at Munich in 1938. When Britain declared war on Germany in 1939, however, Churchill's views became quite popular leading him to succeed Chamberlain as prime minister in May 1940.

Churchill was the man to whom the British people and many in Europe looked to bring solace and comfort in the continent's darkest hour of the twentieth century. His pugnacity and rousing speeches rallied the British to continue the fight during the midst of the almost daily bombing of London by the German Luftwafa, the infamous blitz. He urged his compatriots to conduct themselves so that "if the British Empire and its Commonwealth last for a thousand years, men will say, 'This was their finest hour.' " He firmly believed that while Britain was in a period of darkness, if the people persevered and believed in themselves, the light would return. Churchill was able to convince Franklin Roosevelt to aid England, morally and materially. He established close ties with all Allied leaders in what became known as the Grand Alliance. Yes, Churchill knew that the dark hour would pass and that peace, prosperity, and joy would once again reign. He was a leader, but his life and his work pointed to something greater, the ideals for which he and all free people live. He prepared his people and led them to the light of joy.

Winston Churchill, through his charismatic outreach, pugnacious personality, and inspirational rhetoric, was able to champion the cause as Great Britain moved from the darkness of the Battle of Britain and the blitz on London to the brightness of victory and a new day. Churchill's ability to inspire a nation to move from the darkness of near death to the light and promise of new life serves as an excellent illustration of how God moved the world from darkness to light at the dawn of creation. On this feast of the Baptism of our Lord we honor the action of John the Baptist toward Jesus in the Jordan River, but more importantly we recall our own baptism, which called us to live as people in the light in the face of much darkness.

Although the Genesis account of the creation of the world is familiar to all, we need periodically to read this important story of God's love. We are told that God initially created the heavens and the earth, but the earth was a formless void and darkness covered the face of the deep. Then God created the light. Immediately, God realized the light was good; it was preferable to the darkness. While the text of Genesis does not indicate any pejorative sense of darkness, there certainly seems to be a distinct contrast drawn between the light and the darkness of the world. God intentionally separates the light from the darkness. Since the light is good it is something that we want to seek. Darkness is lonely, quiet, and cold. We generally avoid the darkness. Darkness is filled with uncertainty. Because we cannot see well in the darkness, we often choose not to venture out and discover what it contains. The light, on the other hand, is lively, boisterous, and warm. The light is inviting and thus we seek it with much vigor and effort. God created the light so that we could move from the darkness and seek that which is good.

The creation of the light by God immediately after the heavens and the earth, the first production of God's hand, certainly gives it primacy and significance. Not only did God see that the light was good, he saw a sense of urgency in its creation. The darkness would allow no differentiation in time; without the light the future manifestations of God's creation, plants and animals, and of course human beings, would remain in a perpetual state of indifference. The light would provide vision by which the rest of God's creation could guide its daily existence. Thus, it was absolutely necessary at the outset to create the light so God's plan for the world could go forward. Without the light, the creation story and eventually salvation history would be stunted. The world would have never existed.

Baptism, the premier sacrament that unites us as Christians, is a celebration of one's movement from the darkness into the light. When we are born we enter into the human community — our family, national origin, racial background, and ethnic sensibility. While, as the book of Genesis says, we are made in the image and likeness of God, still something significant is missing from human birth alone. Baptism supplies what we need. We no longer are simply members of the human community. Through baptism we are members of God's family, the Christian community. The words of the baptism formula are very significant. We are baptized, we are brought into the light, through our oneness with God. We are baptized in the name of the Father, Son, and Holy Spirit, that is the Trinity, the God whom we adore. Baptism unites us with God through Jesus Christ and to all who bear the same name of Christian.

The Baptism of our Lord, which we celebrate today, gives us the opportunity to consider many important ideas. First, we should remember the symbolic importance of Jesus' action. As the Son of God, Jesus did not require a ritual cleansing, especially one of repentance that John was performing at the Jordan River. And, even though John protested at Jesus' request for baptism, the Lord insisted that this be done showing that even Jesus could be one with his people. Jesus was willing to experience precisely what he asked his followers to engage. This is certainly an important idea of the feast we celebrate today.

The celebration of the baptism of Jesus is, however, much more than our remembrance of a historical event. More importantly it calls us to recognize both the privilege and the responsibilities we have as baptized Christians. The privileges of baptism, and thereby being a child of God, are numerous, but unfortunately often not recognized or acknowledged. We have the privilege of the name Christian, which designates us as official followers of Jesus Christ. We have the privilege of the Christian community that surrounds us. It seems we rarely consider our Christian name or our membership in a community of faith to be great privileges, but living in a country of freedom and democratic principles, we often take for granted that which is most basic. The church always serves as a great source of strength, but most especially during difficult times in our life. It is the source of our sustenance in many ways. The church is always there for us; we will never be abandoned.

The church provides many additional privileges for us. It helps us to understand and apply the timeless message of scripture to our lives. Unless we can appropriately utilize the New Testament message, then our reading of this sacred book is merely an academic exercise and not one of faith. Thus, it is essential that we take into our hearts what the gospel evangelists, Saint Paul, and the other New Testament writers tell us and make it the structure within which we will live our lives. The church gives us the sacraments, special signs from God that provide us with grace, namely *charis* or gift. The first and premier sacrament, baptism, brings us from the darkness of ignorance of God to the light of Christian revelation. We must rejoice that we have been so privileged. We have been enlightened through our baptism. Now it is time for us to utilize this great privilege and apply it as responsible Christians in the world.

The basic responsibility the Christian life demands of us is to properly and fully live the message of Jesus Christ. Based on our first lesson today from the book of Genesis, this responsibility means we are to transform the darkness present in our lives and those of our brothers and sisters into the light of Christian joy. We do this in general by setting a good example in action and in word. We are to be evangelists to a world that badly needs Christ's message of hope and peace. There is no need to stand on a street corner or go door to door and tell people in an overt way about the message of Jesus. Evangelization is conducted each and every moment of our life by what we do and say. Therefore, we must concentrate our daily activity on removing the darkness and bringing light to others.

Yes, it is our primary responsibility as Christians to transform the darkness of ignorance into the light of the knowledge of Christ. In order to do this well we must continue our own education in the faith. We cannot assume that what we were taught as children (that is a teenager's level of Christian knowledge) is sufficient to adequately provide the light. We would never dare to think we could adequately operate as professionals, whether that is a teacher, attorney, physician, or engineer, without regular updates of our knowledge. Why do many professions mandate "continuing education units" or similar updating systems? These professions realize that to stagnate is actually to move backward. Professionals always want to move forward, to be on the cutting edge, and therefore, they sacrifice time and energy to continually update themselves in their expertise.

In a similar way, the Christian community, especially if we want to help people find the light and all the goodness that comes from it, must continually update and keep abreast of what is happening in our churches. Darkness, as manifest in the many aspects of society today, continues to lurk at our doors. If we do not proactively seek the light the darkness will most assuredly envelop us. It is easy to become lazy and complacent and believe that we can operate on past knowledge and ways of doing things. But such an attitude will not only be harmful to ourselves but will not allow the light to shine. Such an attitude, in the end, will bring darkness back to our world. But, as the first lesson tells us today, God created the light and found it good. Thus we must seek the good and charge forward to the light, as we move daily toward our return to God.

Jesus came to bring the light of truth and hope and dispel the darkness of ignorance and fear. As the prologue of Saint John's gospel says, "What has come into being in him was life and the life was the light of all people. The light shines in the darkness, and the darkness did not overcome it" (John 1:3b-5). Inspired by the ability of Winston Churchill to bring Great Britain from darkness to light in the midst of a terrible world war, let us celebrate Jesus' baptism by remembering the privileges and responsibilities that our own baptism brought us. Let us bring the light of Christ to all we meet, today and to life eternal. Amen.

Epiphany 2
Ordinary Time 2
1 Samuel 3:1-10 (11-20)

Responding To God

We are all familiar with the term "late-bloomers." It refers to people who respond later in life to an invitation and manage in the end to accomplish great things. History has known some famous late-bloomers. Fortunately for us, early or late they followed their special invitation offered by God.

Anton Bruckner was a late-bloomer. Many people do not know the name of Bruckner, but those who listen to classical music certainly know him. Bruckner lived in nineteenth-century Austria as a butcher and part-time organist. He was a very simple man. He always shaved his head and wore old clothes so as not to be mistaken for a person of wealth. Although his life was simple, it was full. Yet, at the age of 41 he heard a performance of Richard Wagner's famous opera, *Tristan and Isolde*. The experience transformed his life. He decided he would dedicate himself to musical composition. By the end of his life he had completed, among many other works, nine symphonies, several of which are still regularly played by orchestras around the world.

The world knows Albert Einstein as a genius in the field of science. This is certainly true, but he did not start out that way. As a boy, growing up in Germany, many people thought him to be ignorant. He failed courses in mathematics; he was very rebellious. As a boy, he showed little evidence of the ability he possessed. Yet, it was Einstein's theory of relativity and similar ideas that brought about the nuclear age in which we now live.

Saint Augustine, one of the finest Christian minds and greatest saints who ever lived, was also a late-bloomer. Augustine wandered about for thirty years trying to find himself. He tried different religions including paganism and the religion of the holy man, Mani, known today as Manichaeism. He was involved in a relationship that produced a son. Eventually, through the prayers of his mother, Saint Monica, he was converted to Christianity. Saint Augustine's response to his conversion is found in a famous line from his autobiography, *The Confessions*, "Late have I loved you, O Beauty ever ancient, ever new, late have I loved you!" Augustine became a bishop and a great scholar. He was one of the most famous men who ever lived.

Each of these men received an invitation. One invitation was to music, another was to science; the third was an invitation to greater service of God. These invitations were always present, because they were gifts from God. Once the gift was found, it became a permanent part of who these people were. The lives of these three famous people present a good illustration of how it is necessary to respond to God. A sense of openness allows one to hear the call in a spirit of courage and conviction and sends the individual forward to do whatever it is that God asks of the person. Our first lesson today asks us to be open to God's call in order to do whatever it is that God asks of us.

The call of Samuel is a biblical story familiar to many. Samuel experiences the call of the Lord, but being unfamiliar with God he does not initially recognize it. On three occasions, as the passage states, God called the young boy to hear his word. Each time Samuel goes to his master, Eli, and asks for guidance. It seems that Eli was also, at least at the outset, unaware of the call. However, when the Lord's invitation is received for the third time, Eli realizes it is God's call and, therefore, says to his young charge, "Go, lie down; and if he calls you, you shall say, 'Speak, Lord, for your servant is listening' " (1 Samuel 3:9).

The Lord then speaks a message to Samuel that I am sure was not expected or wanted. God's message was harsh; punishment would come to the house of Eli. Eli's sons had done evil in the sight of the Lord and the old man had done nothing to stop them. Even with such a harsh message, Eli is still able to proclaim to the young Samuel, "It is the Lord; let him do what seems good to him"

(1 Samuel 3:18b). In other words, Eli accepts what the Lord has brought his way. Even in difficult circumstances he is able to respond in a positive way to the Lord.

As God called Anton Bruckner, Albert Einstein, and Saint Augustine to do great things, and as the Lord called Samuel to listen to his word, so God calls all of us. The question, of course, is how do we know what God wants us to do? How do we know that it is the call of God and not the call of someone or something else? The only way we can know is to be open to the invitation of God, as were the three men in history and Samuel. We must listen for God's voice.

How does God speak to us? People discover the message of the Lord in various ways. Few people today, I suppose, experience the theophanies we hear about in the Hebrew Bible. People today do not wrestle with God, as did Jacob, nor do they encounter the Lord in a burning bush that is not consumed, as did Moses. None of us has ever seen a person taken up to heaven in a fiery chariot, as was Elijah. Even though God does not speak to us in these overt ways, certainly God is calling, but the question is: Are we listening?

God calls us in the events of our lives. Things happen in life, unexpected things, events that bring joy and triumph and those that bring sadness and defeat. The message is not always obvious; we are often confused by what God may be saying. Since the picture is not completely clear, we need to listen as well as observe.

Thus, we need to pray. Most people are quite adept in expressing their feelings to God. We express our praise of God the one who is the source of our strength and sustenance. We give thanks to God for the abundance we have in the many blessings that come our way. We call out to God for our own needs — material and spiritual. We may express our sorrow for what has happened or petition the Lord for our needs. We may even at times express our anger toward God. Still, no matter how beautifully and humbly we may express our thoughts, petitions, and thanksgiving to God, we must listen for the Lord's response with an equal or even greater effort. Prayer is our daily conversation with the Lord. We can never know the Lord's will unless we openly and frequently listen to

God. One day an older, pious woman said, "We have two ears and one mouth and thus we should listen twice as much as we speak." Such wisdom expresses precisely what are prayer should be. Thus, we can know God's call by being open, speaking and listening to God.

Once we hear and believe we know what God is asking, then we must courageously and with great faith go forward and respond. To move from where we presently find ourselves in order to answer the Lord's call takes great courage. When all is settled in our life and we are "in our element," we generally don't want to move. Feeling comfortable is pleasant; why should we change when things are going well? But being too comfortable, if we are not careful, can lead to complacency that draws us into ourselves and takes us away from our Christian vocation to holiness and service to others. Seven hundred years before Christ, the prophet Amos warned the religious leaders of the northern kingdom of Israel against this tendency: "Alas for those who lie on beds of ivory, and lounge on their couches, eat lambs from the flock, and calves from the stall; who sing idle songs to the sound of the harp, and like David improvise on instruments of music; who drink wine from bowls, and anoint themselves with the finest oils, but are not grieved over the ruin of Joseph! Therefore they shall now be the first to go into exile, and the revelry of the loungers shall pass away" (Amos 6:4-7).

Thus, we, like Bruckner, Einstein, and Augustine must be willing to move from our comfortable existence and venture forward, with faith, into the unknown. A certain sense of fear is endemic to the unknown. Few, if any, wish to generate fear for it comes to us too often unexpectedly in ordinary daily life. We do all we can to avoid it. Thus, to overcome the natural fear of the unknown we need faith and trust. Jesus put it well in the gospel: "Do not fear. Only believe, and [you] will be saved" (Luke 8:50). Therefore, to respond to God we must be in conversation with him and open to his call. We must be listening and have trust and faith.

How is the Lord calling you today? Some may be called to take a new job or to move to a different part of the country. Opportunity may be knocking for some and we have the responsibility to respond in some way. Some may be called to a new or changed relationship — to initiate a friendship or something more serious, or to realize that a present relationship is harmful or even destructive and needs to be ended. We must trust the message we have received and act accordingly. We are all called in different ways to deepen our relationship with the Lord. We are called to get more involved with our church to spend more time in our relationship with God and less on the pursuits of the world.

Yes, the call of the Lord is present in our lives, but are we listening? Anton Bruckner, Albert Einstein, and Saint Augustine each received a special invitation from God. They came in diverse ways and were received a bit later in life, but once received and accepted, they transformed their lives and allowed these men to make very significant contributions to society. They, like Samuel in our scripture reading, heard the call of the Lord and responded. They were able to say figuratively or literally, "Speak, Lord, your servant is listening" and then act upon the Lord's words. May we have the faith and courage to do the same! Amen.

Epiphany 3
Ordinary Time 3
Jonah 3:1-5, 10

The Need For Transformation

The Bishop of Notre Dame Cathedral in Paris was known to be a great evangelist and preacher who would reach out to unbelievers, scoffers, and cynics. He liked to tell the story of a young man who, many years earlier, stood outside the cathedral and almost on a daily basis would shout derogatory slogans at people entering the church to worship. He would call them fools and all kinds of names. The people tried to ignore him but it was quite difficult.

One day, the cathedral's rector went outside to confront the young man. The young man ranted and raved against everything the priest told him. After some time the rector addressed the young man, saying, "Look, let's get this over once and for all. I am going to dare you to do something and I will bet you cannot do it." Of course, the young man responded, "I can do anything you propose, just try me!" "Fine," said the priest, "I want you to follow me into the church sanctuary." The man followed the priest, who stopped at the foot of a large figure of Christ on the cross. He said to the young man, "I want you to look at the cross and scream at the very top of your lungs, as loudly as you can, 'Christ died on the cross for me and I don't care one bit.' " So the young man went into the sanctuary, looked at the cross, and screamed as loudly as he could, "Christ died on the cross for me and I don't care one bit." The priest said, "Very good. Now do it again." Again, the young man screamed, but with some hesitancy, "Christ died on the cross for me and I don't care one bit." The priest again complemented the man saying, "You are almost done now. But for good measure, say it one more time." The young man raised his fist, looked at the statue, but the words would not come. He just could not look at the face of Christ and say those words any longer. Then, to the surprise of all who were listening to the bishop's story, he said, "I was that young man. I was that young, defiant man who thought he did not need Christ, but found that I could not live without him."

The angry young man was transformed, it seems, by the power of Christ. He simply could not continue to voice his anger for he could not sufficiently articulate in his mind why he was angry. Similarly, as we hear in our scripture reading today, the prophet Jonah preached to the people of Nineveh who were transformed by his message. They changed and began to follow the dictates of the Lord. We, too, like the angry young man who became a bishop, like the Ninevites, need to be transformed in our lives. We must move from the darkness of ignorance and sin and seek the light of sincerity and truth, for others and ourselves. We must listen to God and be transformed.

We all know the story of Jonah so very well. It is one of the Bible stories that we learn as children. Jonah is told by God to go to the great city of Nineveh and inform the people of their need to repent and transform their lives or God's wrath will come upon them. Jonah, however, refuses and runs away, but God is persistent in his call. The Lord sends a great fish to swallow Jonah. Three days later, the fish spews forth the prophet onto the land. Jonah is now transformed in his thinking.

In our first lesson today, we hear the second half of the Jonah story. Transformed in his thought, the prophet now cooperates with God. He goes to Nineveh and preaches the need for transformation, saying that God will destroy the city unless the people change. Jonah's message is persuasive; the people heed God's warning, proclaim a fast, and put on sack clothing. God, observing the transformation of the people, changes his mind about the planned destruction of the city. Nineveh was saved through Jonah and the response of the Ninevites to the prophet's message.

The message of transformation so clear in the story of the angry young man who became bishop and the preaching of Jonah to the Ninevites is one we must hear as well. By definition, transformation requires us to change. Many people do not like or want change. If we feel comfortable in our lifestyle, place of work, neighborhood, and ways of operating, why would we want to change? In such cases there seems to be no motivation for change. Only when things get out of sync in our life, when we feel things are not going the way we want, do we consider the possibility of change. Change and the ability to be transformed must be an ongoing process in our lives. In order to find transformation we must first have a sense of openness to the will of God in our lives, as we heard in last week's message. We must realize our need for transformation. No one is perfect; no one "has it all together." We need to be transformed in mind, spirit, attitude, and action in order to draw closer to God.

Transformation is multidimensional but it must begin by how we think about ourselves. The so-called "Golden Rule," that Jesus articulated in response to the question, "Which is the greatest commandment?" calls us to love God above all things and to love our neighbor as ourself. We cannot do justice to our love for God or neighbor if we do not love ourselves. Too often in our action-oriented and accomplishment-driven society we do not have a sufficiently positive attitude about ourselves. What we need to achieve is beautifully illustrated in the popular stage play *Man of La Mancha*, a musical rendition of Miguel Cervantes' famous novel, *Don Quixote*. Don Quixote lives with the illusion of being a knight-errant, battling windmills that he imagines are dragons. Near the end of the play, the protagonist is dying and at his side is Aldonza, a worthless prostitute he has idealized by calling her Dulcinea — Sweet One — much to the delight of the howling laughter of the townsfolk. But Don Quixote has loved this woman in a way unlike anything she had ever experienced. Thus, when Quixote breathes his last, Aldonza begins to sing, "The Impossible Dream." As the last echo of the song dies away, someone shouts to her, "Aldonza!" She proudly responds, "My name is Dulcinea." The crazy knight's love has transformed her. Like Aldonza, we need to be transformed to a better appreciation of ourselves. We can achieve this by appreciating our self-worth, made as we are in the image and likeness of

God. Certainly transformation also requires us to change and to be the people God calls us or wants us to be. This may mean changing a few bad habits, transforming the way we do things, and not running away from our responsibilities. We must work to enhance our relationship with God. If we are "right" with ourselves then we are moving in the proper direction for a complete transformation.

Once we have achieved greater self-esteem and have transformed our own personal actions, then we must begin to transform our attitudes and actions toward others. Again, as the golden rule says, we must love our neighbor. Loving our neighbor does not mean we will be good friends with all people, but it does mean that we will demonstrate respect and basic kindness to all. Loving our neighbor, therefore, necessitates for almost all a sense of transformation. Too often today, we focus on our needs and desires; we are insufficiently concerned about others. At times, we perceive that our actions are appropriate, but even then, transformation is at times necessary. A little story illustrates this point quite well.

One day, on his lunch hour, a businessman was strolling through a local park. As he walked, he enjoyed the beauty of the day as he ate a hot dog he had purchased at a local vendor. As he approached a street corner, he encountered a homeless person who asked him for money for food. He ignored the request and continued to walk. As he was heading back to the office he decided he wanted a little dessert. He stopped at a pastry shop and bought himself a chocolate éclair. As he was leaving the store, a young boy came racing down the sidewalk on a skateboard. The man jumped out of the way and, in the process, the éclair fell to the ground. He picked it up but it was filled with dirt and other things; it was simply a dirty éclair. Before he discarded it, he caught sight of the homeless person he encountered earlier, walked up to him and said, "Here, my man, is some food for your hunger." The man continued to walk back to the office thinking he had done his good deed for the day. That night, while he was sleeping, he had a dream. In his dream he was in a restaurant that was very active with many patrons. It took some time, but he finally got the attention of one of the waitresses who took his order. After some time, the woman returned with a piece of dirty pastry on a white plate. The businessman was incensed and said, "I'm a respectable businessman and expect better treatment than this. I want what I ordered." The waitress responded, "Sir, you don't seem to realize where you are. You have arrived in heaven and the only thing you can receive here are things that were sent in advance before your arrival. I went back and checked the records and the only thing we can find is this dirty chocolate éclair."

Yes, there is a need to treat others as we would have them treat us, but for many this will require a transformation, not only in what we do but how we think. When God calls us to transform our lives, we must act; we cannot avoid the Lord. This may cause us some pain; we may have to shift our priorities. We may even have to change direction in our lives. That is precisely what God asked of the Ninevites and because of their willingness to change God relented his planned punishment. Let us learn a lesson from the story of the transformation of the young man who became the bishop and from Jonah's transformation of the Ninevites to the reality of our need for conversion in our own lives. If we can, our reward in heaven will be great. Amen.

Epiphany 4
Ordinary Time 4
Deuteronomy 18:15-20

Contemporary Prophets Speak The Truth

Dorothy Day, a woman who many people today believe to be a prototypical saint for twentieth-century society, was born on November 8, 1897, in Brooklyn, the eldest daughter of John Day, a roving newspaper sportswriter and his wife, Grace. Because of the nature of her father's work, the Day family moved often during Dorothy's youth. In 1906, the Days were living in Berkeley, California, when the great earthquake and subsequent fire destroyed a large portion of the city of San Francisco across the bay. The disaster destroyed the plant of the *Morning Telegraph*, necessitating John Day and his family to move again. They settled in Chicago where John rented a drab six-room flat above a tavern on the south side. When he obtained a permanent position with the Chicago *Inter-Ocean*, his family moved to a nicer home just north of the city.

Like all people, Dorothy Day experienced life with its ecstasies and its problems. Each experience was an opportunity, a challenge, and at times a pitfall. Each experience asked her to make a choice. She could learn, grow through, and move forward from the many experiences of life or she could allow society to conquer her, to retreat inside herself, and shut out the world. In many ways she was a contemporary prophet who spoke God's word by revealing the reality of contemporary life. She forced people to see things in different ways.

At age seventeen, Dorothy enrolled at the University of Illinois on a scholarship from the Hearst newspaper chain. There she attended classes that, for the most part, she found boring, save English, which peeked in her a previous interest in writing. She read voraciously, cutting classes and keeping odd hours in order to satisfy her habit. She was introduced to the ideology of Socialism, which she found to be quite attractive. Each experience of life was an opportunity to grow. She developed a worldview that was socially conscious, outward looking, and open to possibilities.

After two years of college, she returned to New York where she worked as a reporter, first for Socialist and later for Communist newspapers. Life was not easy for Dorothy Day. She lived a "Bohemian" lifestyle, occupying a small flat on Manhattan's upper eastside. She shared her food with the rats that darted through the dingy apartment and with the homeless who slept outside her front door. She barely managed to pay her bills; she was searching and running but never certain as to what the goal was or where it was located. A passing affair ended in an abortion. Another romance led to marriage and to a divorce only one year later. A common-law marriage produced a daughter. She moved about — to Hollywood, Mexico, New Orleans, then back to New York — writing stories, columns, and even a semi-autobiographical novel, *The Eleventh Virgin.*

Floating, drifting, but always questioning and growing, Dorothy came to Washington DC on December 8, 1932, to cover a story for the Catholic weekly, *America.* After her assignment was completed, she went to the Shrine of the Immaculate Conception to pray. As a recent convert to Catholicism, she asked God for direction in her life. She wanted to know the goal and the method to achieve it. It would not be long before God would answer her plea.

When she returned to New York, her friends told her that a middle-aged man had been asking for her in her absence. George Shuster, managing editor of *The Commonweal*, another Catholic weekly published in New York, had sent this man, Peter Maurin, a French émigré to the United States, via Canada, to her front door. Maurin had a new vision for the world, one which he claimed would be its salvation. His plan had three parts: The first was to engage the mind through round-table discussions on the important social issues of the day, led by some recognized expert in the field. The second part was to establish houses of hospitality to shelter and feed the homeless. Lastly, in support of the back-to-the-land movement, he advocated the foundation of farming communes for work and study. Thus in December 1932, an articulate women searching for answers, Dorothy Day, met a man with a vision and plan, Peter Maurin. The result of their relationship was the Catholic Worker movement, which published its first one-penny newspaper on May 1, 1933. It stands as a primary example of the lay apostolate and Catholic Action prominent in the United States of the 1930s.

Dorothy Day is only one example of a plethora of famous twentieth-century people who have been shining examples of contemporary prophets. She, along with the likes of Martin Luther King Jr., Archbishop Oscar Romero of El Salvador, and the combination of Nelson Mandela and F. W. DeKlerk in South Africa, proclaimed a message that was painful for some but uplifting for others. She forced people to squirm, to rethink their lives, both in word and action. She asked uncomfortable questions. Through her actions not only were the poor made visible and better served, but the conscience of society was raised. People were forced to confront their fears, to listen to their conscience. In short, she, like Moses and the great prophets of the Hebrew Bible, challenged people to listen and find the presence of God in a new message.

In a way similar to the life and work of Dorothy Day, Moses, as we heard in our lesson from Deuteronomy, speaks to the people and tells them of the absolute need to listen to the prophets of God. Moses says God will raise up other prophets after him, a message that was certainly a foreshadowing of the many whose names we know. God will place his words in their mouths and they shall speak all they are commanded. God, through Moses, warns the people that they must listen to the message of the prophets. Anyone who does not heed the message will be held accountable to the Lord.

Moses also warns those called to be prophets that they must speak only what God tells them. People are not to presume to speak in God's name. To misrepresent God's message would be blasphemy. Thus, Moses tells the people that one can tell the validity of a prophet by seeing if his words come true. If a prophet's words are not manifest then it is not the Lord who speaks, but rather the man who speaks presumptuously. The people are not to be frightened; God is ever present in the message of the prophets.

When contemplating the concept of prophecy, most people think of future prediction. Certainly Isaiah, Jeremiah, Ezekiel, and all the other prophets spoke in this way. Amos and Hosea predicted the destruction of the northern kingdom; Isaiah and Jeremiah predicted the Babylonian exile. However, the primary reason for prophecy was to proclaim God's disappointment at current conditions as manifest through sinful actions, complacency, and inappropriate attitudes of the ruling elite toward the people of the land.

Today, prophets speak in a similar way, articulating contemporary problems and forcing people to ask difficult questions. While in some ways the words of contemporary prophets look to the future, their concern is with the present reality. Dorothy Day spoke as an advocate for the poor and marginalized during the Great Depression. Martin Luther King Jr. spoke of the injustices against African Americans, thus initiating a peaceful revolution during the American Civil Rights Movement of the late 1950s and 1960s. Archbishop Romero spoke for the poor who were being oppressed by a state bent on power and with little or no concern toward its citizens. Nelson Mandela and F. W. DeKlerk spoke against the injustices of apartheid, a system that not only segregated peoples, but placed one group above another.

Contemporary prophets exist today and they challenge us in many ways. They ask difficult questions, but ones that require our response. When the prophets speak we are generally made to feel uncomfortable. Sometimes we respond by ignoring the message. People don't like to feel uncomfortable and thus it is easy to close our ears and eyes to the message that prophets speak today. But God tells us through the prophet Moses in today's lesson from Deuteronomy that he will hold us accountable if we fail to heed the message of the prophets.

Prophets are not always the famous and those who make our history books. Many people, both famous and ordinary, speak God's truth. Part of the vocation to holiness to which all Christians are called is to listen to the truth and to speak it on behalf of God to a world that is often lost. We may wish to avoid this task, but as

Jonah was tracked down by the Lord to continue his work, so too will God continue to seek us to meet our responsibilities as contemporary prophets.

Confrontation, speaking the truth, being courageous — these are not easy things to do. We all want to be accepted and speaking the truth can, at times, put us at odds with others. But we have a mandate as followers of Jesus to speak and act when things need correction. Paul, in 1 Corinthians 13, tells us that we may have all things, but if we do not possess love we are empty. He concludes, "And now faith, hope, and love abide, these three; and the greatest of these is love" (v. 13). There are several forms of love. The Greeks have given us three: *Eros* or romantic love between a man and a woman, *phileo* or brotherly love between siblings, relatives, and close friends, and *agape,* the love of service. There is, however, a fourth form — tough love. This means mustering sufficient courage to say what must be said and to do what must be done, despite the difficulty or possible pain.

We must be people who love by speaking the truth and we must do so in all the aspects of our lives. We must speak the truth with our families. When a member of our family strays off the right path we must have the courage to speak and to act to correct the situation. It may be a child who is associating with the wrong crowd, a spouse who has lost direction, or a parent who has mistreated a child. We must speak the truth in our place of business. Today, corruption is almost endemic to the corporate structure. Work practices, decision-making, and the treatment of employees are all areas where errors can easily be manifest. When we notice problems in these areas or others do we have the strength and courage to act? We must speak the truth in our society. Oppression, racism, and injustice are observed and experienced throughout the world. When we notice these wrongs do we sneak off, say nothing, or take the easy way out? Can we, on the other hand, muster sufficient courage, strength, and trust, as did Moses, to say the tough word, make the bold move, and take a personal risk, knowing our efforts might not be appreciated?

We must be like Moses, Jesus, and today's prophets and speak the truth. It will not be easy, but then Jesus never said that a

Christian life well led would be a bed of roses. G. K. Chesterton, the famous British writer, commented in his 1910 book, *What's Wrong with the World*, "The Christian ideal has not been tried and found wanting. It has been found difficult and left untried." Let us not be misled. If we live our vocation to holiness well, it will ultimately lead to the cross. But, in the great Christian paradox, it is only through the cross that we will find life. Let us, therefore, be inspired to act and to speak boldly to correct the problems, wrongs, and injustices that we observe. Let us be encouraged and strengthened by Jesus' words, "Know the truth and the truth will make you free" (John 8:32). Amen.

Epiphany 5
Ordinary Time 5
Isaiah 40:21-31

You Are In Good Hands With God

The SS seemed more preoccupied and more disturbed than normal. The idea of executing a young boy in front of hundreds of spectators was no light matter. The commandant of the camp read the verdict. All eyes were on the child. He was extremely pale, almost calm, and he bit his lip. The gallows threw its shadow over him. This time, the Lagerkapo refused to be the executioner. Three SS soldiers replaced him. The three victims were seated next to each other on chairs. A single noose was placed around each man's neck at the same time. The two adults cried, "Long live liberty!" The young boy, however, was silent.

"Where is God? Where is he?" yelled someone behind me in the crowd. When the sign was received from the camp commandant, the three chairs were tipped over by the SS soldiers. Total silence reigned throughout the camp; on the horizon the sun was setting. "Bare your heads!" was the order from the commandant. All in the crowd were weeping. The commandant continued, "Cover your heads." The two adults were no longer alive. Their tongues, swollen and with a blue tinge, hung from their mouths. But the third rope, that bearing the young man, was still moving, for he was still alive. For more than half an hour the young man struggled, with his feet between heaven and earth, life and death, enduring a slow agonizing death before our eyes. We were forced to stay there and watch him the entire time he was still alive. When I passed by him, his tongue was still red and his eyes were not yet glazed. Behind me, I again heard someone cry, "Where is God now?" And then from another part of the camp came the answer: "Where is he? He is here — he is hanging on the gallows."

This powerful true story, told by Holocaust survivor, Elie Wiesel, speaks of the presence of God in those who suffer, in those who seem to have been defeated. The ability to find God in such horrific conditions was precisely the challenge placed before the Hebrews in exile in Babylon. As Isaiah tells his fellow Hebrews in today's first lesson that God's greatness is omnipresent and the Lord is ever faithful, so we in our day must have confidence that God is present at all times, both the good and the bad. We must have confidence that we can live comfortably in the hands of our Lord.

The middle section of the long book of the prophet Isaiah, chapters 40-55, were written at a time of great distress for the Hebrew people, a time, like Wiesel's account, where it appeared God had abandoned his people. Isaiah proclaims God's word to the Hebrews in exile in Babylon. The numerous warnings proclaimed by Isaiah himself, Jeremiah, Obadiah, and Habakkuk had not been heeded. As a result, the Hebrew religious leaders and other influential people of Judaic society found themselves in exile away from their homeland. They may have thought that God had abandoned them. The situation seemed very bleak. Most assuredly, the people were disheartened, if not convinced, that God had deserted them and their fate was permanent.

However, the message of God as proclaimed by Isaiah is not one of warning or doom, as had been proclaimed earlier, but rather one of hope. Logically speaking, one might assume that God's anger or frustration at the inability of his people to maintain the covenant would distance the Lord from his people. From the outset of their exile, God, through the prophet, spoke lovingly to them that they were not abandoned. The prophet proclaims, "Speak tenderly to Jerusalem, and cry to her that she has served her term, that her penalty is paid, that she has received from the Lord's hand double for all her sins" (40:2).

In today's first lesson, Isaiah speaks of the close proximity of God by describing how the Lord is attentive to the actions of his people. The prophet speaks of God who lives in the heavens and brings ruin to those rulers of the earth who think themselves more important than the Lord. It is God who controls the destiny of nations. The nation was planted, but almost immediately the people acted in ways that were inconsistent with the Lord's plan. God's wrath will blow upon a people and they will wither. Nations and the rulers will be carried away as a tempest carries away the stubble. Thus, it is necessary for people to abide by the dictates of the Lord.

Then, in a more positive tone, Isaiah speaks of the greatness of God encouraging people not to be downcast. He says, "Lift up your eyes on high and see ... He who brings out their host and numbers them, calling them all by name; because he is great in strength, mighty in power, not one is missing" (v. 26). In other words, God is with the Hebrews in their exile. They might not understand at the time, but God will not abandon the people. If the Hebrews believed that the Lord was hidden, that God had disregarded the people's plight, the prophet assures them this is not true. Isaiah states, "Have you not known? Have you not heard? The Lord is the everlasting God, the Creator of the ends of the earth. He does not faint or grow weary; his understanding is unsearchable" (v. 28). God gives power and strength to those who are weak and vulnerable. Those who have faith and wait for the Lord will be renewed in strength. Isaiah is very clear, "They shall run and not be weary, they shall walk and not faint" (v. 31b). Yes, God will be present to the people even in the most trying of times.

The experiences of the Hebrews in exile and Elie Wiesel in the Nazi concentration camp serve to challenge us to find the presence of God in all situations, both those that are positive and encouraging and those that are troubling and difficult. Life grows more complex on a daily basis in the twenty-first century. We never seem to be less busy, only more, never do we have fewer responsibilities, only greater. We are so involved with other things that too often God gets lost in the mix. Sometimes we even become estranged from God. Possibly, in our confusion, we may think God is absent — that God has abandoned us. We can feel at times like the Hebrews in exile, as Isaiah describes them, or as the Jews during the time of the Holocaust. This situation might prompt us to go in search of God, perceiving that God is somewhere else, that he is not present with us at the time. However, God is ever present; there is no need to go anywhere to find God. A short story illustrates the point.

There once was a man who had grown weary of life. Bored and looking for something to do, he decided to leave his own hometown, his ancestral village, to search for the perfect Magical City where all would be different, new, full, and very rewarding. On his journey, he found himself in a forest. He settled down for the night, took out his backpack, and began to eat his dinner. Before he went to sleep for the night, he carefully took off his shoes, and pointed them in the new direction toward which he was going. Unknown to him, however, a jokester came during a night while he was asleep and turned his shoes around. When the man awoke the next morning he carefully stepped into his shoes and continued onto the Magical City. After a few days, he arrived at his destination. It was not quite as large as he imagined, in fact it looked somewhat familiar. He found a familiar street, knocked at a familiar door, and met a familiar family. There he lived happily ever after. The story is clear; there is no need to leave your own situation to find the presence of God. All we need to do is be open to the power and presence of the Lord and God will do the rest.

Unfortunately, however, too often we are closed off to God. We don't think God could be concerned about our problems or situations. We perceive our situation to be too small for God's concern. We may feel that we must find a new environment for God, but as Elie Wiesel's true account and our reading from Isaiah demonstrate, the power and presence of God is everywhere. We may think that God is disappointed with us and, thus, rather than reveal himself and reach out, he would rather punish us. In other words, some people live in fear of God. A poignant story demonstrates the fallacy of such an understanding of God.

There once was a young boy who consistently came home from school late. There was no good reason for his tardiness and no amount of discussion and warning from his parents seemed to help. Finally, in desperation, the boy's father sat him down and said, "The next time you come home late from school we are going to give you bread and water for your supper, and nothing else. Is that clear, son?" The boy looked directly into his father's eyes and nodded in the affirmative. He understood perfectly. A few days later, the boy came home even later than usual. His mother met him at the door but didn't say anything. His father met him in the living room, but he said nothing as well. That night, however, when they sat down together for dinner, the boy's heart sank when he saw his father's plate filled with food and his mother's as well, but his own plate contained only a single slice of bread. Next to the plate was a lonely glass of water. The boy stared at the bread and the glass of water. This was the punishment his parents had warned him about. The father waited for the full impact to sink in then quietly he took the boy's plate and placed in front of himself. He then took his own plate and placed in front of his son. The boy understood what the father was saying through his actions. His father was taking upon himself the punishment that he, the boy, had brought upon himself by his own delinquent behavior. Years later, that same boy recalled the incident and said, "All my life I have known what God is like by what my father did that night."

Yes, God is ever present, but we must be open to the power and goodness of God. We may think that God could back out on us, as the Hebrews perceived God had abandoned them during the days of the infamous Babylonian exile. Yet, God, like the famous British poet, Francis Thompson's, immortal, "Hound of Heaven" leaves no stone unturned in a diligent search for souls. Isaiah is clear — God strengthens us in our weakness and lifts our eyes to possibilities. The Pauline author puts it this way: "If we have died with him, we will also live with him; if we endure, we will also reign with him; if we deny him, he will also deny us; if we are faithless, he remains faithful — for he cannot deny himself" (2 Timothy 2:11-13). In short, we must go to God and rest in his company. Amen.

Epiphany 6
Ordinary Time 6
2 Kings 5:1-14

No Litmus Test For Jesus

United States society in 1917 was one filled with much fear and misunderstanding. The end of the Progressive Era and its Social Gospel message of reform, the onset of World War I, and the Bolshevik Revolution raised anxieties in the minds of many Americans. One significant manifestation of this fear was the rise of xenophobia; Americans grew wary of outsiders. The nation, which was built on the sweat and blood of immigrants, now turned its back on these very same people. Beginning as early as 1882, ideas of immigrant restriction had been circulating with the passage of the Chinese Exclusion Act. A decade later, the Immigration Restriction League, founded in Boston in 1894, argued that the best way to keep out "undesirables" was a literacy test. The campaign bore no real fruit at the outset as initiatives passed by Congress in 1896, 1909, and 1915 were vetoed by presidents Cleveland, Taft, and Wilson. However, in 1917, a literacy test bill was again passed and made law over the veto of Wilson. The United States had created a situation where, in essence, immigrants had to pass a litmus test to gain entrance.

The immigration policy of the United States in the wake of World War I, which was capped with the passage of the Johnson-Reed National Origins Act in 1924, presents a situation all too common in human history, personally and communally. Similar situations have existed throughout human history, as we hear clearly articulated in our first lesson today from 2 Kings.

Naaman, a commander of an alien army group, held power and influence, but because he was a leper he was ostracized by all.

Not only were people afraid, due to the contagious nature of this affliction, but people were considered cursed if they fell victim to this malady. Thus, while he was a man of influence, Naaman had no real opportunity because he could not pass the litmus tests that society placed before him. Hebrew society marginalized lepers as did the nation of Aram, from which Naaman came. Victims of leprosy were to be shunned by all, for they would render a person ritually impure if any physical contact was made.

Yet, as we hear in the reading, Elisha, the prophet of God was not in any way afraid of Naaman, but rather offered him a solution to his problem, a cure for his affliction. Initially, Naaman was not impressed by the prophet of God; he wanted some miracle cure. But he was convinced that there was no need for God to act in powerful and miraculous ways, but rather simple and ordinary bathing could be equally effective. Thus, Naaman's cure demonstrates that God has no particular litmus test for people. All that is necessary is that they have the ability to trust and to do what God asks. All are acceptable; none will be rejected, even those outside Israel. God shows no favorites or partiality; there is no litmus test for the Lord.

As the Father showed no partiality toward Naaman, a man afflicted with leprosy, an outsider from the community of Israel, so Jesus of Nazareth accepted all who came to him. No one was rejected; all were accepted. As one who understood human nature very well, Jesus realized human frailty and the tendency we have to make judgments on people in order to measure them. In other words, Jesus understood that we often require people to pass a litmus test before we find them acceptable.

The gospels provide many examples of how Jesus reached out to all. Jesus asked no litmus test for one's physical condition. Saint Luke (17:11-19) describes how Jesus cured ten lepers. Due to purification laws, lepers were ostracized from Jewish society, literally forced to live outside the city. Jesus was not concerned with such laws; what was important to him was meeting the needs of those who asked his assistance. Thus, he did as they asked and cured them all, including one who was a foreigner. Immigrants to Israel and those outside the Jewish community were also rejected by the people of Jesus' day, but again this was no obstacle to the Lord. When a Canaanite woman asked him to cure his daughter he fulfilled her wish, noting that the woman's great faith was the reason for his action (Matthew 15:21-28).

Jesus broke all the taboos of his day by speaking not only to a foreigner, but a woman. His conversation with the Samaritan woman surprised even his apostles, but, as always, Jesus used this incident to teach his apostles the value of being inclusive (John 4:1-42). Again, Jesus demonstrated that he had no specific test that a foreigner must pass in order to gain his attention or help.

Jesus reached out to his own people, but most especially those who, for one reason or another, had been brushed aside by the ruling elite. The Pharisees and scribes often accused Jesus of associating with tax collectors, those who were seen as collaborators with the dreaded Romans, and "sinners." But Jesus gave no apology for his outreach to these people; on the contrary, in some ways he sought them in a preferential way. He chose a tax collector, Matthew, to be a member of his inner circle. He often went to their homes to dine and celebrate. When his actions were questioned, he responded forthrightly, "Those who are well have no need of a physician, but those who are sick; I have come to call not the righteous but sinners" (Mark 2:17).

Jesus synthesized his teaching on acceptance when he said, "Here are my mother and brothers! Whoever does the will of God is my brother and sister and mother" (Mark 3:35). For Jesus all who were willing to follow him were members of his family. Yes, Jesus never required a litmus test for anyone — nor should we!

The Christian community needs to hear the message of Jesus and rethink how it treats people, both as a church and individuals. Acceptance and tolerance must be trademarks of our day-to-day existence, but unfortunately these important virtues are not the hallmarks that characterize our lives. On a communal level we must reject attitudes like those present in early-twentieth-century America and welcome the stranger, the orphan, the widow, and those who are stereotyped as "not welcome."

Too often in our contemporary society we classify the poor, certain races, ethnic groups, or religious denominations with the tag "to be avoided." This pattern has been a persistent problem with human society, but that does not mean it should be tolerated. On the contrary, systemic prejudice in our world can only be eliminated when people first recognize its existence, understand its sinful nature, and resolve to change institutions, laws, and patterns of operation and belief. Such changes do not happen overnight, but as was dramatically demonstrated by the American Civil Rights Movement of the 1960s and more recently, the work of F. W. DeKlerk and Nelson Mandela in South Africa, systemic racial segregation and injustice can be transformed.

The transformation of society into one that is more tolerant and accepting must begin, however, on the individual level and move upward. As the expression goes, one must think globally but act locally. Thus, individual Christians must make the ofttimes perilous inward journey, see the prejudices and ways of exclusion that we practice in our personal lives, and then make every effort to change. We exclude people, consciously and unconsciously, by their appearance, ethnic or national origin, religious persuasion, economic prosperity, or level of education. Whether we realize it or not, the people we encounter, even on a regular basis must often pass a litmus test to be found acceptable. While our admission requirements are not as obvious as passing a literacy test, they are, at times, even more restrictive. Some people are in and others are out in our view of the world. This attitude, however, is inconsistent with the message of Christ who welcomed all, but preferentially sought those who needed him most.

The Christian life is filled with many challenges, most of which we probably would choose to avoid. Yet, it is through the great challenges of life that we learn the most significant lessons. When we are forced to review how we treat others, how we set barriers before them, we come to the realization that we miss so much by excluding others. Diversity is the spice of life, but we will never know how sweet the taste of this diversity will be if we are not willing to take a chance on others. Let us, therefore, not be compromised by the way society categorizes and excludes groups and individuals, but rather break through the barriers that institutions, governments, and even churches place before others. Let us be like Elisha who sent his messenger to Naaman and through his action brought not only healing, but additionally, the power of God. Let us as well take up Christ's work to be a physician to those who need us most. Let us do as the author of the letter to the Hebrews suggests: "Do not neglect to show hospitality to strangers, for by doing that some have entertained angels without knowing it" (Hebrews 13:2). Amen.

Epiphany 7
Ordinary Time 7
Isaiah 43:18-25

The Renewal Of Life

There once was a tree that lived happily in a big forest with many other trees. Occasionally, some of his brother and sister trees were cut down and the tree grieved, but when he discovered that his friends were reborn into some beautiful object that helped human beings, he no longer wept but actually looked forward to his turn to become something beautiful. Before long, a woodcarver came and examined the tree. The carver looked at the tree and imagined a beautiful figurine that could be made from its fine wood. The tree was delighted thinking that someday it would stand in a museum where people from all over the world could come and enjoy its beauty. The tree was so excited it jumped for joy, but just as it did the carver's initial blow came to the tree causing a huge gouge in the wood. The wood-carver looked at the tree and thought that it could no longer serve his function, so he moved on to another tree.

Over the next few weeks and even months, various other woodcarvers came to the forest, looked at the tree but regretfully shook their heads saying, "It is a pity. Such beautiful wood and exceptionally fine grain but now it is good for nothing but to be thrown into the fire." The poor tree wept. All around him he saw his fellow trees being made into beautiful objects but he was good for nothing except to be chopped up and burned. He would die and never live forever as he had hoped.

Then one day, a new carver appeared in the forest. He walked up to the tree sat down and looked at it with great concentration. After some time, he left and went away. Over the next several days, the man returned each day looked at the tree, but said nothing. Finally, one day the man did speak: "I see it now, the shape that you were meant to be." And then the man began to carve. He worked day and night with great passion to see the figure come before him. The tree did not understand what was happening. He had heard over and over again that he was ruined and could never be beautiful but as the new carver continued his work, he began to sense something remarkable was happening. He felt new life surge through his being and finally, one day he emerged, a dancer, caught in precisely the proper moment that the contours of the damaged piece of wood dictated.

The man took his new masterpiece to a museum where all began to marvel at its beauty. Some said the flaw in the tree forced the artist to be more inventive than usual if he had worked with perfect materials. The tree really did not care. All he knew was that he had been renewed, reborn as a dancer, and he danced away to the delight of all who passed by.

The tree learned that it was necessary to move on, not to dwell on the past, but rather to place one's faith in the future. If the tree had concentrated on what happened with the first blow from the original carver, that first mistake, it would never have become a beautiful object to behold. Similarly, God, through the prophet Isaiah, tells the Hebrews in exile and all of us by extension that we must move beyond the past and look to the future. God looks at us today, not yesterday. So too, we must not concentrate on the past, but look to the present and future for others and ourselves.

As we recall from two weeks ago, the middle section of Isaiah, chapters 40-55, was proclaimed to the Hebrews during their infamous fifty-year Babylonian exile. Thus, today's first lesson, drawn from this section of the prophet's words, articulates a similar pastoral scene — the need to not concentrate on the past, but to move to the future. God, speaking through the prophet, is very clear: "Do not remember the former things, or consider the things of old. I am about to do a new thing; now it springs forth, do you not perceive it? I will make a way in the wilderness and rivers in the desert" (Isaiah 43:18-19). God will provide the proper route that will allow us to renew our lives. This certainly must have been a comforting message to the Hebrews since, I suspect, many may have felt lost, as if they were in the wilderness. A sense of lifelessness, like the dryness of the desert, must have been part of the daily experience for those in exile. But a way out of the desert will be provided and the dryness of the land will be vanquished. God will give drink to all his people (43:20c).

God, through Isaiah, then reminds the people of their past. Israel had grown weary of God, for the people had not honored God with sacrifice nor provided any burnt offerings, frankincense, or sweet cane. On the contrary, what the people gave God was the burden of sin; they had wearied God with their iniquities. Yet, even with all of this, God is still able to say to the people: "I, I am he who blots out your transgressions for your own sake, and I will not remember your sins" (43:25).

The concepts of renewal and rebirth, as articulated by the prophet Isaiah, are experienced annually in the rebirth of our world. Many parts of the world experience the delight of spring that brings a sense of hope as it brings new life, color, and vitality to our world. The deadness of winter is vanquished by the brightness of spring. What the world does naturally is a bit more difficult for humans who must overtly strive for renewal in rebirth. This absolute necessity of life will only happen through our effort and initiative; we cannot find renewal or rebirth by simply assuming it will happen. On the contrary, we must be proactive to find a special renewal that is necessary for our world and ourselves.

The image of spring, coupled with the message of Isaiah and the story of the tree should challenge us to seek renewal in our lives. We must first seek renewal in our human relationships. We must work harder and be more persistent in those relationships that are most important and fundamental — with our spouse, children, parents, and other close relatives. If a relationship has been damaged or strained, it needs our attention. If we have been neglectful toward others, we must do what is necessary to meet our responsibilities.

Some may require renewal in our work, both our occupations and the things that keep us busy on a day-to-day basis. Why do we do what we do? Are we working for ourselves alone or for the common good? Is our daily work a nine-to-five period of time that simply puts food on the table and pays the other bills or do we find relevance and satisfaction in our efforts? Can we say we are making a difference? The attitude we take at work is often critically important to transfer what might otherwise be a humdrum and monotonous task into one that has life and becomes a ministry toward others.

Possibly we need to renew our personal health. Most of us take our health for granted until something goes wrong. As God told the Hebrews through Isaiah in today's first lesson and as the tree learned, it is necessary to forget the past and move ahead. With respect to our health this might mean to eat better, sleep a bit more, and exercise more regularly. In short, it means taking care of the body that God gave to us and to be stewards of our health. We need to do the best with what God has given to us. Only in such a way will we be able to maximize our potential as workers in the vineyard of the Lord.

There is no question that all of us need to renew our lives of faith and especially our relationship with God. This is precisely the renewal that Yahweh sought with the people of Judah. God acknowledged the sin of the people, yet the past was to be forgotten; the transgressions and sins of the people were to be remembered no more. Jesus had similar ideas as clearly demonstrated in the New Testament. We recall Jesus' encounter with a woman "caught in the act of adultery" (John 8:21-11). Jesus did not condemn the woman but told her to go and sin no more. In other words, Jesus was telling her to forget the past and move on to the future. In a more general sense, Jesus understood the human tendency to be trapped by the past. Thus, when Jesus raised his friend Lazarus from the dead, he told those who witnessed this great event, "Unbind him, and let him go" (John 11:44b). God wishes for us to live in freedom. We must let go of our past transgressions against others and forgive those who have transgressed against us. The Lord's Prayer says it all: "Forgive us our trespasses as we forgive those who trespass against us."

Sometimes we are hesitant to let go of the past in any way. When this happens we are held back, whether we know it or not, and do not allow ourselves to go forward. It is as if we had a ball and chain attached to our leg that weighs us down and slows our progress. We need to break the chain and not allow the weight of the past to impede us any longer.

To find the courage to renew our lives and not be fearful of letting go are not easy prospects. A true story about the great American inventor, Thomas Alva Edison, can show us what the goal should be. In December 1914, Edison's laboratory was virtually destroyed by a fire. Although the damage exceeded $2 million, the buildings were only insured for approximately $250,000, because they were made of concrete and thought to be fireproof. Much of Edison's work went up in that spectacular December blaze. When the fire was raging, Edison's 24-year-old son, Charles, was frantically searching for his father among the chaos. He found him calmly watching the scene, his face glowing in the reflection and his white hair blowing in the wind. Charles commented, "My heart ached for him. He was 67 — no longer a young man — and everything he knew was going up in flames." The next morning, Edison looked at the ruins of his laboratory and exclaimed, "There is great value in disaster. All our mistakes are burned up. Thank God we can start anew." Amazingly, only three weeks after the fire, Edison delivered to the world the first phonograph. Thomas Edison understood the need to let go.

After the woodcarver's initial mistake, the tree thought all was lost, but he learned that with patience great things were possible. It was necessary to let go of the past in order to reach for the future. Similarly, the Hebrews needed to let go so God could guide them to a new day. We, too, must let go and God will provide us with a new day as well. Do we have the faith necessary to drop the past and move on to the future? Only you can answer! Amen.

Epiphany 8
Ordinary Time 8
Hosea 2:14-20

Reconciliation — The Heart Of Love

Have you ever taken a course of action or held a particular attitude, all the while thinking that it was correct and then never giving it another thought? That is what happened with Ludovico Gadda, Pope Leo XIV. Ludovico was born in a small Italian town, like many of the popes, all from Italy, who have occupied the Chair of Saint Peter since the time of the Council of Trent in the sixteenth century. It seemed that Ludovico was destined for ministry and priesthood from his earliest days. He was ordained and lived a very traditional life as a parish priest. He lived by the canons and doctrines of the faith. Ludovico was good at what he did. Thus, he was made bishop of the diocese. Later he was moved to a larger metropolitan area and was made archbishop. Still later he was made a cardinal and finally he was elected pope. The people in Ludovico's hometown were not surprised by the course of events.

Upon assuming the Chair of Peter, Ludovico, who took the name of Leo XIV, was invested with much power and authority. The power he held was beneficial to some but it was highly detrimental to others. Like all of us, the pope had an agenda. He took a course of action; he held certain attitudes and opinions. The problem was that he never reflected on his actions and attitudes. He never considered the possibility that he was hurting others by what he did or thought.

What would it take him to change? For Ludovico it would be a bout with serious illness. Chest pains landed the pope in the hospital. Doctors told him he needed heart bypass surgery. The thought of such major surgery placed the pope in a more contemplative mood. He began to think about his life and what he had done. He began to realize that he might have hurt others. He knew that he needed to change, to find healing, forgiveness, and reconciliation. But for Pope Leo XIV, it would be too late. His inability to look into his heart would prove fatal. The very people he had hurt before he had the opportunity to change his ways would assassinate him.

So goes, in summary, the last of Morris West's fictional trilogy of novels that describes popes and faith. The name of the book is *Lazarus*. Morris West's tale illustrates the important message of our need to look into our hearts, see if wrong has been done and then seek forgiveness and reconciliation if needed, but always knowing that forgiveness and God's love are ever present, all we need do is be open. God will do the rest. In today's first lesson from the prophet Hosea, we hear a message of God's invitation to be reconciled, but we must respond.

Hosea proclaimed God's word to the northern kingdom of Israel some 750 years before Christ. Like his associate, Amos, Hosea spoke of God's displeasure with the people, namely the religious elite of Israel. Whereas Amos complained of social injustice, railing against the oppression of the poor and the complacency of the rich, Hosea's message is one of scandal and idolatry. At the outset of the book, Hosea is told to marry Gomer, "a wife of whoredom." This marriage is a metaphor for how Israel abandoned Yahweh and sought its sustenance in idolatrous conduct, especially association with the Baals. The prophet speaks of God's disappointment at the ingratitude of the Hebrews. After all God had done for them — calling the people, making them a covenant or chosen race, rescuing them from slavery, providing the law, giving them victory over their enemies, and settling the people on the land — still the people seek other gods than Yahweh.

In today's lesson specifically, Hosea, after speaking of future punishment, proclaims another message from the Lord. God will give the people another chance; he seeks reconciliation with them. God will speak tenderly to Israel and give her new vineyards. God will provide hope. The people will be renewed as they were after their escape from bondage in Egypt. Additionally, God says through the prophet that he will once again be husband to Israel; the name of Baal will be removed. God will make a covenant to abolish the things of war and create peace. The people will lie down in safety. God will once again take Israel as his wife: "And I will take you for my wife for ever; I will take you for my wife in righteousness and in justice, in steadfast love, and in mercy. I will take you for my wife in faithfulness; and you shall know the Lord" (Hosea 2:19-20). In a very real way, God is holding out hope that Israel will once again return and be the nation that it was intended to be. Reconciliation is always possible. God has made the first step; now Israel must respond.

When considering the concept of reconciliation from the perspective of the church, most folks, I suspect, think of Lent. Surely it is an important theme of this most holy season of preparation that lies ahead of us. Reconciliation must be an ongoing daily effort — our need to return to God, and to receive forgiveness, while, at the same time, reaching out to others as God has reached out to us. We must forgive others, starting with ourselves.

The prophet Joel writes, "Rend your hearts and not your clothing. Return to the Lord, your God, for he is gracious and merciful, slow to anger, and abounding in steadfast love, and relents from punishing" (Joel 2:13). God continually seeks our return. The Lord wants us and thus leaves no stone unturned in a diligent search for us. Like Francis Thompson's epic poem says, God is the "Hound of Heaven" who seeks our souls. We must be open to his search; we must cooperate. God will not come where he is not welcome. God's favor rests on those who call upon his name. We have been granted this great privilege because the Jews did not deem God's plan acceptable.

Saint Paul puts it this way in his letter to the Ephesians: "In former generations this mystery was not made known to humankind, as it is now been revealed to his holy apostles and prophets by the Spirit: that is, the Gentiles have become fellow heirs, members of the same body, and sharers in the promise in Christ Jesus through the gospel" (Ephesians 3:5-6). As inheritors of God's great gifts, we must be open to the invitation of reconciliation that he places before us. To take any other route would mean losing the opportunity of a lifetime. We must respond in love to the God who first loved us.

The New Testament is filled with many stories and images about the need to be reconciled. We recall when Peter asked the Lord how many times it was necessary to forgive, thinking seven times would be more than sufficient. But Jesus said to him, "Not seven times, but, I tell you seventy-seven times" (Matthew 18:22). Of course, Jesus' response in essence says that we must be able to forgive an infinite number of times. As God stands willing and ready to forgive us, so in a similar way we must be ready to forgive others. Some may fear that they have responded too late to Jesus' invitation, but the parable of the workers in the vineyard (Matthew 20:1-16) tells us that it is never too late to accept God's invitation. Many of us, like the workers in the parable who accept the invitation early in life, seem to think we have received an affront if we do not get more than those who come in at a later hour, but the boundless and great mercy of God extends to all people. As the parable states, if God chooses to be merciful to others, that is not our concern. We are to do the best we can and leave judgment up to God.

It is certainly true, God is just waiting for us to return. God is like the father in the parable of the prodigal son, who patiently waits for his son, never giving up hope that he will one day return. There is nothing that cannot be forgiven, nothing that cannot be overcome by God's love. A dramatic example of this is the drama played out in chapter 21 of Saint John's gospel. We recall in the early morning hours of Good Friday Peter fulfilled the prophecy that Jesus had articulated at the Last Supper only a few hours earlier. After denying the Lord three times he was devastated and wept bitterly (Luke 22:62). He realized he'd betrayed his best friend. After the resurrection, Jesus allowed his chosen chief disciple to redeem his earlier denials for three affirmations of love. John wrote, "When they had finished breakfast, Jesus said to Simon Peter, 'Simon son of John, do you love me more than these?' " (John 21:15b). When Peter responded in the affirmative, Jesus repeated the question twice more and received the same response. Certainly, Peter had to understand Jesus' reason for asking and how reconciliation was in a very real way affected at that moment. Even if we deny the Lord, Jesus will welcome us back with open arms.

As God has been merciful and compassionate toward us, we must be merciful and compassionate to each other. People make mistakes; it is part of being human. Thus, sometimes we will hurt or offend others and others will hurt us. We must move beyond this initial step, admit our mistakes, the errors of our way, our sins, and then we can begin to move forward. We cannot live in the past. Holding a grudge against others keeps them at a distance for no logical reason. Can any of us imagine if God acted in such a way with any of us? What would we do if we felt that God was selective in his forgiveness and reconciliation? God's message of love and reconciliation goes out to all people for all times. If we are to be followers of Jesus, then our attitude and actions must emulate what he has taught us. We should never follow the example of the elder boy in the prodigal son story. He held a grudge against his brother and, it seems, his father as well. On the contrary, reconciliation is necessary not only to create harmony, but also to allow us to grow so we can be the people Lord calls us and wants us to be.

In Morris West's novel, *Lazarus*, the protagonist discovers too late his need to be reconciled. His sudden death leaves reconciliation unattained; an open chasm will never be filled. Let's not wait until it is too late but rather act now, knowing that Jesus is waiting for us to accept his invitation. This special call from the Lord is aptly depicted in a famous painting and a popular verse of scripture that provides both the challenge and the answer for us. In the National Gallery of London, there is a painting by Hans Holbein with which many are familiar. Jesus stands in a garden and he is knocking on the front door of a little cottage. Everything is normal in the scene except one small but important detail. There is no doorknob for Jesus is knocking on the door of our hearts. What the painting shows pictorially, Revelation describes: "Here I stand, knocking at the door. If anyone hears me calling and opens the door, I will enter his house and have supper with him, and he with me" (Revelation 5:20).

Yes, the "Hound of Heaven," our God, is knocking on the door of our hearts. Let us today respond to the knock of the Lord; let us open the door to our hearts and find reconciliation. Let us have dinner with Jesus and he with us, today and to life everlasting. Amen.

The Transfiguration Of Our Lord
(Last Sunday After Epiphany)
2 Kings 2:1-12

Commissioned For Christ

On a warm and sunny early June day in 1943, John Francis Laboon, "Jake" to his friends, stood with his Naval Academy classmates on Warden Field; it was graduation day. These men were the class of 1944, but because of World War II raging in both the Pacific and European theaters, and thus need of their presence in the fleet, the class was "accelerated" one year in its training. A rough and tumble young man from the steel town of Pittsburgh, Jake had come to the academy in the summer of 1940. He excelled in athletics. During his tenure he earned the honor of an all-east selection as tight end on the academy's football team and led the lacrosse squad to the national championship in 1943, by his selection as an All-American defenseman.

The athletic heroics and even the regimen of the Academy would have to be memories, however, as it was not only graduation day, but the date the class was commissioned for service as officers in the Navy and Marine Corps. Jake and his classmates raised their right hands and took the oath of office from the Secretary of the Navy, pledging themselves to service of country and "to defend and protect the Constitution of the United States." Jake had been training for this moment for three years — academically, professionally, physically, and spiritually. Now was the hour for him to accept his commission, apply the talents and gifts he had nurtured and acquired, and to do the work for which he had been trained.

After graduation, Jake reported to the Naval Submarine School in New London, Connecticut. After a short training period, he was sent west to Pearl Harbor to his assignment onboard the *USS Peto.*

As a junior officer, he distinguished himself in completing five war patrols, and winning the Silver Star for gallantry when he rescued a downed naval aviator in Japanese-held waters. In June 1946, Jake was transferred from the *Peto* and three months later, with the whole US military in stand down after the war, he resigned his commission in the Navy. God was calling Jake Laboon to another commission.

In 1949, after contemplating the diocesan priesthood for a couple of years, he entered the Jesuit novitiate at Woodstock, Maryland. He was ordained a priest in 1956 and two years later in 1958, after having finished a doctorate in theology, received permission from his religious superiors to return to the Navy as a chaplain. Beginning with his first duty station at Patuxent River Naval Air Station, Jake Laboon served as a Navy chaplain, completing an illustrious career. He traveled far and wide and met many people. Some of his most noteworthy duty stations were a return to his alma mater, the Naval Academy from 1966-1969, chaplain to the staff, Commander-in-Chief US Pacific fleet from 1972-1975, and just before his retirement in 1980, service as force chaplain, Commander-in-Chief US Atlantic Fleet.

Upon retirement, Jake took up a new commission when he joined the staff of the Jesuit retreat house staff at Manresa on the Severn in Annapolis. With the Naval Academy visible from his bedroom window, Jake Laboon touched the hearts of thousands as a retreat master and confessor. In 1988, he was assigned as pastor of St. Alphonsus Church in Woodstock. There, after a short illness, he died. Because of his wide-ranging and high-profile assignments, as well as his dedication and commitment to God and country, Jake Laboon was without question the best-known and most widely respected chaplain in the US fleet. The commissioning of the *USS Laboon* in 1994, only the second American ship ever dedicated in the name of a chaplain, demonstrates his contribution and the appreciation of others. Jake Laboon was a man who accepted his commission, applied his talents, and served God and country.

Jake Laboon followed the call of the Lord. Over the course of his life, he served his country, God, and then most prominently God and country as a chaplain in the United States Navy. He took the baton as a Naval officer and priest and ran with it a good leg of the relay race of life. His inspiring work now allows that same baton to be passed to many others in the service of their nation, church, and God. As we celebrate the Transfiguration of the Lord, when the three "super apostles," Peter, James, and John are privileged to witness the physical transformation of Christ, we see how these men were commissioned by Jesus to go forward and continue his work. We, in turn, contemporary apostles of Lord, are called to do the same.

Although he has no book of prophecy in his name, Elijah was one of the great prophets to the northern kingdom of Israel. His ministry was significant and it centered itself about rooting out evil in the hearts of people. His commission began as a mission of mercy and compassion. He was sent to the widow of Zarephath (1 Kings 17:8-16) to assure her that God had noted her faith and that she and her son would not die due to the great famine in the land. Elijah was next sent to challenge King Ahab and his wife, Jezebel. He knew what was in their hearts and tried to help them see the errors of their ways, but they would not listen. Next, the prophet was sent to challenge those loyal to Baal. Elijah proved Yahweh's superiority over Baal and then had all the prophets of the false gods slaughtered (1 Kings 18:20-40). Lastly, Elijah was once again sent to Ahab to inform him of God's displeasure at his action in wresting Naboth's garden from its rightful owner (1 Kings 21:1-29).

In today's first lesson, as the mission of Elijah draws to a close, we hear how his commission was passed on to his successor, Elisha. Elijah had done well in his ministry; he, like Jake Laboon, had run his leg of the race well. Now it was time for him to pass the baton and Elisha was ready. As we heard in the reading, three times Elijah tells his young protégé that he is to stay while the master moves on, but the young disciple wants to share with his master, the prophet, in all respects. His devotion to Elijah is laudable, but possibly more importantly is his desire to follow in Elijah's footsteps. He requests a double portion of the prophet's mantle, a sure sign of his desire to continue the prophetic ministry. When Elisha witnesses the prophet's rise to the heavens on a flaming chariot, he knows his wish shall be granted for he has the promise of God.

Elisha willingly accepted the commission that God gave to him. In fact, in a very real way he sought the commission. He wanted to serve Yahweh, to be his agent among the people. He must have realized his ministry would not be easy. On the contrary, if the experience of his mentor, Elijah, was any example at all, it would mean his future life would be very difficult. It would require him to go places he might not want to go, to encounter people and situations that he might wish to avoid, to perform tasks that might be distasteful and very difficult. He confidently continued to seek the Lord. Elisha wished to be God's prophet, his messenger in a troubled world.

Like the commission of Elisha, today's celebration of the Transfiguration of our Lord is a special time for us to consider our own commission to be holy people and to do God's work in this world. We recall the story of the Transfiguration event. Jesus took his three so-called "super apostles" to the mountain and there he was transfigured before them. Some scripture scholars believe that this event was actually a post-resurrection story that was placed at this point in the synoptic gospels for effect. The fact that all three synoptic writers, Matthew, Mark, and Luke, narrate this event — one of the few so mentioned by all three evangelists — is clear evidence of its significance. What happened on that mountain? Jesus was, for a short period of time, transformed in his external appearance. The scene must have been quite surreal. More importantly, however, what happened to Peter, James, and John? This is the central question.

Most assuredly, the three apostles were transformed as well, but on the inside to a new and permanent understanding of Christ and their role in his kingdom. From this time forward, these apostles could no longer see Jesus as a mere human being, for they realized they had been chosen to witness this apparition for a special reason. They were being prepared for their future commission. They were to teach their brothers and the other faithful about what they had seen and heard. They were, thus, commissioned to go forward and proclaim the message of Christ. As surely as Jake Laboon received multiple commissions to country, God, and God and country, and as Elisha took the mantle of Elijah, so we must take our responsibility as baptized Christians to go forth do God's work in our world.

Since Christ's work would not be completed before he left the world, he prepared the apostles for their future work in furthering the kingdom that he initiated. When Jesus sent the apostles forward to finish the task, they had all the assistance they needed. As the Acts of the Apostles (2:1-11) says in describing the Pentecost story, Jesus fulfilled his earlier promise and sent the Holy Spirit. It was the Spirit of God, who dispelled doubt and fear in the hearts and minds of those first disciples. The Spirit was very powerful, giving the apostles and others the ability to do things which they were not educated to do, namely to speak many foreign tongues. Most importantly, however, it was the power of the Spirit that empowered the apostles to accept their earlier commission and go forward to complete Christ's work. Jesus knew that the task would be difficult. Twelve followers and a cadre who would follow them could not do it. The work would take all God's children and thus the gifts given to accomplish the task were many. Saint Paul tells us in 1 Corinthians 12:3-13 that we have received multiple gifts. All of the gifts, however, have one source — the Holy Spirit — and all have one ultimate purpose — to complete Christ's work on earth.

We have all been commissioned and, like Jake Laboon, the commissions probably have been multiple. Possibly, we did not know it at the time but our baptism was our first commission. We became a member of the body of Christ. Baptism gave us some great privileges, such as the name Christian and the opportunity to experience the power of the Christian message in our lives. The commission of baptism also gave us responsibilities, the most important of which is to be builders of God's kingdom on earth. There are many other commissions. Marriage is a vital commission. Married couples are commissioned to act in Christian love and mutual fidelity, and to work together always, two acting as one. Many professions have commissions. Doctors take the Hippocratic Oath;

attorneys swear that they will uphold the law and fight for the rights of their clients with all their skill. Teachers agree not only to impart knowledge, but also to give good example. Graduation is a commission. Graduates finish one aspect of life, but they begin a whole new adventure. That is why such events are called commencements. Graduates must take the skills that have been honed and tested and the new ones that have been recently acquired and use them in their new work, in order to one day make a positive contribution to human society.

Jake Laboon heard God's call in his life, first to naval service, later to the priesthood, and still later to a new commission to the service of both God and nation. He was a limited person, as are all humans, but he was one who accepted his multiple commissions, applied his talents, and did his best to do what God asked of him. Our own commission will be different, but it has the same purpose. Christ's mission was incomplete when he left our world. We, the Master's disciples, must complete his great work. Let us, therefore, accept our commission, as professional, as student, as parent, but most especially as Christian. Let us apply our talents and gifts and do what we can to complete Christ's work. Let us build the city of God this day! Amen.

Sermons On The First Readings

For Sundays
In Lent And Easter

God, The Good Ally

Ken Lentz

Ash Wednesday
Joel 2:1-2, 12-17

Let The Shofar Sound!

The school bell rings. The noonday siren sounds. The church bells call the faithful to worship. In the fifties, the wail of the sirens urged American citizenry to take cover from a potential imminent atomic attack; children took position beneath their desks and those at home headed to the bomb shelter in the basement.

The book of the prophet Joel urges the trumpeter to sound the shofar, translated "trumpet," (v. 1) to warn that "... the day of the Lord is coming, it is near...." The "shofar" was usually a ram's horn but it could be the horn of any clean animal except that of a cow. It was used in the feast prescribed in Numbers 29:1, the feast of New Year's Day, "Rosh Hashanah." The shofar, sounding mornings and evenings except on the sabbath, called the faithful to prayerful preparation for the great feast.

Most experts agree that Joel was a cult prophet who felt himself aligned to the postexilic temple rebuilt in the Persian period, probably between 400-350 BC. A plague of locusts and drought are signs pointing to the imminent catastrophe. The day of the Lord will hardly occur unnoticed. God's judgment will be accompanied by an army that will "scorch the earth" (2:3-9) following earthquakes below and chaos in heaven above (2:10). Jewish scriptural tradition pointed to a time between the present era and the era to come. At that "kairos" point, "the sun shall be turned to darkness, and the moon to blood" (2:31). Joel's warning is mirrored in Isaiah (13:10, 13) and the prophet Zephaniah accentuates Joel's gloom-and-doom message with distress, anguish, ruin, and devastation (1:14-18).

Modern disaster films do a good job at communicating Joel's point. Joel's day of the Lord is in our time heralded by the shofar sounding an all-out nuclear war, a global warming catastrophe, or a meteor heading straight for New York City. Today's shofars are sounding in the Middle East, in pest and genocide-ridden Africa, and in the crime-infested dark ghetto corners of American cities. For some reason, Joel assumes that his people can hear the shofar. The glitz and glamour, the fast pace driven by cell phone communication, and the violence and hedonism promoted by television and film make it difficult for Americans to hear the blast of the shofar.

Ash Wednesday is the moment to turn up the shofar's volume. The noise and rush of Shrove Tuesday is over. The day that begins the journey of Lent has begun. The excess of Mardi Gras is silenced. The day to clean up the party trash left on the carnival streets has come. It's time to begin the shadowy and solemn walk through the dark streets of Jerusalem to the place of death and execution. The shofar sounds the wake-up call. It's time to get down to the serious business of repentance, fasting, penance, confession, and amends. The shofar sounds the beginning of the march to the hangman's noose. It's not a pretty picture.

However, the shofar sounds again! It has a different ring, a different tone! Oh yes, the terrible day of the Lord is coming! There is no escape! Now the shofar strikes a new note: "Yet even now, says the Lord, return to me with all your heart, with fasting, with weeping, and with mourning! ... Return to the Lord, your God, for he is gracious and merciful, slow to anger, and abounding in steadfast love, and relents from punishing" (Joel 2:12-14). Hear the new song! Your God relents from punishing!

Whether symbolically or actually, Ash Wednesday is the day to place the ashes upon our foreheads. Symbolically or actually, we step forward to the altar to confess our repentance and our desire to show God and our communities that we are willing to have our hearts cleansed.

First of all, we confess that we really want to be better human beings, that we want to love God and love our neighbors. We would gladly rend our garments if that would do any good but, more importantly, we are willing to rend our hearts. Our desire must be sincere. The road to a broken marriage is usually paved with insincere promises.

A pastor once visited a parishioner just returned home from the hospital. He noticed a picture on her wall. "I know that young man," he said. "He's a bagger at the supermarket. He always has a smile on his face and he is friendly and courteous to all of the customers." The parishioner replied, "That's my nephew, Andrew. He's in a heap of trouble. He was caught three times in three different towns driving under the influence of alcohol and in possession of illegal drugs. He's in a halfway house now awaiting sentencing. Pastor, would you mind visiting him?"

When the pastor arrived at the halfway house, Andrew was sitting outside in the garden on a bench with his head held low. The pastor wondered about the reception he would get. Had the aunt alerted Andrew about the visit? The pastor walked up and started, "Hello, Andrew, your aunt asked me to visit you...." Andrew sprung to his feet and wrapped his arms around the visitor. He sobbed and heaved without apology. Without the need for Andrew to verbalize his intentions, the pastor knew that Andrew had made a decision to change his life.

With the support of his new friend, Andrew completed a short time of incarceration, managed to travel to and from his place of employment without benefit of an auto license for one year, complete the obligations of parole, retrieve the right to drive, find a lovely lady to marry, and repeat his marriage vows at a garden wedding presided over, of course, by his pastor friend. Andrew became an electrician and was quickly promoted by his company to the rank of foreman. He embraced a new life as a husband and a father. Drugs and alcohol were no longer in the picture. His repentance was sincere. He heeded the call of the shofar. He stepped up to receive the ashes on his forehead and unabashedly wore his new life on his shirtsleeve.

Secondly, we rend our hearts before God's Ash Wednesday altar as a sign of willingness to accept God's grace. In penitential humility, we return to the Lord who is gracious and merciful. We will show all people that the God of grace is our God.

During the Spanish-American War, Colonel Teddy Roosevelt commanded a regiment of "Rough Riders" in Cuba. He was closely attached to his men and was quite concerned when many of them became ill. He heard that Clara Barton had received a supply of food for the soldiers in Teddy's area. Roosevelt immediately requested that she sell a portion of it to him for his sick men. He was troubled when his request to buy the supplies was denied.

Roosevelt went to Clara personally and asked, "How can I get the provisions I need? I must have proper food for my sick soldiers!" Clara Barton replied, "Just ask for it, Colonel. It's yours for the asking." "Oh," said Roosevelt, "that's the way it is. All right then, I hereby ask for it." The food was immediately sent to the hospital where the Rough Riders lay sick.

It takes humility and grace to wear the ashes.

Thirdly, the penitent are those who see the cross behind the veil of Lent, beyond the shadows of Good Friday. A minister, shortly after he moved into the parsonage in a country parish, visited one of his families for dinner. By the time he said his good-byes, a snowstorm had covered the countryside. The host family suggested that he stay the night. He politely turned down the invitation, knowing that the way back to the parsonage was only about three miles. He cautiously traversed the snow-covered road. The headlights of his car were reflected in the densely fallen snow and visibility was effectively nonexistent. He barely managed to stay on the road. After some minutes of travel, he realized that he had missed his turn and had no idea about his location. He peered forward into the night and was sure that he would at some point veer off the path. Suddenly, he realized that there was a light ahead of him beyond the wall of snow. He drove slowly toward the light until the light was above him directly to his right. He opened the window and recognized a barnyard light he had passed before. He knew where he was and returned to take the turn he had missed.

The day of Ash Wednesday is not too early to fix one's compass on the cross. Like the North Star, the cross atop the hill of Calvary beckons us forward.

A painting adorning a sixteenth-century altar in a thirteenth-century church close to Hamburg, Germany, portrays the donor of the painting climbing a trail, staff in hand. Atop a hill in the distance to the left of the painting is the cross. The hill is cast in dark shadows. The traveler must pass through the darkness ahead. But the outline of the precipice is clearly visible. There is a source of light beyond and behind it. The traveler must press forward into the gloom, but he and the viewer see the brightness beyond.

Ash Wednesday is the portal through which we pass to begin our Lenten journey. We pass slowly around the plots, the betrayal, the condemnations, the suffering of the one who beckons us follow him. We have six weeks to make the journey. Will we reaffirm our devotion to him or will we have failed him when the cock crows three times? To which signal will we respond? The signal of the shofar or the signal of the cock? The shofar once accompanied the victory at Jericho. Now it calls us forward to the light. Jesus was victorious; he descended the lower hill in order to ascend to the light above. Bathed in light that is almost blinding, the angels call us forward to him. Amen.

Lent 1
Genesis 9:8-17

Troubled Waters

A man from Johnstown, Pennsylvania, died and went to heaven. Saint Peter was directing the activities and explained to him, "Each Friday we have a get-together for the new members. To break the ice, every new member must make a speech to all the others here, on any subject desired." The man from Johnstown said, "I think I'll talk on the Johnstown flood." Saint Peter replied, "I think it's all right but I'd better warn you; Noah will be in the audience."

The story of Noah's ark has its origins in ancient history, but the story itself did not take on its present form in the literature of the Hebrews until the time of a literary renaissance during the reigns of David and Solomon about 1000 BC. The writers of the story seem to have recast an ancient story told by the Sumerians and Mesopotamians. In fact, there is a tablet dating from about that time found in the Tigris-Euphrates river valley that tells the story of a man named Utnapishtim who, having been warned by one of his gods (Ea), builds an ark and experiences the same adventure as Noah in the Old Testament version.

There are striking differences between the Genesis account and the other ancient-world traditions. The Hebrew account uniquely confesses that there is only one God and that this one God is not capricious but judiciously measured in his interaction with humans. The Hebrew God causes the flood in order to accomplish his righteous purpose. Unlike the ancient gods of Israel's neighbors, he displays solicitous concern for his human creatures. His justice demands that he punish the wicked people of the earth, but his attribute of mercy is manifested in his act of salvation for Noah and his family in order that the human race might be continued. Israel's God, in the story, wants to spare the innocent and extend his mercy not only to a few righteous humans but to the entire creation.

The story of Noah and the ark is not only the story of a just God but also of a gracious God. The story is used over and over again in nursery schools across the land. Many children are familiar with the famous ark and all the beautiful animals that were saved from the waters of the flood.

According to the story, all of humankind was confronted by the horror of a universal deluge, and all humans were destroyed by waters that were more than troubled (they were catastrophic) except Noah. His confrontation with watery death led to the victory of a fresh start on planet earth and the experience of reconciliation with a God who did not give up on his project humanity.

Noah did not save himself. He had no greater ability to tread water than anyone else. In fact, he had no idea about how to build a ship. God was the engineer in the project. Without the intervention of God, Noah would have drowned along with all the other rats. Noah's righteousness would have been of no avail in the swarming and swirling waters. A lot of good people went down with the *Titanic*. All of us, the good and the bad, are threatened with extinction in the troubled waters of our lives.

In a totally unpredictable way, for Noah and the animals, the waters of destruction turned out to be the waters of salvation. The gray clouds parted to reveal a silver lining, which issued forth into a glorious rainbow! And the animals were included!

One account (not in the Bible) reports a conversation that Noah had with a gorilla boarding the ark. Noah asked, "Where is your mate?" The gorilla answered, "I was hoping to meet her on the ark. I have heard that a cruise is a good place to find a wife!" That silly story makes a point. The flood story is about the salvation of all life on earth. Somehow it all worked out; the gorilla species is with us today. The gorilla did more than meet his mate. He met his future; he met his salvation. The whole creation was back on track heading for its destiny. The gorilla would see the lamb lay beside the lion.

In classic theological constructions, the ark story is the second of four covenants with God. The first is the covenant with Adam and Eve: They would have dominion over the works of God's creation. The second is with Noah: God would not destroy the earth with water again. The third is with Abraham: God would guarantee that Abraham's descendents would survive and prevail. The fourth is with Moses: God gave to Israel a sacred charter to guide them.

Is that it? No. There is a fifth covenant: the new covenant, the New Testament, the new salvation wrought in the person and ministry of Jesus Christ. Whosoever believes in him will not perish but have everlasting life.

God has placed a rainbow in our sky as a sign that floods would never again cover the whole earth. The rainbow is a bridge over troubled waters. The rainbow of the Old Testament has become the bridge of the New Testament. Jesus is indeed the bridge over the troubled waters of our lives.

A true story about the Nazi occupation of Denmark records the plight of Danish Jews. Just as they did in all their "conquered" lands, the Nazis tightened their grip slowly on the Jews of Denmark. Finally, the Jews learned that they were to be rounded up on Rosh Hashanah, the Jewish New Year. They had only two days to flee and disappear. Seven thousand were arrested and placed in internment camps. Five thousand who were able to hide or flee miraculously survived the war. One group went by boat in the middle of the night across the Oresund Straits to ports in free Sweden. It is hard to imagine the immensity of their fear as they boarded those boats, as they crossed the choppy water in the dead of night, as they anticipated detection at any moment by Nazi scouting boats. They reached the other side — they reached safety, new life, and salvation.

We all know what it's like to venture into troubled waters. Sometimes we willingly place our boats into the water. We begin courses at college; we give up the security of an old job for the uncertainty of a new career; we take marriage vows; we charter a course for parenthood. Sometimes we begin a journey that we do not wish. A relationship begins to spiral downward; we lose our job; the physician spots cancer in our body; a loved one suddenly is lost to death.

In the beginning, the embryo church sailed in choppy seas. She was persecuted, mocked, accused of being disloyal to the state, and charged with barbarianism. But she survived and prospered.

The liturgical name of the portion of the church where worshipers sit is the "nave," derived from the Latin word for ship whence we get our word, "navy." The meeting place for worship reminds us that we travel as a community of travelers, a great company of sailors, past, present, and future, of every race, age, and class.

Many churches in northern Europe display ship models in their entries or in their naves. There are about 1,300 church ships hung in Denmark alone. They were donated by sailors' groups for decoration, perhaps given in memory of departed loved ones, or perhaps given as a thank offering for survival at sea. They also serve as a metaphor for the universal church. Those on board the ship of the church must weather storms, waves, and tumult. But the ship of the church will reach the shore beyond; the church will weather the storm; the church will come to safe harbor.

The mast of the ship is the cross. Our Lord is at the helm. As he stilled the storm on the Sea of Galilee (Mark 4:35-41), so will he guide us through the tempests of our lives.

A newly ordained young pastor at his first parish in rural northwest Ohio was encouraged by the enthusiastic support of the youth group. He enrolled himself and some of the high school students in a seven-day sailing trip in a 55-foot ketch in the Bahamas. The trip sounded like a horizon-expanding experience for himself and the students, among whom none had ever seen an ocean.

All went well until Betty, one of the adult counselors, on the way to Miami, bravely rose in the darkness of the morning in the host home in Atlanta to brush her teeth; not wishing to disturb the sleepers in the house, she brushed with shampoo from a tube that felt like a toothpaste tube in the dark bathroom. In mid-afternoon, Betty and the others arrived at the Port of Miami to board the boat. Betty was not feeling well.

The group gathered in the cockpit of the vessel, aptly named *Shark VII*, to hear the captain's briefing. Betty was putting up a brave front. The high school students sat in the hot sun and learned about port and starboard, aft and forward, galley and head. The boat at dock bobbed gently up and down. The sun, reflecting off the water of the marina, increased its intensity. The young pastor began to feel queasy in his stomach. The captain began to speak about seasickness. He explained dramatically that seasickness is only a figment of the imagination. The pastor was glad to hear the good news but began to wonder about his increased light-headedness and creeping feelings of nausea.

The freshly indoctrinated crew left the Port of Miami and thus began the pastor's personal odyssey of nausea, disorientation, and life below deck flat on his back. Regular doses of seasickness meds left him sweetly semi-comatose. He survived on hope. He hoped that Betty would not die. Early the first morning, the boat weighed anchor off an island with a lighthouse. The lighthouse crew sent a longboat for those who wanted to step on dry land. The pastor, Betty, and some others jumped in. The waves leaped from the pages of *Moby Dick*. The pastor considered a long life at the lighthouse. Betty was getting worse. She and the pastor returned to the ketch and convinced the captain to set sail for a clinic.

Betty was encouraged to eat; she needed strength for the journey to the physician. The crew from the soybean fields of northern Ohio offered her a tuna fish sandwich made from a miraculous dehydrated substance in a can. Betty's condition seemed to worsen. The captain allowed only a short stop at the clinic.

Five days later the seafarers finally anchored again offshore in a beautiful cove. All on board were still alive. They were sticky from saltwater, smelly from lack of showers, traumatized by the oil-scented un-air-conditioned cabin, weary of food taken from tin cans, wounded by an attack of sand fleas, wrapped in dark or red burnt skin, overcome by the summer Caribbean heat, but alive!

They searched for a place to conduct devotions. Someone suggested that they sing "Amazing Grace."

Through many dangers, toils and snares ...
we have already come.
'Twas grace that brought us safe thus far ...
and grace will lead us home.

The novice seamen seasoned by six days upon the deep sang words of gratitude. There are few people from Christian cultures who cannot identify with those words and who cannot sing some of that hymn when lamenting bagpipes squeal and kilts swirl.

Noah made it safely over the sea. He celebrated with a little strong drink. He had a right to celebrate. He and a zoo-full of people and animals beheld God's mercy under a clear, sunny sky. God had not withheld his promise.

We are those who have been drowned in the waters of baptism. We have been taken by the chaotic waters. But we have also been raised up because on that day God called us by name and adopted us as his own. He made a promise. He will not withhold that promise. Amen.

Lent 2
Genesis 17:1-7, 15-16

The Divine Deal ...

The priest challenged the rabbi at lunch: "Rabbi Cohen, when are you going to eat a piece of this delicious ham?" The rabbi answered, "I'll make a deal with you, Father Laughlin. If you get married, I'll eat the ham at your wedding."

Deals. The owner of a house wants to sell it. She picks a realtor. In return for 6% commission, the realtor will find a buyer. The papers are signed. The deal is struck. The realtor has promised to represent the seller. A potential buyer seeks the help of the realtor. Naturally, the realtor will want to sell his listing. But the realtor must also be loyal to the buyer. What does the realtor do if he knows about a better house listed by another realtor offered for less money? Does he remain loyal to his client the seller (a loyalty putting more money in his pocket) or does he decide to take into consideration the interests of the buyer? The deals get messy.

Made With Abraham

God once made a deal with Abraham, a man of nineteenth century BC called by God to go up from Ur of the Chaldees to a new home that God would show him. According to one Old Testament line of thought (the P source), the covenant with Abraham was the third of four "dispensations." Following the dispensation of the creation and the covenant with Noah, God made a deal with Abraham, after which God made a deal with the nation of Israel at Sinai.

God's deal with Abraham, a new era, was marked by the change in Abram's name. Abram ("may God be exalted") was changed to Abraham ("the father of many nations").

The deal was somewhat one-sided. Abraham had no responsibility to God in exchange for God's blessing, except perhaps to say "thank you," head in the direction to which God pointed him, and introduce the practice of circumcision to his male descendents. God's sign that he would follow through with his part in the deal would be the pregnancy of Sarah, Abraham's wife, a laughing matter that would turn dead serious.

The deal was more like a call. God called Abraham to a glorious future rife with milk and honey in a place called Canaan. Abraham's response to God's offer would be simple gratitude and a willingness to go after the dream and to keep the dream alive.

Perhaps Abraham also had the charge to proclaim the goodness and power of the god named "El Shaddai" (God Almighty).

In some ways, the call of God to pastors and priests who are beckoned to enter the land of parish ministry is similar to the call of God to Abraham.

Dietmar Linke was a pastor called into church ministry in the former DDR. At Christmas 1983, he and his family were ordered to leave the DDR. The record of his "criminal activity" began when he was the pastor of his first congregation in the East German town of Meinsdorf. He noticed that the Jewish graves in the town cemetery were not cared for. He decided to organize a week of presentations and public discussion focusing on the theme, "Jews and Christians." The state accused him of propagandizing in behalf of the country of Israel and called him an agent for "outside interests."

He and his wife later participated in an effort to promote world peace by organizing small discussion groups that invited writers from the West to present their thoughts.

Pastor Linke and his wife incited the authorities to overt action when they participated in a human chain of lighted candles that extended from the American embassy to the Soviet embassy in East Berlin in the early morning of World Freedom Day, September 1, 1983.

That straw that broke the camel's back led to expulsion from their own country. In obedience to his "call," Dietmar Linke had to endure public accusations by the authorities, the relinquishing of his driver's license on several occasions, and the unannounced entry into his home by security police.

Complaints by the authorities against him were made to the leaders of his denomination, his children were harassed in school by their teachers, and hate letters were sent to his home. The strategy of the security police worked. Pastor Linke was forced to request permission to leave the country. He was ordered to leave the country within a month.

Like Abraham, he left his "Ur of the Chaldees" to enter unknown country. Once "safe and sound" in West Berlin, he had to wait two years to receive a parish assignment because of another "deal" between the western and eastern judicatories of his denomination. His loyalty to his God who called him forth to venture into a land of uncertainty led to the "milk and honey" of satisfaction that he had kept his part of the bargain. Abraham and Sarah were to find rest in the promised land in a burial cave near Hebron.

Fulfilled In Jesus

The priestly narratives of the Old Testament spoke of the four dispensations, but Irenaeus, an early church father, spoke of the four "covenants" made with Noah, Abraham, and Israel at Mt. Sinai, and, fourthly, with humankind through Jesus of Nazareth.

Irenaeus was coached by Saint Paul's letter to the Galatians: "... Now the promises were made to Abraham and to his offspring; it does not say, 'And to offsprings,' as of many; but it says, 'And to your offspring,' that is, to one person, who is Christ" (Galatians 3:15-18). Paul, the rabbi, taught that the consummation of the promise to Abraham was, in fact, Jesus Christ.

Jesus is the way and the leader to the promised land. Perhaps he is also the promised land himself! When we find him, we find the milk and honey, the peace and the fulfillment to which God calls us. Ignatius, another early church father, said "Apart from Jesus we have not true life."

The promise to Abraham was that he was to be the "father of many nations." If Jesus is the one who fulfills the promise of salvation to many nations, then Christians need to think broadly and boundlessly.

A Catholic priest once told of an incident in an ecumenical study group in the Detroit, Michigan, area. The incident took place during the time of the Detroit riots of 1967. It seems that some folks clandestinely painted the statue of Jesus in front of Sacred Heart Seminary. Morning daylight revealed a black Jesus. A few nights later, white teenagers, with a bucket of white paint, rendered Jesus Caucasian again.

Some faculty members and students of the seminary recognized the potential for misinterpretation by the community. The times demanded a statement from the seminary. Again, for the third time, the paint buckets were employed. The faculty members and students went to work at 4 a.m. to return Jesus to the black race. Unfortunately, some neighbors, unaware of the plot, called the police. Only when the perpetrators were apprehended, did the boys in blue recognize their police chaplain and rector of the seminary, Msgr. Frank Canfield and friends. The vandals were released and Jesus remained black for a very long time. Ministerial and ecumenical groups regarded the riots as a wake-up call to begin aggressively the work of reconciliation and racial integration in the Detroit area.

Not all Christians celebrate the season of Epiphany but all Christians celebrate the story of the magi who came from the east to pay homage to the Christ Child. They were guided by a star. Maybe it was Halley's Comet that shot across the sky in 11 BC. Maybe it was a brilliant conjunction of Saturn and Jupiter that occurred in 7 BC. Maybe it was the star named by the Egyptians, Sirus, the dog star, which rose at sunrise with extraordinary brilliance. At any rate, it was not too surprising for the scientists of the day, the magi, who in this case could have been members of a priestly class, the Medes of Persia, to regard unusual stellar phenomena as signaling the birth of a new king. It is noteworthy that the popular legend about the three kings gives them precise identities. Melchior was an old man with a gray beard; Caspar was young and ruddy;

Balthasar was swarthy, perhaps even black, with a newly grown beard. Epiphany means "manifestation." The Christ Child was manifested or revealed to foreigners, to the nations. The Christ Child had not come just to redeem the nations but to redeem the world, the "nations." To Abraham was given the promise, that he would father "many nations." His seed would be a beacon and a leader to many nations, perhaps a savior to lead "many nations" into a promised land hardly imagined by even Abraham himself.

With Benefits

According to the theology of Paul, Abraham became a "father" of millions. His "seed" would become a blessing to all those who proclaimed Jesus as Lord, thus participating in Abraham's faith. The future benefits of the contract God made with Abraham would accrue to countless millions. Paul might say that the investment of faith (or "trust") "deposited" by Abraham has been paid out to many beneficiaries. An Old Testament scholar, Gerhard von Rad, put it in his commentary on Genesis, "Abraham's call [was connected] with the hope of a universal extension of God's salvation beyond the limits of Israel [the covenant with Abraham has a] timeless validity...."[1] "... In you all the families of the earth shall be blessed" (Genesis 12:3).

The blessing given to Abraham is the blessing of faith joyously celebrated by all Christians who step onto the trail with Abraham's (spiritual) descendents who follow behind him on the way to the glorious promised land.

Most Christians might agree that believers are "grandfathered" into the list of beneficiaries on the day of their baptism. Once a group of American Presbyterians went to Scotland to enjoy a retreat. One day, between sessions, some of them began to stroll through the gardens of the retreat center to do a little exploring. Presently, they came to a stream spanned by a timeworn bridge. They failed to see the warning sign and began to cross the bridge. A gardener in the distance began to shout. Too far away to hear what he was shouting, one of the Presbyterians shouted back, "It's okay! We're allowed to be here. We're Presbyterians!" The gardener shouted back, "I'm no carin' aboot that, but if ye dinna get off the bridge, you'll all be Baptists!"

Presbyterians baptize infants and Baptists only baptize believers, but the practice of baptism is a good time to remember the divine deal. Some ministers use a shell to baptize, the sign of the blessing that comes from the water. Perhaps a candle will be lit from the Christ candle, the sign of the blessing transmitted from Christ, Abraham's "seed."

Sometimes oil or water is traced on the forehead of the baptized, replacing circumcision, the mark of adoption by the resurrected Christ, again, the "seed" of Abraham. Faith is at the center of baptism, the faith of those who present the child at infancy, or the faith of those who profess their faith before their adult baptism. Saint Paul links our baptismal faith to the faith of Abraham. "Abraham believed God, and it was reckoned to him as righteousness" (Romans 4:3). God's deal offered to Abraham was undeserved. Abraham was not a good guy and his faith did not entitle him to God's grace. His faith was his trust in God almighty who made him an offer. He accepted the offer. He believed.

Any deal we make with fellow humans involves an element of trust. The bank has to trust us to make the mortgage payments and we have to trust that the bank will not foreclose on our property without following the stipulations of the contract.

God's deal is rock solid. He will not withdraw his benefits. Furthermore, God will not force us to love and obey him. He will not back out of the deal but he allows us the freedom to reject his offer. Such a deal! Amen.

---

1. Gerhard von Rad, *Genesis: A Commentary* (Philadelphia: The Westminster Press, 1961), p. 195.

Lent 3
Exodus 20:1-17

God, The Good Ally

A group of American tourists once listened to a story told by their Jewish guide. The guide, Moshe, claimed that his story would explain why the commandments were published on two tablets of stone. Moses came down from the mountain with a tablet of stone listing some of the commandments. He first met a group of Kenites. "Do you want the commandments of God?" he asked. "What do they say?" asked the Kenites. "Thou shalt not kill," replied Moses. "Thanks, we think we'll pass," responded the Kenites.

Next, Moses encountered the tribe of Hittites. "Would you like the commandments?" asked Moses. "What do they say?" "Thou shalt not commit adultery," answered the prophet. "No, thank you very much, we'll move on," retorted the Hittites.

Moses came to the camp of the Israelites. "Here are God's commandments," he said, "would you like to have them?" "How much are they?" they asked. "Nothing. They're free," answered Moses. "Fine, we'll take two," they replied.

God, The Good Ally Of Israel

Actually, the Kenites, a clan of the Midianites, are thought to be involved with the encounter of Moses and his exiled followers and sooner or later also confessed Yahweh as their God. It is thought that Sinai was a holy mountain for the Midianites before being "discovered" by the Hebrews.

At any rate, Moses met God in a terrible but wondrous way on the top of the mountain. God chose to ally himself with the Hebrews and made an offer. Through his spokesperson, Moses, he extended his special favor and the gift of the rules of life uniquely to the band of slaves who had made a run for it out of captivity in Egypt. The Hebrews had already experienced the favor of God. Without his aid, freedom for them would have been unthinkable.

So God deepens his relationship with Israel by proposing, "You shall be my people and I shall be your God." The giving of the law to the people constitutes a contract. It is not a law that is conditional which spells what will happen (the penalty) if the law is broken but it is an absolute law: "Just don't even think about disobeying!"

Another way to classify a law is to determine whether the law is a parity contract, a contract made between two equal partners to the agreement. For example, there was once an old farmer with an ill temper who married late in life and was lucky enough to win a young lady for his new bride, probably a girl who was naive or desperate. After the wedding, he drove his wife home in a wagon pulled by a mule. Suddenly, the mule stopped. The groom said, "Now, that's one," and he hit the mule with a stick. Later the mule stopped again. "Now, that's twice," said the man and he hit the mule again.

Later the mule stopped for the third time. The old geezer said, "Now, that's three" and he shot the mule between the eyes. The new bride protested, "Now, honey, that wasn't necessary. The mule was doing the best it could — you should not have shot it!" The old farmer pointed his finger at his new bride and said, "Now, that's one!" The marriage contract between the farmer and his bride was obviously not a parity contract.

Likewise, the law given by God is not a parity covenant, but it is a unilateral contract. It is a law between a much superior party to be subscribed to by a weaker party, which has been aided or rescued by the superior party. In the ancient Middle East, a superior party, perhaps a king, might save the hide of the inferior party, perhaps a vassal. The weaker recipient of the favor gladly agrees to the conditions of the contract because of (usually extreme) gratitude.

But, of course, the usual categories can't possibly illuminate precisely the covenant between God and the Hebrew refugees. God here reveals an otherworldly grace not capable of human desire nor effort. At first glance, it might appear that God, in effect, said,

"Look at what I did for you; now you do this for me!" God didn't really make any kind of offer. He saved the hides of the Hebrews and now he offers an additional gift, guidelines for living life; for loving him, for loving those within the community, and for loving those who would become Israel's neighbors. King David later would be chastised by the prophet Nathan because he took for himself another man's wife. Even today, Iraqis invaded in their home by American soldiers searching for insurgents or the weapons of insurgents will be offered a cup of tea.

God's gift and his unique partnership with the desert rats was nothing that could be turned down by sane human beings. The God of Sinai was proving himself to be a good ally. He was a keeper. The loyalty of the Israelites waned to and fro for centuries before the words of the prophets recorded after the return from the Babylonian exile proved that at least some of the remnant remembered the pact in the wilderness.

Good For The New Israel

The event of Jesus marked the birth of the new Israel. The pact with God at Sinai, incorporating God's goodness extended to the people in the wilderness, was taken off the shelf. Jesus came to endorse the contract and its stipulations and to elaborate upon them, "Do not think that I have come to abolish the law or the prophets; I have come not to abolish but to fulfill ... You have heard that it was said to those of ancient times ... But I say to you ..." (Matthew 5:17 ff).

Volumes have been written on the application of the commandments in today's world. Even the elaborations of Jesus are hard to apply in the twenty-first century. What does it mean to "love one's enemies," according to Jesus, and how could one possibly refrain from looking at another man's wife with lust? (Matthew 5:28).

Admittedly, it's not difficult for modern Americans to avoid making "graven images." Our graven images are anything that is other than Paul Tillich's "ultimate concern."

A man began to lose his commitment to his church congregation over a period time. His attendance at church dropped; he stopped making a yearly pledge and occasional checks in the offering plate diminished to zero. First-class letters sent to his address were returned "no forwarding address."

He was not angry at the church council and was not offended by changes in worship. He had no bone to pick with his pastor. He just didn't find church "exciting" anymore. Devotion to orthodox Christianity cramped his style. He decided to move on. He sought more interesting friends, more exciting "diversions," and the thrill of less respectable activities. One day he appeared suddenly again at worship. "Jack," the pastor exclaimed, "you've been gone a long time. Why did you come back?" Jack answered, "I've been missing the trumpets in the morning!" What will it be? A sexual lifestyle without responsibility? The big bucks? The stimulating social life with the local community "movers and shakers," the "in group"? Yuppie cars, yuppie wines, yuppie clothes? Or will it be the "trumpets in the morning"?

What about taking God's name in vain? Some good folks cuss a lot and some bad folks use correct English as they gossip and share the latest "insider stories." John Otwell, a Canadian Lutheran theologian, once put it this way, "Much more serious than the mindless swearing or cursing of the modern age is the tendency of believers to use God's name to bless their many personal causes and concerns. The truly blasphemous taking of God's name in vain is that which uses God and the Bible to justify racial discrimination, aggressive war, and a host of other things that are contrary to God's revelation in Christ."[1]

There is also the issue of going to church on Sunday. The Israelites were taught by God how to remember that God created them and all that exists. The creation account notes that God rested on the seventh day. Likewise, the people of the God of Sinai were to rest on the sabbath in order to devote their thoughts and prayers to gratitude for the creation.

The people of the new covenant (Christians) also celebrate a sabbath, the first day of the week, to devote time, prayers, and praise to the proclamation of the resurrection.

It is difficult to imagine that God would condemn to hell anyone who must work on Sundays. How does one obey the commandment to observe the sabbath in an industrialized economy? Many churches offer worship opportunities on Saturday or Wednesday evenings.

A tourist found his way one morning to the Sistine Chapel in Rome. To his dismay, the chapel was closed that day because it was the feast day of Saints Peter and Paul. He turned to negotiate his way through the crowded streets in the direction of Saint Peter's Basilica. A group of children cornered him between parked cars and a wall. They stuck a newspaper in his face. He thought that they wanted a handout, but they were not persistent. They quickly ran away from him. A few steps later, the tourist discovered that his wallet was missing from his front right pocket. He retraced his steps back to the entrance to the Sistine Chapel and looked on the ground where he remembered he had taken out his wallet. Another man asked, "What are you looking for?" The tourist answered, "My wallet!" "The children took it," explained the local Roman.

The tourist went to the police station and wrote the same report seven times. There was no carbon paper. He called his office in California and asked his secretary to cancel all of his credit cards. A friend in Rome loaned him the cash he lost in his wallet, his spending money for the next two weeks in Europe. His friend also told him about the bands of Gypsy children trained by adults who send the children forth to prey on the unsuspecting. The hapless tourist received his wallet in the mail several weeks later, credit cards intact but cash missing. A note from the Italian police said that the wallet had been simply tossed into a rubbish container.

The children of Israel were to thank God for his favor by refraining from stealing. In fact, even possessions that accidentally fell into the hands of others were to be returned to their owners, even if the owners were an enemy. The children of the new covenant must apply the law to identity theft or the theft of one's reputation caused by loose tongues or the theft of pension security by unscrupulous corporation leaders. The theft of a wallet by street children is a small matter compared to the potential for theft and unimaginable grief and chaos in the wake of technological and electronic theft in modern America.

What about the commandment not to kill? Innocent civilians die in the Middle East every day. The world stands at the sidelines while thousands die of genocide and starvation in Africa. The media nonchalantly announces the latest numbers of those killed by suicide bombers in between exhaustive reports about the latest movie star scandal or a politician's faux pas. But, in truth, a commentator's slip of the tongue about black female basketball players or the words of hip hop that belittle gender also embody murder.

Some who observe American culture have become increasingly concerned about the passing of civility. In 1996, Jonathan Alter wrote a piece in *Newsweek* in which he lamented, "... vicious politics, abominable manners [and] a dangerously atrophied civic spirit."[2] Mr. Alter still optimistically believed that people say "thank you" on the bus and "excuse me" on the stairs. But there are still the cell phones that ring at the movies, the car driver behind that won't allow time for the car in the lane to her right to move in front of her, and the clerk at the checkout counter who regards the buyer as though she were a robot or some other inanimate object. The commandments are more than the sum of their total; they are guidelines for living in a community.

When God is our ally, his commandments (not "suggestions," according to a popular television commentator) are the backup system for the law written into our hearts. After all, we already know the difference between right and wrong. If the gift of the law were not enough evidence for our partnership with God, then there is more: His Son died on the cross for us, thus bestowing the greatest gift of all from our strong ally — entrance into the kingdom where rules will not be needed. For the ancients, graven images were poor divine allies.

The God of Moses spoke from the mountain; he did not threaten. He gave the people of Moses a great gift: the gift of the law. If the law were taken seriously, it would go well with the Hebrew people. Now the law has been fulfilled in the person and work of Jesus. The law helps us to get along with one another but it cannot save us: only God's Son can do that and he did. Amen.

---

1. John Otwell, *Proclamation: LENT: Series B* (Philadelphia: Fortress Press, 1975), p. 31.

2. Jonathan Alter, "Cheering the Nice Capades," *Newsweek*, June 15, 1996, p. 50.

Lent 4
Numbers 21:4-9

Hope Lifted Up

It was a mystery. Hezekiah, the twelfth king of Judah, the father of Manasseh, asked around about the mysterious bronze snake, named Nehushtan, on display in a corner of the temple. Encouraged by the prophet Micah, Hezekiah wanted to restore and strengthen the monotheistic religion of his forefathers. The veneration of such a "graven image" was inconsistent with the worship of the one God, the God of Abraham and Moses. No one knew the origin of the thing. Hezekiah didn't research the matter. He ordered that the snake be destroyed. That was the end of idol worship on the side within the very walls of the temple.

Much later, some Jewish rabbis took the dusty case records out of the files and more earnestly did the research. They concluded that the destroyed bronze serpent had something to do with the plight of their ancestors in the wilderness. The historical records revealed that the Hebrews in the wilderness had camped for a long time at a place called Kedesh, a place about fifty miles south of the land of Canaan. The people of Moses were losing their fascination with the spectacular rescue event orchestrated by God and executed by Moses.

The more the monotony and bleakness of the wilderness dampened their spirits, the louder was their cry to return to the "good old days" in Egypt. Their desperation finally expressed itself in a bold plan to attack and enter Canaan from the south. Moses was not convinced but reluctantly agreed to send a couple of spies to check out the strength and the position of the enemy. Most of the spy party advised against the attack, citing the greater stature of the

Canaanites and their military strength. But the bravado of Joshua and Caleb convinced Moses to attack. The Hebrews were routed and quickly broke camp and headed east on the king's highway and tried to enter Canaan from the east, finally to enter the promised land from the eastern side of the Jordan.

Hope Lifted Up In The Wilderness Time

What about the bronze snake? Between the time of the failed conquest of Canaan from the south and the decision to head east, the Lord sent an army of poisonous serpents to attack the faithless people. The people recognized the error of their ways and quickly repented and confessed their apostasy. God told Moses to place a bronze serpent upon a pole as a sign of their deliverance from the serpents. In faith and trust, the people looked at the serpent and were delivered from the jaws of death.

Later they would remember that God and his grace were manifested in three gracious signs: the manna, the pillars of fire by night and smoke by day, and, thirdly, the bronze serpent. The bronze snake in the temple was not there to encourage veneration but it had been there to remind the people of God's mercy and deliverance in the wilderness. In retrospect, the time in the wilderness had been a good time.

Two brothers drove down the once-familiar highway toward their childhood home. They stared silently at the changes wrought by time. If they had not known the name of the roads, they could never have relied on their memories of where to turn and when. The town that they entered had been their home for twenty years and many years had passed since they left it.

Their parents had died at a retirement home in the Sunbelt and it was the boys' job to take care of the details at the house in the north. It had been locked up for the winter some months before. As they drove into the driveway, they had the eerie sensation that time had reversed itself and that their mother was waving at them from the kitchen window.

The back door key still required just the right twist to make it work, and the throw rug still bunched up when they pushed open the door. They stepped into the kitchen, looked around, and years of memories were revitalized. They both sat down at the kitchen table with tears in their eyes and sighed, "Home." It was a moment of grace.

The invocation of memory sometimes smooths down the rough spots and highlights the good times, the moments of laughter, the moments of family solidarity, the tender moments of forgiveness, obstacles surmounted, and challenges met. Perhaps that was the real purpose of the bronze snake in the temple, to remind the people of the hope God raised for them in the wilderness, their home for forty years.

Hope Lifted Up In Our Time

So what does a snake in the wilderness have to do with us? According to the gospel writer, John, who quotes Jesus, there is a connection: "... just as Moses lifted up the serpent in the wilderness, so must the Son of Man be lifted up, that whoever believes in him may have eternal life" (John 3:14-15).

Jesus predicted his own elevation upon the cross. The Greek word implies that Jesus is not to be identified with the snake, but it is in the "elevation" (or the ascension of Jesus) that there is salvation. The Hebrews looked on the bronze snake because they *wanted* to believe (they repented — they already believed) and we look upon the person on the cross because we "believe" in his work of salvation. The Jews looked at the elevated snake and they were rescued from death; we, the believers, look at the crucified Christ and we are likewise delivered from sin, death, and the devil.

Visitors to Jerusalem today go to the Church of the Holy Sepulchre to see an enclosed marble chapel many believe marks the spot of the tomb of Jesus. At the other end of the structure are the remains of the hill of Golgotha, barely visible behind stone walls. The visitor is offered the opportunity to "see" the place where the cross was raised, raised to inspire abiding faith.

Emperor Constantine came to the Roman throne at the beginning of the fourth century in part through his spectacular victory in his face-off with Maxentius in northern Italy. Constantine, a non-Christian, prayed for victory in the afternoon before the battle. He had a vision, a cross of light in the heavens accompanied by the inscription, "Conquer by this!"

God appeared in a later dream and commanded him to use the sign of the cross in all encounters with his enemies. Constantine prevailed, relocated the Roman capital to Byzantium, sent his mother, Helena, on a trip to the Holy Land, and convened the first of four Christian ecumenical councils at Nicaea in 325 AD, a meeting which began the process to define the orthodox Christian faith. The hope, literally "lifted up" in Constantine's battles, paved the road for the Christianization of the western world.

Sometimes, God lifts up hope for his creatures when humans desperately seek hope. In the case of the Hebrews in the wilderness, however, the "chosen people" were driven to the search for hope by God's punishment. Perhaps the story implies that they were heading in a hopeless journey of abandonment of the God who had delivered them from slavery. God hit them with a two-by-four. The fiery snakes were only a foretaste of their future fueled by reckless apostasy. Only more "fiery snakes" awaited them in a future of godless destitution given over to self-indulgence and pride.

Recourse to the faith of Sinai drove the people to cast their eyes upon the bronze snake of healing. Hope was restored and the road to the promised land was rediscovered.

Today's people of God are not safe from the temptation to backslide. A well-known gambler answered the altar call at a revival. The preacher asked him to burn his cards and his gambling equipment in front of witnesses as a testimony to his conversion. He answered, "I can't do that because if I did, what would I do if I backslid?"

Lent is the time to confess our propensity to abandon life in and with God. When we're "in the money," we forget whence material blessings come. We forget our promises to share with others. We complain if we're losing the battle to keep up with the Joneses. Manna and water are not enough. We want to drink the best wines, own the high-end automobiles, and live in spacious homes with at least three televisions and an entertainment room with stadium seating. What God gives to us is ours, we believe, not God's things given to us to share with others in God's name. Perhaps unemployment and health crises are God's "fiery snakes," snakes of grace lifted up to drive us back to our senses.

The girl, Helen Keller, was taken hundreds of times by Miss Sullivan to the well with the pump. Her tutor held Helen's hands beneath the flow of water and patiently spelled out the letters, w-a-t-e-r, on Helen's palm. Poor Helen, totally dumb, blind, and deaf, just didn't get it.

Suddenly, one day, the child grabbed the hand of her teacher and in turn spelled out the word, w-a-t-e-r. The months of patience paid off. Why did it take so long for Helen to recognize the freedom and grace offered to her by her teacher? Why does it take so long for the drug addict to make that life-saving decision? Why does it take so long for many to discover the life that faith in God offers? Later, Helen Keller said of herself, "I was a no-thing living in a no-world and I did not know that I was."

We struggle and hobble along in lives that are only half-lives. We are, in part, "no-things" living in a "no-world" and we do not know that we are.

The young man, Augustine, lived a life of hedonism and abandon until, alone in a garden in Milan, prompted by a soft voice, he began to read the letter of Saint Paul to the Romans. His eyes fell upon the words, "let us live honorably as in the day, not in reveling and drunkenness, not in debauchery and licentiousness, not in quarreling and jealousy. Instead, put on the Lord Jesus Christ, and make no provision for the flesh, to gratify its desires" (Romans 13:13-14). Further inspired by Ambrose, the bishop of Milan, the young man gave up his concubine and became the Bishop of Hippo, perhaps the greatest Christian thinker the world will ever know.

Augustine was driven by the fiery poison of his loose living to gaze upon the Christ on the tree and "put on the Lord Jesus Christ." The young North African replaced the destructive fire of reveling and licentiousness for the fire of faith in Christ. It can happen to anyone: a felon in prison, a corporate head who turns from greed to compassion for his or her employees who depend upon the company pension, a runaway teen who returns to the love of the parental home.

God revealed his love in the bronze serpent in the wilderness. God revealed his love again in the man on the cross. "For God so loved the world that he gave his only Son, so that everyone who believes in him may not perish but may have eternal life" (John 3:16). Amen.

Lent 5
Jeremiah 31:31-34

The Last Compact

A man, seriously ill in the hospital, requested a visit from his pastor. "Pastor," he said, "if you pray for me and I recover, I will give $25,000 to the building fund." The pastor prayed and the patient recovered completely. The pastor tactfully tried to remind his parishioner about the promise. Stonewalled, the minister put it on the line, "Jim, you promised to give $25,000 to the building fund when you became well." "Did I?" answered the newly recovered man. "Well, that should give you some idea of how sick I was."

Broken contracts — promises not kept — it's part of the human experience. It's a part of the human story in the Bible.

Take a look at Father Abraham. God made a deal with him. The deal was signed with the blood of animals that were cut in two. (People now use printed paper contracts and ink.) The cut carcasses were then placed back together again and after the sun had set, and an eerie darkness had fallen over the place, "a smoking fire pot and a flaming torch" were passed between the pieces (Genesis 15:17).

The smoking pot and the flaming torch represented the presence of God and in this way Abraham entered into a personal covenant relationship with God. God promised Abraham that he and his descendents would possess a great land, become a great nation, and become a blessing to the peoples of the earth.

Abraham and his tribe, his flocks, and his tents moved south from Haran to Canaan. But Abraham had reason to believe that God had reneged on God's side of the contract. Abraham had no sons with his wife, Sarah. The proxy son by his Egyptian maid did not qualify as "descendent," but God showed good faith. God provided for a son from the elderly Sarah. Abraham had reason again to doubt God's intentions when God commanded the father to sacrifice the son. The command turned out to be a test of Abraham's trust in God and the deal was back on the road again. But Abraham's descendents ended up in hopeless slavery in Egypt. Now for sure, the contract with God had come to a dead end. No promised land. No great people. No blessing to anyone except the Egyptian tyrants who were, understandably, quite proud of their new tombs.

But wait — the story is not over. After a lengthy pause, God sent Moses to save the day. Moses led his people out of Egypt. Moses led his people through the Red Sea and no one even got a foot wet. (Did you see the movie?) According to one account, God renewed his covenant with Israel in a ceremony at the foot of the mountain. The Ten Commandments, guidelines for living, sweetened the deal. Moses led his people to the east side of Jordan, poised for the entry into the promised land. Moses received a glimpse of the land promised to Abraham, passed the baton to Joshua, and died. Joshua "fit the battle of Jericho."

The history of the chosen people in the promised land is not a pretty sight. The people of Israel and Judah vacillate and backslide and stumble on the way to their destiny. The prophets come and go. The united kingdom under Saul, David, and Solomon flowers briefly. The kingdom divides into two. The kingdom in the north, Israel, is wiped out by the Assyrians. Enter the prophet Jeremiah stage right. Either before the fall of Judah in 586 BC, or perhaps during the fall or after the fall, Jeremiah brings up the matter of the contract with God. Before the imminent fall of Judah at the hands of the Babylonians, Jeremiah warned the people that they were like a clay pot. If clay pots are damaged and if they leak, they are destroyed. The people of Judah were a damaged clay pot and it would have to be smashed in order that a new people might be formed (Jeremiah 18:1-11).

Jeremiah was a visionary. Regular contracts can become null and void, but contracts with God? No way! Perhaps the contract could be saved. Perhaps the contract could be edited a bit. Jeremiah gets a glimpse of the rewritten contract. He noted, first of all, that the reworded contract would be written on the hearts of people. The new revised contract would not be carved in stone. It would be inscribed into human hearts. Tablets of stone exist outside human flesh and bone. The renewed contract would be part and parcel of people; not over against them and judging them but *inside* them, stitched and woven into their very bodies and souls. From the post-resurrection point of view, one would say that the meeting with God at the mountain of Sinai has been supplanted by the meeting with God at the hill of Golgotha, at the cross.

The fire and glory of the majestic God at the top of the mountain has become God the human suffering on an instrument of torture and slow, painful death. It's not a pretty picture, seeing God on the cross. A professor of church history once sat at dinner in Berkeley, California, with a professor of comparative religions. The world religion professor revealed that he was a Buddhist. The history teacher asked if his children would become Buddhists as well. "I don't know," said the Buddhist, "they are searching. My daughter went with a Christian friend to a church and was appalled by the sight of the suffering Jesus upon the sanctuary cross. 'How gross!' she said."

Perhaps that young girl could not relate to the suffering of a man hanging on a cross because she, herself, had yet to experience the suffering and pain that comes with the package we call "life."

The year 2007 was the 400th anniversary of the birth of the German composer, Paul Gerhardt. After completing his preparation for the Lutheran ministry, he was assigned to the parish of Mittenwalde, a small town near Berlin. There he comforted the populace, victims of the ravages of the Thirty Years' War. Gerhardt experienced in his lifetime the unholy violence of destruction and man's inhumanity to man. In his hymn, "O Sacred Head Now Wounded," he contemplates the violent passion of the Christ upon the cross. Gerhardt knows about the suffering of the man, Jesus, because he too has seen it all. (It is a minor miracle that he lived to be 69 years of age.) Therefore, he recognizes the abuse and scorn, the pale agony for what it is, because the violence of first-century Roman soldiers was repeated by plundering soldiers in his own century.

However, Gerhardt, though seemingly obsessed by the pain and suffering of life at times, saw beyond the event of the cross the splendor of the heavens beyond. Gerhardt praised "patience," as a gift from God that enables the traveler in the world to persevere in the face of earthly travail. Spiritual patience drives one to trust in the passion and death of Jesus. Like Gerhardt, C. S. Lewis experienced the pain, isolation, injustice, hunger, thirst, and exposure of WWII. The memories of the war haunted his dreams for years and he believed that death would be better than to have to endure another war. For him, the Christian could only experience real happiness when one realizes that "the crown is not permitted without the cross...."[1]

Secondly, Jeremiah proclaimed that the new contract would not be taught by neighbors to neighbors. What does that mean? It means that the element of judgment of the goody-goody two shoes upon the lower-life common "sinners" would be ruled out. One's relationship with God would be henceforth between the sinner and God. In the Protestant tradition, that means that the pastor or minister does not have the right to do the judging, but as a fellow "priest" in the "priesthood of all believers," he or she would only announce God's mercy upon the penitent sinner. In confession, the priest or the pastor does not bestow the forgiveness but only passes the forgiveness on from God. No longer can the kettle call the pot black. The new covenant announced the demise of the spiritually elite. In the scramble to find righteousness, it's always comforting to note that one is ahead of someone less righteous. In the era of the new covenant, all are equally fallen from God and all are equally restored to God through the work of Christ.

Thirdly, Jeremiah presses forward to his grand conclusion: "... [the Lord] ... will forgive their iniquity, and remember their sin no more" (Jeremiah 31:34). Could the matter be stated anymore plainly?

There's an old story about a college swimming coach who tossed and turned in his bed on a hot summer's night. He arose and crossed the small campus to the swimming hall. He knew the building well and did not turn on the inside lights. He mounted the diving board and stretched his arms to each side. The moon shone brightly that night and cast his shadow upon the opposite wall. His shadow caught his attention; it reminded him of a cross. The sight gave him pause. He stepped back off the diving board and realized that there was no water in the pool. The custodian had drained the water out during the day in order to do some repairs. The coach later related to others the incident and said, "I was saved by the cross."

From the point of view of the Christian believer, Jeremiah announced a salvation that he may not have totally comprehended. God spoke through him about God's unbounded and unconditional forgiveness. If Jeremiah's vision gave hope to those in captivity in Babylon, how much more is the boundless hope that fills our hearts and lights the path of our journey to the kingdom beyond the dark cross of Golgotha? In hope we enter the final week before Passion Sunday, eager to see the light at the end of his "way of sorrows." Amen.

---

1. C. S. Lewis, *The Joyful Christian* (New York: Touchstone, 1977), p. 214.

Passion/Palm Sunday
Isaiah 50:4-9a

Who Is Isaiah's Servant?

A man had three small children, all three old enough to enjoy the activities of Halloween. A coworker at the office of the father volunteered to visit his home on trick or treat night and bring sweets for the kids. The father's colleague appeared at the door dressed up as "the little green man," with an ugly green face and long, knotted, twisted hands protruding from a long coat that effectively disguised the identity of Daddy's friend.

At the appearance of the mysterious stranger in the entryway of the house, the kids ran for cover. The little green man grunted and moaned and held extended the bags of candy. One boy ran quickly from behind the couch to retrieve the gift. The other son bravely ran forth from behind a chair followed by his sister cowering behind mom's skirt. All three siblings retreated to the safety of their shelters to await the departure of the ghoul into the darkness of the night. The drama of the visit was repeated the following year.

A few months later, the father advised his friend at the office that the kids were already anticipating the appearance of the little green man, due to knock at the door six months hence! The conversation of the children revealed fear and anxiety about the spooky man's coming. Father and friend decided that the green creature would visit one last time and take off his mask in the presence of the children and reveal the familiar friend who often sat at the family table. The mystery was solved and fearful anticipation directed to other riddles in the lives of three imaginative children.

The Old Testament lesson for Passion/Palm Sunday embodies a mystery about the identity of the "servant of the Lord" (certainly not the little green man) proclaimed by the prophet Isaiah in four passages.

The "servant of the Lord" texts are included in the section of the book of Isaiah probably written to those in exile in Babylon after 586 BC. Who is this "servant"? Guesses about his identity range from the nation of Israel itself, to an individual with a mission *to* Israel, to a new Israel awaiting birth in the future, to a future figure who stands (or will stand) at the threshold of the dawn of a new day. In accordance with Israel's sense of community, the servant could be both individual and nation. The nation is made up of many individuals but the nation is also one; one nation, though comprising many people, stands as one entity in its dealings and history with God.

Whatever the identity of Isaiah's servant, the servant has marked qualities.

First of all, the servant is *confident*. This is the most notable trait, according to Krister Stendahl, writing while he was Dean of the Divinity School at Harvard University. The text "expresses the confidence of the servant as he faces conflict and enemies. It is a song of trust in God's help and vindication in times of ridicule and accusations."[1]

Stendahl points to verse 4, "The Lord God has given me the tongue of a teacher, that I may know how to sustain the weary with a word." The servant is not a teacher who is unsure of the material he/she presents and the servant is certainly not one who is intimidated by the students. But the servant is also not one who is arrogant and superciliously holds in contempt the ignorance of those before her. The confidence of the servant is strength: "The strength is organic, the strength of a healthy heart, not the strength of stone or steel — or plastic."[2]

Martin Luther stood before the assembled powers of the emperor, princes, and cardinals to declare, "Here I stand!" His stand came from the heart; his knees quivered and his legs wobbled. He wished to be safe and sound at home, at the Black Cloister with friends and family and students in familiar Wittenberg. But his heart compelled him; his discipleship compelled him to stand before earthly powers to make his confession. He modeled the confidence of the servant of Isaiah; he stood before his adversaries on the certain and solid ground of the truth. His teacher was God's word; his confidence flowed forth from the dayspring of the almighty.

Secondly, Isaiah's servant *listens*. "Morning by morning [the Lord God] wakens — wakens my ear to listen as those who are taught" (v. 4). One thinks of Jesus who is reported by the gospel writer, John, to have said, "... for the words that you gave to me I have given to [my disciples] and they have received them and know in truth that I came from you ..." (John 17:8).

The student learns by listening. "Faith comes by hearing." An American studying in Germany was "adopted" by a German family who invited him to spend his weekends with them. Using a book of devotions developed by Zinzendorf and the Bohemian Brothers, "Losungen," the family, father, mother, and three children began each day at breakfast with Bible readings, commentary, and prayer. The discipline was repeated at lunch, at dinner, and again at bedtime. The American student learned a lot of German in the process but also learned about the discipline of daily devotions. He also learned some Latin because the head of the household, a religion teacher by profession, regularly injected the ancient language of Rome into his spontaneous digressions. "Faith comes by hearing."

The "school" of the American theology student served hard rolls and jam with coffee, cabbage rolls, and mid-afternoon cake. The school of Isaiah's pupil was the "school of hard knocks." Jesus, too, "gave [his] back to those who struck" him and endured the pulling out of his beard and faced insult and spitting. The servant does not justify his sufferings by thanking God that he was tested and strengthened by the affliction; the soldier survives the boot camp because he or she is convinced that the rigors of life under the drill sergeant will save his or her life in the midst of combat. But the servant endures his trials and tribulations because God is with him and sustains him. In the midst of adversity, he listens to the voice of God. God speaks to him "through" the challenges that his role calls forth.

One of the greatest compliments that a pastor or priest can receive is that he or she is a good listener. How greatly is the parishioner supported and nourished when the listener makes the troubled or grieving sheep of the flock feel that she or he is the most important person in the world when the pastor gives his or her undivided attention to the words of the one who has been hurt.

Thirdly, the servant described by Isaiah *lives for others*. The world listened in shock as the horrendous story of the shootings at Virginia Tech in April 2007 captured a national television audience. Liviu Librescu, a 77-year-old Jewish engineering professor who survived a concentration camp in Europe, listened to the gunfire from the adjoining classroom. He ordered his students to jump for their lives out of the second-story windows of their classroom. The last student out the window saw his professor using his frail body to hold the door closed to keep out the intruder, Cho Seung-Hui. The students survived. Librescu did not. At his funeral in Israel, his son wept as he honored his father who had given his life for his students.

It would be difficult, even for a skeptic, to deny the connection between the servant of Isaiah and Jesus. The violence of Mel Gibson's movie, *The Passion of the Christ*, if anything, vividly dramatizes the assault against the pacifist, Jesus of Nazareth. If the reading of the passion accounts in the gospels do not offend the sensitivities of the reader, Gibson's movie will.

It's not just that an innocent, loving man is shredded by the torture instruments of the Romans. We, the onlookers, know that he has wound his way down the Street of Sorrows willingly, giving his life that we may enter into the happy kingdom of God, judged suitable for life with God because of the sacrifice of Jesus. Someone once said that God's prophecies are consistent. It would be hard to deny that Isaiah didn't somehow have a vision of a future servant who would die for others. His people were in servitude and exile in a foreign land. Their servitude as a people is reduced into one individual who would give a grand meaning to servanthood. That must have given them hope. Their servitude directed them to a vision of servanthood *par excellence*! They modeled a gracious act of divine history already on their horizon. Perhaps their ordeal in exile would lead to a better world — a better world for them and for all nations. Perhaps those most intuitive saw in the servant of God a glimpse of something wondrous ahead.

Fourthly, Isaiah's servant *knows he is vindicated*! What sustains the servant? He knows that God is with him. He knows that there is some kind of meaning in his humiliation at the hands of his adversaries. He also knows that he is vindicated. He knows that he is guiltless of the charges thrown into his face. He knows that the highest supreme court in the universe, the court of the almighty, has already judged him guiltless and acquitted.

As Paul put it, "Who will bring any charge against God's elect? It is God who justifies" (Romans 8:33). That was Paul's number 1 message: God is the one who justifies. Human courts may be fair or unfair. A mother-in-law may choose to forgive or hold a grudge forever. International courts may prosecute a criminal dictator but the sentence may be light or execution may be carried off clumsily (Saddam Hussein). God judges perfectly, but that is no comfort to those who see the bumper sticker, "Jesus is coming back and, boy, is he ticked off!"

We humans seem programmed to expect the worse. It is only human to expect that God judges like we do: The good guys should get a fair shake and the bad guys should go to hell in a handbasket.

Now comes Paul's number 2 message: "For we hold that a person is justified by faith apart from works prescribed by the law" (Romans 3:28). God finds us "not guilty" because of the vindication of the servant, Jesus. The vindication of Isaiah's servant, of God's Son, is charged to our account. In him are we all vindicated!

A young mother called her pastor to make an appointment. In the privacy of his study she explained that she was plagued by anxiety. She feared that she was unacceptable to God. She felt unworthy, useless, an absolute failure in the eyes of God. Her fear was an obsession and it had a negative impact upon her marriage, upon her daily life, and upon her performance at the office where she worked.

She sought psychiatric treatment. After a number of sessions with her psychiatrist, he suggested that she consult her pastor. The pastor phoned the therapist who stressed the importance of the pastor's involvement in order to help her to realize that God accepted her and loved her. The psychiatrist asked the pastor to work with him on a team basis.

The weekly sessions with the pastor soon revealed that she was oppressed with guilt. She was a bad daughter, a bad mother, a bad wife. Furthermore, she was not worthy of God's love. She was a faithful worshiper but church services only served to remind her of her guilt and deepen her despair. The sermons, the liturgy, the hymns, and the prayers all reminded her of her unworthiness and her sin.

Each session became devoted to a revisit of the worship on the previous Sunday. The sermon, the lessons, and the hymns were re-examined. When she sang the hymn, "Amazing Grace," she heard no grace. She heard the words, "wretch," "lost," and "blind."

The pastor discovered that she had been raised in a church served by her childhood pastor who engaged in pulpit slamming and condemnation. As a child, week after week, she was reminded that she was a worm, a wretched excuse for humanity marked by festering sin wounds. Surely she was fit only for the eternal fire. It took almost a year of weekly meetings, but she finally was able to integrate the gospel good news into the fabric of her soul, heart, and mind. She slowly climbed upward from hatred of herself to acceptance. She learned that she was vindicated. She was pronounced "not guilty" by God because of her newly found trust in a loving God and his servant who transferred his vindication to those in exile, those in bondage to the law, those, like her, lost in low esteem.

So who is Isaiah's "servant"? Like the little green man, he is the one who unmasked himself, who shoved the dark curtain aside to show God's unfathomable, unconditional love, the love of perfect justice, the love that finds the lost, gives sight to the blind, and opens the gate for those in self-imposed exile. Amen.

1. Krister Stendahl, *Proclamation: Series A* (Philadelphia: Fortress Press, 1974), p. 9.

2. *Ibid*, p. 21.

Maundy Thursday
Exodus 12:1-4 (5-10) 11-14

Thanks For The Memories!

The dark of the night began to turn to the gray of morning. In the clouded distance could be heard the cries of mothers and fathers discovering the lifeless forms of their firstborn sons. The elders rushed from one adobe structure to another. "Quick!" they whispered, "pack the unleavened dough! Finish the lamb! Grab what you can! Now is the moment! Follow Moses to the sea while the Egyptians are preoccupied with their tragedy."

Hurriedly and silently, the dark shapes of men, women, and children passed under blood-marked lintels into the allies of their ghetto. Guided by their leaders, they rushed to the road to the sea. Not even a dog barked at them.

Their flight was the culmination of days of bargaining between their leaders and the Pharaoh. Threats of Moses had become realities: Frogs, gnats, boils, hail, locusts, flies, and diseased cattle had failed to persuade the king to release the slaves of Israel. Even some of the slaves themselves were not convinced that Moses' signs and wonders were all that extraordinary. The deaths of the firstborn caught Pharaoh's attention long enough to give the slaves a head start for the wilderness. The stumbling of the people through the Red Sea looked as though their efforts would lead to a watery grave as they looked over their shoulders and saw the Egyptian war machine close on their heels. But the chariots were caught in the muddy waters. The people struggled up upon the dry land and turned their footsteps in the direction of their meeting with destiny at Mount Sinai. They left behind the days and decades of digging clay, kneading the moistened clay with small hoes, shaping the clay into bricks, drying the bricks, and lugging the bricks to the construction sites. The unimaginable suffering, the drudgery, the heartless blows of the taskmasters, the deaths of the fainthearted under the merciless sun, all of it was left behind with those who began to bury their dead.

Freedom was born; a nation was born; a promise and a pact with the God of Moses accompanied them to the promised land. It began on that fateful night that would be called to mind in the countless homes of families gathered around roasted lamb and bitter herbs. In the following centuries, once a year on Passover evening, the youngest member of the family would ask, "Why is this night different from all other nights?" The adults conducting the proceedings of the evening would answer, "This is the sacrifice of the Lord's Passover, for he passed over the houses of the people of Israel in Egypt, when he slew the Egyptians but spared our houses" (Exodus 12:27).

The most important question of the evening is not merely a question about an event in history. The questioner does not ask, "Why *was* that night different from all other nights?" but "Why *is* this night different from all other nights?"

In the first place, the celebration of the Passover is more than a celebration of *history*. It is the celebration of freedom from slavery for the slaves and their descendents. "They were freed and *we* are freed with them." "When God saved them, God saved us!" Holy Moses! Holy were his people! Holy are his people today!

The text from Exodus 12 records more than memories. In the first place, they are more than memories about *us*. For those old enough to remember the *You Are There!* series hosted by Walter Cronkite, the text lures the reader into the action of the exodus. Christians must be careful not to mock and offend their Jewish friends with hokey presentations of the Seder meal on Maundy Thursday evening in the fellowship halls. Yet, those "Christian" renditions of the Seder meal make a point: Christians, the new Israel, have also been invited to tag along in the exodus out of Egypt. The salvation of the Israelites is repeated in the salvation extended by Jesus to the faithful in the upper room. It's the same God. It's the same deliverance from the destroyer that plagued the ancient Semites, today named sin, death, and the devil.

Christians express the Jewish awareness of inclusion in their salvation story when they ask, "Were you there when they crucified my Lord?" Of course, we were! How pitiful are the disclaimers who insist that the Jews killed Jesus! Hitler cheered the productions of the *Oberammergau Passion Play* depicting the Jews as sneering monsters with horns protruding from their heads. Modern Oberammergau productions omit the horns and depict only a portion of the crowd shouting, "Crucify him!" Modern textual research suggests that only some of the temple elite conspired against Jesus.

Contemporary Jews of faith join in the trek out of slavery. Contemporary Christians see themselves hammering the nails and thrusting the lance. Many are the contemporary Christians who sit at table in the upper room receiving the spiritual body and blood of our Lord on Maundy Thursday.

Secondly, the exodus memories are more than memories about *family*. Whether we march in the line of those headed for Sinai or join in the line of those headed for the communion rail, the focus is on family.

A group of Christian students decided to host their own version of the Jewish Seder meal. They asked a local rabbi to join them. The students stuck to the script religiously and reverently. The rabbi suddenly spoke up and offered a suggestion. "Don't be so stiff and formal!" he urged them. "When we do it, we say a prayer, then talk or laugh a bit, then we have a glass of wine, and after more conversation we say another prayer. It's a bit of a family thing. If you keep going the way you're going, you'll be done in twenty minutes."[1]

Those who have joined hands around the Seder meal have felt the power of the family circle. The Passover was moved later in Jewish history to the temple, but today it is back where it belongs: in the family circle.

The American family has taken many hits. In the mid-'80s, American sociologists defined the family in American culture as "a place where one is unconditionally accepted ... a place of love and happiness where you can count on the other family members."[2] But alas, by the middle of the nineteenth century, "... the network of kinship has narrowed and the sphere of individual decision has grown."[3]

The sense of "family" has also diminished in the church family. Exceptions to the rule are the small country churches where the entire membership joins in prayer at worship and then joins in "fellowship" around a buffet table laden with salads, sandwiches, pastries, coffee, and powdered drinks. The northern European model of worship attended by individuals and occasional couples entering and leaving with no "Hellos" and no "Good-byes" is repeated in staid mainline American churches.

"The family that prays together stays together" is a rule often confused but rarely practiced. Holy communion, rooted in the Jewish Seder, is a family affair. Nuclear families come forward to the altar and rub shoulders with the greater family, the community of believers gathered together in baptism and then nourished together by the bread and the wine (or grape juice). Continuous communion underlines the family theme.

The congregational family also acknowledges the "communion of saints" in the third article of the creed. The observance of Maundy Thursday also brings about two billion members of the universal Christian family to the same altar of Christ who feeds his earthly family and pours out upon it the power of his blood. But there is more: Keep on adding the countless hosts of those past, present, and future, who stand before the throne of the Lamb in heaven.

Thirdly, the exodus memories are more than memories about *our future*. From the biblical point of view, history is linear. It runs in a straight line. The Jews gathered around the Seder table to look back and see themselves tagging along behind Moses and the elders herding them toward the Red Sea and the safety beyond. Christians "remember" at the Lord's table not only the Jesus who sat and sits at the head of the table but looks forward to the heavenly feast to come.

An American exchange pastor was finishing up his tour of duty in a town near Hamburg, Germany, when the planes plowed their fiery way through the twin towers of the World Trade Center in New York on September 11, 2001. One of his German colleagues phoned him that evening to ask if he would share the message at a special prayer service scheduled the following evening. The American agreed, finished the conversation, and then went into the parsonage library to look for a text. On the desk he found a framed quote from Dietrich Bonhoeffer:

> *Wonderfully protected by benevolent powers*
> *Comforted, we await what may come*
> *For God is with us in the evening, in the morning*
> *And most certainly in every new day.*[4]

Bonhoeffer wrote those lines shortly before his hanging at the hands of the Nazis.

The church was packed that evening; there was standing room only. After the service, two young girls with tears in their eyes approached the American pastor. "We are so sorry about what happened yesterday in America," they said and handed the pastor two red roses. A few weeks later, when the guest pastor celebrated communion and said his farewells to the congregation, there was a sense of being bound together that would not have been as strong had the events in America not taken place. The visiting pastor and the members of the German congregation confessed to one another, "We are family!" But it was a family with a common past and a common future. Fiery chaos in New York could not stop the migration of brothers and sisters in Christ, holding hands, assisting one another in the journey to God's future. The physical realm had too little power to delay the coming of the kingdom.

The event in the upper room preceded the event of Golgotha by only a few hours. Christians everywhere were in that upper room and accompanied the Nazarene upon the *Via Dolorosa* to the place of execution. When Christians stand or kneel at altars around the world, their thoughts are more than memories. Their collective back flash brings tears. It brings joy. It brings anticipation. It is accompanied by a sense of unity ... unity with all believers of all times and places ... indeed, a sense of unity with all people for whom Christ offered his body and his blood. Amen.

1. Reginald H. Fuller, *Proclamation: Series B Holy Week* (Philadelphia: Fortress Press, 1975), p. 39.

2. Robert Bellah, et al, *Habits of the Heart* (New York: Harper & Row, 1985), p. 87.

3. *Ibid*, p. 89.

4. Dietrich Bonhoeffer, *Wiederstand und Ergebung* (München or Muenchen: Christian Kaiser Verlag, 11. Auflage, 1962), p. 275 (author's translation).

Good Friday
Isaiah 52:13—53:12

A Death On A Long Friday

After dying in a car crash, three friends went to heaven for orientation. They were given the privilege of spiritually attending their funerals. They were each asked, "What would you like your friends and family members to say about you?" The physician answered, "I hope they will say that I was one of the great physicians of my time and a loving family man." The second deceased person, a schoolteacher, replied, "I would like to hear that I was a wonderful wife and teacher." The third auto victim thought for a moment and then replied, "I would like to hear my friends say, 'Look, he's moving!' "

Humor helps us face the inevitable: our last resting place will be the coffin! We pray for a quick and painless death, perhaps a sinking into a deep, silent sleep. Such, however, was not the death of the servant of God described in the fourth servant song of the prophet Isaiah. "... he poured out himself to death ..." (53:12) but not before he was "wounded," "crushed," "bruised," and "led to the slaughter." Not a pretty picture.

Let's get to the point. The early church recognized Jesus in this prophetic image. In Acts 8 we read the story about Philip who was sent by an angel running down the road on the way to Gaza to catch up with an Ethiopian official who had just paid his respects at the temple in Jerusalem. Philip, perhaps huffing and puffing, managed to stop the official's chariot and caught the Ethiopian reading from the book of Isaiah.

Philip asked him, "Do you understand what you are reading?" "Of course not," replied the eunuch. "How would I be able to understand the words of some old Jewish prophet?" Philip replied, "Well, the one who was led to the slaughter like a sheep was my master, Jesus!" Philip's testimony leads to an instant baptism.

A pastor giving a children's sermon described a large, black animal growling, spitting saliva, and flashing its teeth, blocking the path in front of a hiker in the dark forest. "What was it?" asked the pastor rhetorically. One little girl frantically waved her hand, "It's Jesus! It's always Jesus!"

From the post-resurrection point of view, the suffering servant in Isaiah's song is Jesus. For Isaiah and his readers it was the nation of Israel, perhaps, or maybe an individual who gave his life as a guilt offering. (This is the only Old Testament passage that suggests that a person can give his life as a guilt offering.) But Christians would have to jump through hoops to convince themselves that this fellow described by Isaiah says nothing about Jesus.

This is Good Friday. We have to talk about death. Death is not regarded by most of us as "good." Good Friday is good because it was a Friday that led to salvation for many. The Swedes call it "Long Friday" because he who suffered and those who loved him and watched perhaps thought the agony and torture would never end. Mel Gibson's film, *The Passion of the Christ*, certainly dragged out the horrendous ordeal.

What made that Friday so long? There was a death that Friday. *It was the death of an innocent.* In his hymn, Johann Heerman, the seventeenth-century German pastor, asks, "Ah, holy Jesus, how hast thou offended?"[1] Heerman could tell the difference between guilt and innocence. He saw his town burned to the ground by plundering soldiers, buried his young bride, buried most of his pestilence-stricken townspeople in 1631, and died in 1647 after enduring throat disease.

Like his pietistic contemporaries, he certainly did not regard himself as an innocent, but praised and proclaimed the innocence of Jesus, his personal Savior. When Heerman found it impossible to forgive the bloodthirsty soldiers of Tilly, Jesus could and did. When Heerman wrestled with the visitation of the plague upon his people, Jesus saw a reason for the suffering of good people, a reason that Heerman would have to wait to see "then, face to face." While Heerman wept at the grave of his young wife, Jesus received her into the joy of the kingdom. Jesus was no fallen angel; he was God's beloved Son. He was absolutely obedient to his Father in heaven. His was the death of an innocent.

Methodist Bishop Gerald Kennedy reflected in one of his books on a picture taken during World War II.[2] It was a picture taken when some Jewish people were driven from the Warsaw ghetto by Nazi soldiers. Down in the front of a group of captured Jews was a little boy with his hands up and a look of uncertainty and fear on his face. A Nazi soldier was standing behind him with a gun pointed at the head of the boy. The youngster had an expression on his face which seemed to say, "What is going on here? What are you doing to me? What have I done?" For Kennedy, the photo portrayed also that moment when Jesus was betrayed in the garden. The boy was betrayed by his fellow human brothers. Jesus was betrayed by those for whom he died. Innocents are murdered even by those they love.

A pastor received a phone call at the office. A young single lady in her early twenties was senselessly killed by two intruders in her home. The murderers broke into the home to seek revenge upon the girl's mother who had fired them at their place of employment the day before. The mother was not home so they killed Janet, the daughter, instead. The pastor wept with the mother, prayed with her, decided upon the details of the funeral service, and delivered a sermon marked by anger over the wanton senseless murder of a gifted and energetic young lady facing a promising future. It was the death of an innocent. There was a death that Friday. *It was the death of a happy person.*

Soon after Janet's funeral, the pastor called upon an elderly woman named Martha. Martha had been somewhat frail and weak her entire life, even in her childhood. But she lived a long life, well into her eighties. She and her husband loved the Lord and dedicated their lives and their energies to the work of the church. On the day that the pastor visited her, she shared with him her awareness that she was about to go home to Jesus. She asked the pastor to preach on her confirmation text, Isaiah 43:1 at the funeral service, "But now thus says the Lord, he who created you, O Jacob, he who formed you, O Israel: Do not fear, for I have redeemed you; I have called you by name, you are mine."

The pastor reflected upon the two funerals. If there have to be the deaths of innocents, then why couldn't all those deaths be like Martha's? Martha was ready for death. She was happy. Unexpectedly, she had beaten all the odds. She fooled the prophets of doom and gloom. She had a happy marriage. She had loving children. She sat on her couch in her modest apartment and bounced her grandchildren on her lap. She served the church. The congregation was grateful. She would have served gladly without the accolades. Martha's death was the death of a happy person. So often do we experience the blessed "passing" of elderly people who lived for others.

Instinctively, we know that Isaiah's servant of the Lord gave his life for others joyfully. Did he not know that "he was wounded for our transgressions, crushed for our iniquities; upon him was the punishment that made us whole, and by his bruises we are healed"? (Isaiah 53:5).

Have we solved the enigma of Martha's death, the one to whom a long life was given so that she could experience the joy of serving others? Perhaps — there was a death that Friday. *It was a death unto life*. Perhaps here we can begin to solve the enigma of Janet's death.

The servant of the Lord, Isaiah's servant, was vindicated. "See, my servant shall prosper; he shall be exalted and lifted up, and shall be very high" (Isaiah 52:13). Janet's life was cut short; years of adventures were taken from her. But in spite of the pastor's anger at her funeral, he commended her to the God of mercy and grace, the God of life.

Look at the servant on the cross at Golgotha. In an earlier sermon in this series, we examined an altar dated from the end of the fifteenth century in the rear of St. Peter Church in Buxtehude, Germany. It was commissioned and donated to the parish of Buxtehude by the nephew of Meister Halephagen who wanted to honor the memory of his uncle. Meister Halephagen was a learned and loving priest and teacher who gave from his personal estate to help the poor of the city. His trust still supplies the needs of the underprivileged in that community.

In the painting, one sees Jesus bearing the cross to Golgotha. He is surrounded by a crowd of people, soldiers, faithful disciples, and tormentors. He peers straight out from the canvas into the eyes of the onlooker. "Look upon these proceedings; gaze upon your Lord who loves you, O sinner!" The eyes of the beholder of the painting are directed to the left of the picture, following the path to the top of the hill. The peak of the mount is shrouded in darkness and shadows. It is a dark death to which the Lord advances. But, look, the top of the hill is starkly outlined against brightness beyond! There is a suggestion of bright mountain peaks and trees behind Golgotha; the path seems to wind its way above and beyond the tip of the hill! The servant is vindicated! There is light and life beyond the grave. The story does not end on the cross.

Once a well-dressed man casually strolled down a busy city street. He stopped to take a closer look through a window displaying the scene of Good Friday, dominated by three stark crosses set against a grayish-black sky. The figure on the center cross, tragic and lifeless, brought an emotional tear to the viewer's eyes. A small seven-year-old boy, standing there as well, spoke to the gentleman, "Do you know what that is all about, mister?" "No," replied the gentleman. The boy, in his own words, told the story from the gospels. The man nodded agreement and started to continue down the street. The youngster ran after him. The man stopped and waited. The boy breathlessly blurted out, "Hey, mister, wait! He rose on Sunday. He's alive!"[3]

The death of innocents presents a gnawing dilemma. The children of Iraq, the everyday inhabitants of the Middle East, the women of Darfur, those who struggle in the midst of human need and tension in America's ghettos: These are the innocent. The beginning of peace and resolution for us can only be achieved when the more fortunate of us act to reach out to the victims of our planet. Good Friday was a long Friday. Our Fridays are long, as well. Will the injustice and violence and exploitation ever stop? Good Friday turned out to be good because it ended and dawn appeared on the horizon of the lives of the faithful. Death on a long Friday will find its defeat in the victory of the Sunday to come, the Sunday already achieved by the servant, the Sunday that waits to greet us as well. Amen.

---

1. "Ah, Holy Jesus," words by Johann Heermann, *Lutheran Book Of Worship* (Minneapolis: Augsburg, 1979), #123.

2. Gerald Kennedy, *The Preacher and the New English Bible* (New York: Oxford University Press, 1972), p. 134 ff.

3. Earl C. Willer, *A Treasury of Inspirational Illustrations* (Grand Rapids, Michigan: Baker Book House Company, 1975), p. 44.

Easter Day
Isaiah 25:6-9

Death Meets The Lord

The writer quoted in Isaiah 25 promises that an unlikely victory will occur. An unlikely victory had already occurred in his tradition when Goliath, the hero of the Philistine army confronted David, a young sheepherder. It didn't look like an even match. Goliath was a seasoned warrior, six cubits and a span tall, covered with a coat of mail and bronze helmet, and armed with a shaft with an iron spearhead that weighted six hundred shekels. He taunted the Israelites for forty days before David asked Saul to let him give it a try. Saul didn't have any better idea so he said to David, "Go for it!" David's first, smooth stone, launched from a sling, sank into Goliath's forehead, and Goliath fell face down dead (1 Samuel 17).

David was lucky. A comedian who thought that wrestling was a hoax lasted only a few seconds in the first round. Boxers and kickboxers who are evenly matched last longer.

The unknown writer, whose poetic eschatological thoughts are injected into the book of Isaiah (according to most scholars), predicts the death of death. "[the Lord] will swallow up death forever." The death of death is only a part of God's plan to usher in God's universal kingdom. The new earthly headquarters of the kingdom will be Jerusalem, a new center for peace and harmony between Jews and the Gentiles. The united peoples of earth will sit together in fellowship at a heavenly feast featuring the best wine imaginable and choice fatty meat usually reserved only for the gods.

Easter is the time to celebrate the fulfillment of that part of the prophecy that envisions the victory of life in God over its archenemy, Death (with a capital "D").

Martin Luther said it well in his hymn, "Christ Jesus Lay In Death's Strong Bands":

It was a strange and dreadful strife
When life and death contended;
The victory remained with life,
The reign of death was ended.
Holy Scripture plainly said
That death is swallowed up by death,
Its sting is lost forever.[1]

C. S. Lewis put the thought in modern language when he noted that Jesus is the David who knocked the wind out of the greater Goliath, Death. "[Jesus] is the 'first fruits,' the 'pioneer of life.' He has forced open a door that has been locked since the death of the first man. He has met, fought, and beaten the King of Death ... This is the beginning of the New Creation: a new chapter in cosmic history has opened."[2]

The American culture works overtime to sanitize the reality of death. People don't die anymore; they just "pass" and they are not dead; they're just "gone" and one imagines they'll be back soon. Our funeral directors use a whole new vocabulary to soften the blow when they meet with survivors. The funeral staff member who does the cosmetic work happily stands in the wings to listen as the visitors exclaim, "Why, it looks like Harry is just sleeping!" or "Doesn't she look great!" That's why many clergy prefer that the coffin be closed before the funeral service begins so that the worshipers can better focus upon the hope of the resurrection. Many members of the family dread that moment when the coffin is closed because they are unwilling to accept the finality it signals.

A German theology professor once wrote a letter to a gifted student snatched by the Nazis out of the classroom to serve as a pilot in the Mediterranean. The young man had shared in a letter his fear of certain impending death. The mentor wrote:

Death is in fact an enemy, a contradiction ... Does it not sever and destroy the bonds of life and friendship? Does it not take away the best of our youth and shatter

> *the lives of thousands of others? Is it not really an unnatural disorder, as the Bible portrays it? ... In death I am really and irretrievably and in actual fact at my end.*[3]

No Christian can begin to win the struggle against death without first realizing the finality of death. A curious friend of a deceased man was invited by the mortician to linger after the funeral service to view the embalming process in the back room. To his horror, the friend recognized the remains on the embalming table. He didn't even know that his friend, Gus, had passed away earlier that day.

As he watched the embalming process, the friend realized that Gus' sleeping days were over! He was really dead. His spirit, his soul, his body, his mind, his memory, all of it! His life was gone. Gus was not immortal. He had really come to the end of his rope. There could only be one hope.

Back to Isaiah 25 — "... he will swallow up death forever." It appeared that poor Gus was the loser in the bout against Death. So was the flyer on the Mediterranean front. He was shot down but not before he read the rest of the letter from his professor.

> *In death I am really ... at my end. But at the same time I am one whose history with God cannot stop, since I am called by my name and I am the friend of Jesus. The Resurrected One is victorious and I stand within his sphere of power. [He] receives me on the other side of the gloomy grave.*[4]

We can't hope to win any fights against Mr. Death. Gus lost out. So will all of us. Someone was victorious in our stead. There is only one who went up against Death and won the match. We can, in faith, take his extended hand and rise up victorious with him who, at our baptisms, called us by name. He never forgets that name! That name, on God's list, becomes our ticket out of the land of Death.

Christ has taken the sting out of death. A man went to his pastor, time after time, and promised that he would never drink again.

The pastor said that he would accept the pledge only one more time. The vow was made. In the late evening the man appeared and said that he must be allowed to have a drink or he would die. The pastor quietly told him to go home and die. The next morning the man came with a brightness in his face and said, "I died last night." He who was raised into new life from the grave on Easter is available to help us die in many circumstances. That is the glory of the resurrection.

The Berlin Wall was a horrific barrier. It separated Germans from Germans, brothers and sisters, children and parents. It was in place long enough for one culture to be divided into two cultures. After it came down during those dramatic days in November 1989, people from both sides who spoke the same language painfully realized in the ensuing months that they had become different. On one side was wealth, democracy, and materialism; on the other side was a people who had learned to live unto themselves into their private lives with far less material resources, and, perhaps an intensity of faith and a desire for peace that left the free world behind in the dust.

But the wall came down! In the years since the "fall," the two peoples have become one again. The incarceration is a memory that belongs to the past.

A rebirth, of sorts, has occurred. In Christ, a rebirth has already begun to turn the world into a future to which Christ calls and pulls us.

After the devastating fires of the summer of 1988, many Americans thought that Yellowstone National Park would never be the same again. In spite of the expenditure of millions of dollars and the efforts of 25,000 firefighters, the fire raged on and the whole nation began to lose hope. Finally, it ended in smoldering blackened ruination.

The serious observer, however, noted that a resurrection began to occur within days of the end of the fire. It was observed, for example, that only a few animal inhabitants, relatively speaking, perished; within days, there was luscious grass to eat in burned out regions and by spring, the new meadows created by the fire were ablaze with new vegetation that could have never discovered the light of day had the fire not destroyed competing vegetation. In other words, the Yellowstone disaster was really only nature at work, thinning out the herds, giving new seeds a chance to do their thing, renewing and continuing the process of creation. The death of Yellowstone turned out to be the birth of Yellowstone.

Nature reminds us that death can lead to life: Small cedars straighten themselves after a heavy snowfall; the daffodils and the tulips spring from the ground out of the melting snow in the spring; the butterfly breaks forth from its coffin, the cocoon; the human body mends itself unceasingly and only reluctantly falls to the mat when, in many instances, we abuse it with junk food, lack of exercise, or cigarettes.

The benefits of God's decisive action in Christ abound. He who died on the cross and rose from the grave encourages us to seek new life and reach for the ring of hope in all circumstances.

In the movie, *Empire of the Sun*, young Jimmy Graham was living in Singapore with his parents when the Japanese suddenly took the city while Jimmy was at boys' choir practice in the church. When the confusion of the attack began, he ran home to find that his parents were already gone. He was taken by the Japanese to an internment camp in Japan. There he modeled the life of Christ as he ran errands between the American and English prisoners, kept hopes up with his cheerful demeanor, and befriended a Japanese boy stationed at the air base next to the compound who met Jimmy at the fence. He was well treated by the Japanese and the English prisoners, and he was badly treated by the Japanese and the English captors. He confided to the chaplain through tears that he could no longer remember the faces of his parents. He witnessed the beheading of his Japanese friend, accused of fraternizing with the enemy. He found his surrogate mother deceased in bed. He saw a bright flash of light on the horizon one day.

Soon thereafter, the Japanese guards abandoned the camp and the surviving prisoners, while moving in caravan away from the camp, were overtaken by the American liberators. Jimmy and the other orphaned children were placed in a makeshift orphanage. One day a group of hopeful parents came to find their children.

Jimmy's parents saw him in the assembled crowd. He stood listless, inanimate, empty, looking but not seeing, with a 1,000-yard stare. His mother came up from behind him and rested her hand on his left shoulder and whispered, "Jimmy?" Jimmy had become Jim, a man, but he was like a dead man. His mother passed around him to his front; she looked into his gray eyes and slowly hugged him, only as a mother could. The camera zoomed in for a close-up. The viewer sees a tear run down his cheek. Jimmy is alive; he has been reborn. He is resurrected.

What does the prophet say? "Then the Lord God will wipe away the tears from all faces" (v. 8). "And he will destroy on this mountain the shroud that is cast over all peoples, the sheet that is spread over all nations; he will swallow up death forever" (v. 7).

The tears were taken from those who rejoiced on the first Easter morning. Their friend, their teacher, their Savior, was raised from the dead. But it was only the beginning. There is still the feast to come. Amen.

---

1. Martin Luther, "Christ Jesus Lay In Death's Strong Bands," *Lutheran Book of Worship* (Minneapolis: Augsburg, 1978), p. 134.

2. C. S. Lewis, *The Joyful Christian* (New York: Touchstone, 1977), p. 65.

3. Helmut Thielicke, *Death and Life* (Philadelphia: Fortress Press, 1970), pp. xxi, xxii, and xxv.

4. *Ibid*, pp. xxv-xxvi.

Easter 2
Acts 4:32-35

What Is Our City?

In the text from Acts 4, we get a glimpse of life in the Christian community after the resurrection event. The text offers some answers to the question of T. S. Eliot:

> *When the Stranger says: "What is the meaning of this*
> *city?*
> *Do you huddle close together because you love each*
> *other?"*
> *What will you answer? "We all dwell together*
> *To make money from each other"? or "This is a*
> *community"?*[1]

What makes the church community different from other communities?

In the first place, we read that "... the apostles gave their testimony to the resurrection of the Lord Jesus ..." (v. 33). Luke's mention of the testimony of the apostles recalls the earlier testimony of Paul himself in his first letter to the Corinthians, which he was passing on the message about the good news that he had already received from fellow apostles (1 Corinthians 15:1-2). If the scholars are right, the description of the community provided by Luke in Acts 4 was of a community harboring apostles proclaiming the good news perhaps twenty years after Paul proclaimed his good news to the Corinthians. And Paul said that he was somewhat late in the chain of communications. Here we see evidence of a tradition already perhaps three or four decades in place. The leaders of the Christian communities recognized that their job was to keep proclaiming the resurrection of Jesus. The implication is that the early church communities shared the earmark of resurrection proclamation!

This suggests that there is some credence to the claims of some Christian communities today that they possess an "apostolic succession" of one kind or another. Most Protestants today reject such lists of bishops or church leaders that trace the proclamation of the good news physically from one leader to another backward all the way to Peter, but all Christians agree that one mark of the continuity of the Christian church is the faithful passing on of the apostolic good news that "He is risen! He is risen indeed!"

Four great ecumenical councils beginning with the one in Nicaea in 325 and ending in Chalcedon in 451 went to a great deal of effort to dot the "i's" and cross the "t's" of the good news, just to make sure that the succession of teachers in the church would keep it straight. The early church adopted Sunday as its day of worship in order to keep the resurrection event at the center of the story of Jesus.

A young American student at the University of Heidelberg in Germany was discussing theology in one of the local student taverns one evening with two German students who attacked his naive take on scriptural witness. How could he possibly believe in the resurrection of Jesus? A few days later, the American learned that one of his good friends, whose father was a church superintendent, also rejected the resurrection. The friend was committed to a career as a pastor in order to promote social causes. The American was rattled. Didn't Saint Paul say once that faith is futile without the resurrection component? (1 Corinthians 15:17-19).

The American embarked upon a mission to read up on all the latest scholarly German commentaries on the five accounts of the resurrection (the end of the four gospels and 1 Corinthians 15). He discovered that his friends had not done the same and had not, for example, read the latest material written by Wolfhart Pannenberg, the popular New Testament scholar who advocated the historicity of the resurrection of Jesus. Pannenberg and other contemporary scholars applied the tools of historical research in their examination of the resurrection accounts and concluded, "If Washington crossed the Delaware to surprise the Hessians at Trenton on Christmas Day night, then Jesus was also raised from the dead!"

Providentially, the chain of gospel delivery has not been broken, thanks to leaders like Augustine (who battled the heresies), Pope Gregory the Great (who sent missionaries to Britain and Ireland), Benedictus XI (who returned the church to Trinitarian teaching in 1305), Martin Luther, the Wesley Brothers, and Dietrich Bonhoeffer. However, most of us did not sit at the feet of any of those stars. We received the message passed on in catechisms, hymns, liturgies, and prayers. More likely, we received it from parents, Sunday school teachers, pastors, priests, or college professors. Whether born and raised in a church community or grafted in later in life, we went into the community through the door of faith. In spite of the weaknesses and foibles of human vessels, we caught the vision of a glorious, life-changing assertion, that Jesus died on the cross for us and was raised from the dead to lead us as well into a glorious future. That future (and present) is already accessible and at hand in the community of believers where testimony to the resurrection of Lord Jesus is given.

Actually, the power and vitality of the church can only be at maximum strength when the message of the church is about the resurrection. A member of a church in Michigan enjoyed the frequent company of his pastor at his home in the evenings. He loved to talk religion but he didn't waste the pastor's time talking about the resurrection. He initiated serious discussion about the height of candles in the sanctuary and the protocol dealing with the most holy sacred lighting of them by the acolytes. He was annoyed when the congregation called a new assistant pastor who was shorter than the senior pastor. It just didn't look right! That was his religion. It was a poor substitute. If the early community mentioned in Acts 4 talked about candle height or proper vestments or a church building drive, it's not noted. We do know that the "apostles gave their testimony to the resurrection of the Lord Jesus" (v. 33).

What makes the church community different from other communities? The Christian community is the place where resources and gifts are shared. "No one claimed private ownership of any possessions, but everything they owned was held in common" (v. 32). Furthermore, they sold their lands and houses and "laid (the proceeds) at the apostles' feet, and it was distributed to each as any had need" (v. 35).

In an American capitalist society, it might be considered a bit radical to cash in one's equity and bring the money to the church council for distribution. But there are models. We think about the Amish communities, the Kibbutz communities of Israel, Native American communities, and cults (dangerous or not).

Few congregations, if any, are communal. There are many congregations that enjoy an attitude of sharing: hot dishes delivered to the doors of the ill, trucks pull up when someone needs help with a move, younger parishioners transport the elderly to the supermarket or to the physician's office, benevolence dollars are distributed to the local and national churches to feed the hungry and provide homes for the homeless and the abused. The spirit of sharing is alive and well in many parishes and congregations.

Few congregations are like the small church upon which a lot of oil was discovered. As the money rolled in, the forty members attended a special meeting to decide what to do. Deacon Brown made a motion that the money be divided equally among the forty members and, "furthermore," he suggested, "I move that no new members be taken in."

The embryo church of Acts 4 took to heart the new command of Jesus, "that you love one another. By this everyone will know that you are my disciples, if you have love for one another" (John 13:34-35). There are Christian communities who place the greatest emphasis on saving souls, and rightly so. But the decision of the penitent to accept Jesus as one's Lord and Savior is a decision to accept his call to discipleship. Step one: Accept Jesus as Savior. Step two: Go forth to serve in his name. You can't have one without the other. The many sales of Rick Warren's book, *The Purpose-Driven Life*, prove that many people are searching for purpose and meaning in their lives.

For Christians, the purpose-driven life is the life that is given to Jesus who said, "Take up your cross and follow me" (Matthew 16:24). It is troubling that it sometimes appears that leaders of megachurches seem to imply that big churches are an expression of the "real" church because of the great numbers of "members" who worship there. One thinks about pastors and priests serving in small rural churches where spectacular numerical growth is not possible. The "glory" of the church is not large edifices with the best sound and lighting technology, but it is the loving and the sharing and the sacrifice of the community of faith. The church that follows the model of Acts 4 is the church that shares and serves, and that means more than giving out a few turkeys at Thanksgiving. A beloved Catholic priest in the Detroit area always ended his visits with an admonition, "Remember to pray for the poor." His parish also gave to the poor. Charity begins at home. It's not surprising that congregations that share their collective good fortune with each other also have impressive ministries to those outside their doors, in their neighborhoods and beyond.

The community model embedded in Acts 4 stood on the two pillars of proclamation and loving one another. There is a small congregation in eastern Arizona in a mining town that saw its glory days pass about a half-century ago. The parish has about 125 members and there are usually at least 125 people at Sunday services. When the pastor announces that the choir will sing, about half of the congregation stands up and approaches the altar. When the offering looks a little meager, the president of the congregation stands up and tells the ushers to pass the plate again. Closing prayers are long and detailed and cover those facing surgery to those who are worried about the kids to those who are about to go on a trip. The "refreshments" after the service include cakes, sandwiches, hot dishes, meatballs, gelatin dishes, and several kinds of beverages. In other words, it's a Sunday lunch and it's time to visit with one another and catch up on the latest happenings within the community. If someone should mention that they resemble the community described in Acts 4, they would be embarrassed. What if a stranger would confront the people? "What is the meaning of this city? Do you huddle close together because you love each other? Or do you dwell together to make money from each other?" The people in that community would say, "There's not much money to make from each other. We just enjoy each other's company. We share our mutual woes and joys. And by the way ... we meet up there on the ridge at 5 a.m. to greet the Son on Easter morning."

That community is an Easter community. It is a sharing community. Enough said. Amen.

---

1. T. S. Eliot, "Choruses from 'The Rock,' " *The Complete Poems and Plays* (New York: Harcourt, Brace and Co., 1952), p. 103.

Easter 3
Acts 3:12-19

Three O'Clock At The Temple

A church caught on fire. An elderly man came running to join the others who had come to throw water. After the fire was under control, the minister said to the old gent, "Why, John, this is the first time I've ever seen you at church!" John replied, "This is the first time I've ever seen this church on fire."

Many have reduced the number of visits to the neighborhood church. They are, perhaps, tired of unpolished, irrelevant sermons. Perhaps the worship is done by rote and boring, not inspirational, but dull. Maybe the welcoming mat is gone. A lady went to church. She parked her car. Someone said, "You took my parking place." She took a seat in the third row, right on the aisle. The stare she got from the man next to her said it all, "You took the place of my wife who will soon come to sit." After services, she went to the fellowship hall to get a cup of punch. As she finished off the last cup in the bowl, someone said, "You took the pastor's cup of punch." The visitor went into the church to look at the altar cross. She looked up at the crucified one and thought, "But you took my place!"

Peter and John went one day to the temple at three o'clock in the afternoon to pray. The story starts at the beginning of chapter 3 in the book of Acts. They watched as a lame man was laid at one of the gates. As Peter and John passed him, the man asked them for a handout. Peter responded, "I have no silver or gold for you but I have something better: In the name of Jesus, stand up and walk!" The man's ankles and legs responded; he stood up and, dancing, accompanied Peter and John into the temple.

A *miracle* — it happened at the temple; it happened at church; it happened at three o'clock in the afternoon. There were witnesses that day milling around on a great stone porch built by Herod the Great facing the Mount of Olives. The lame man must have raced around throughout the temple compound showing off his new strong ankles and legs. The visitors recognized him; he had been laying at the gate for years. There was no doubt, the man once paralyzed was running around making a nuisance out of himself.

It was clearly a miracle!

Can miracles still happen at church? Charismatic Christians witness to speaking in tongues and dramatic healings. But there is more: Worshipers weep as they receive the body and blood of Christ. Sometimes those who exit the services exclaim to the pastor or priest, "You were talking to me today, pastor," or "You touched my heart!" Sometimes a man or a woman will make a silent vow to make amends with a neighbor or a parent or child. Sometimes guilt or doubt is exorcised from the soul. It happened at three o'clock in the afternoon. It can happen at the eight o'clock mass or the 10:30 service of praise.

A point was made — at the temple — at three o'clock. Peter expressed bewilderment about the astonishment of the people. The witnesses have missed something. Have they not heard about the raising of Jesus, the man from Nazareth? "It's a new world! The promises of God to Abraham and Isaac and Jacob have been fulfilled in Jesus! You remember Jesus, don't you? He's the one you consigned to death when Pilate the governor wanted to acquit him! He's the innocent man you sent to the cross! But know this! That very man you murdered has given new life and hope to the lame man at the gate! What do you think about that?"

There was a little soul searching that day. Maybe people don't want to search their souls anymore. That's why they avoid church on Sunday morning. Some have found other "churches" that omit references to sin, death, and the devil. People can go to churches that accept credit cards, which only preach positive messages complete with references to fluffy white clouds floating in bright blue skies. The choirs sing numbers from Gershwin or Rogers and

Hammerstein or simple "praise" songs inviting audience participation. They want to praise, praise, praise God and drown out God's word of judgment. Soul searching is discouraged.

There was a challenge — at the temple — at three o'clock. Peter lets his listeners off the hook. "You didn't know what you were doing. You didn't know that you were murdering a man who willingly took the bullet for you! But now you know! Look at this lame man now whole and leaping and dancing! The man you killed was raised from the dead with great power. It is that same man who gave back life and hope to this poor soul! God had it all planned out! It was not a coincidence! God has made good on his promises to the fathers, to the nation, to Israel! Look at this man once lame and know that the God who healed this hopeless piece of humanity can also heal you! Repent! Make up your minds! Get on the bandwagon! Follow the risen Savior! Enter the land of hope and restoration!"

There is a museum in Berlin that documents the attempts of Germans entrapped behind the wall in the German Democratic Republic to escape to the west. Some of them tunneled under the wall. Others hid in the beds of trucks or brazenly crashed through the wall. A few daringly floated over the wall in hot-air balloons. Some simply made a run for it.

Many were shot or killed on the spot or captured. Some simply vanished, their fates still unknown. One documented incident records the efforts of three men to dig a tunnel from the basement of a small house near the wall. They dug a passage twenty inches in diameter and about sixty yards long, under three rows of barbed wire. The digging was slow. The men took turns shoveling the dirt in front of them behind to be transported back to the house that became filled with sandy dirt, in closets, in dressers, in cupboards, in the rooms from floor to ceiling. When the tunnel was finally finished, seven women, four men, and two children wiggled their way through the tunnel to freedom.

Peter challenged the people standing on the porch of the temple that day to accept the courage and power of the living Christ to move the obstacles between them and the kingdom from before them to behind them. Is God the punitive God who needs to be appeased? Move that god behind you. Is God the God who operates on merit? Move that god behind you. Pride, human effort, pretentiousness, power games, worldly success (or the appearance of success)! Move that dirt to the back. Clear the way! Go with God! Love God; do not fear him! Love God; love your neighbors! Follow the risen Lord!

"Repent!" said Peter. "Make up your minds!"

A film was made in 2005 based upon the book, *Tsotsi*, about a boy in South Africa who runs away from home because of the cruelty of his father. Tsotsi survives by living with orphans in giant construction pipes near the city. He becomes the leader of a band of thieves and is able to get his own "place" in the township. The boy in the group nicknamed the "teacher" accuses Tsotsi of going too far and abandoning "decency" when a robbery gets out of hand and a victim is killed. Consumed by a fit of anger, Tsotsi beats up the teacher.

He goes to a good neighborhood, steals a car, and later realizes that there is a baby in the backseat. He decides to keep the baby and takes it to a young widow for feeding. He returns to the baby's house to fetch toys. He does not allow a fellow thief to harm the baby's father who is in the house at the time of the toy raid.

His love for the baby initiates a transformation. He apologizes to the teacher. At the moment of confrontation with a helpless cripple in an alley, he decides not to take the cripple's take for the day. He wants to help the young widow. Moved by the widow's love for him, Tsotsi agrees to take the baby back to its parents. On the way to the house, he is curiously moved by the sight of several baptisms in the river.

In his attempt to return the baby, Tsotsi fails to avoid a confrontation with the police. The baby's father persuades the police not to harm him and Tsotsi is taken into custody. Tsotsi's fate is not known but the viewer of the movie knows that Tsotsi has been redeemed. The plight of those weaker than he (the baby, the young widow, the teacher, the wheelchair-bound beggar) has moved him to compassion. He has left his life of crime and the hatred for his father behind. He goes to jail but he goes as a free man, a man who has been liberated by love.

There are many accounts of Paul, Peter, and other apostles recorded in the book of Acts that demonstrate the power of the risen Christ in the lives of his first-century followers. The Easter season is not only the time to celebrate the resurrection of Christ, but it is also the time to remember how the power of the risen Christ was visible and manifested in the life of the early church. At the gate of the temple at three o'clock in the afternoon, a lame man was restored and healed! Those who witnessed the miracle of restoration were challenged by Peter and John to embrace the power of new life. Perhaps the pastors and priests of today's mainline churches cannot preach as inspiringly as Peter but perhaps, on the other hand, today's seekers do not see the love of the community that can transform them. Their eyes are not open; their hearts are turning to leather. Perhaps they are looking for the wrong kind of miracles. They may go to the temple but they are looking for the wrong kind of miracles. Too bad. They are dragging their feet when they could be dancing for joy. It's three o'clock. It's time to go to the temple. Anytime is a good time to go to the temple to see what God can and has done, but Peter and John went at three o'clock in the afternoon. Amen.

Easter 4
Acts 4:5-12

Salvation Has A Name!

There's a story going around about a college student who stayed up all night preparing for his zoology test. He entered the classroom and saw ten stands each with a bird on it, each bird covered with a sack with only the legs showing. The professor instructed the students to use the legs to identify each bird by name, habitat, genus, and species. The perplexed student, sitting in the first row, was consumed by despair. All legs looked alike. Enraged, he approached the desk of the professor and exclaimed, "What a stupid test! How could anyone identify birds by looking at their legs?" He threw the unmarked test on the teacher's desk and headed for the door. The professor was taken by surprise. He didn't know the names of all of his students so he called after the young man, "Mister, what's your name?" The enraged student pulled up his pant legs and said, "You guess, buddy! You guess!"

Birds are named. So are students. Salvation, also, has a name. The name is Jesus.

It is a name that involves risk. Acts 4 continues the story of Peter and John who healed a lame man one afternoon at the temple in Jerusalem. The healing of the man, handicapped since birth, caused quite a stir. In fact, in a short time, according to Luke's account, about 5,000 people were positively impressed by the incident. That's when the Sanhedrin, the ruling legislature of the Jews, decided to take action. They thought that they had taken care of the Jesus question. They coerced Pilate into executing the man responsible for arousing the passions of the people and jeopardizing the *status quo*. The followers of Jesus were going around healing people in the name of the man, a man branded as a criminal, whom they thought they had removed from the scene. The Sanhedrin had the authority to arrest Peter and John but they had no authority to put anyone to death. It appears that the court wanted to intimidate Peter and John; usually a stay overnight in jail is sufficient.

Peter and John were not only guilty of healing a lame man. (It could always be claimed that it was a trick.) They were pushing the envelope further by claiming that Jesus wasn't really dead. In fact, he was raised from the dead, and his post-death new life had the power to turn nature's laws upside down. The Sadducees were upset because they didn't believe in the resurrection and the rest of the lot were upset because Peter and John were taking the idea too far! Jesus was alleged not only to have been raised from the dead; he was in the position to confront people, to force people to make a decision for or against him, and lead people into a new kingdom!

Peter and John's "gospel" was threatening. Only the high and mighty leaders of the nation had the right to make religious proclamations! Peter and John were lowly fishermen, ignorant people "of the land." How dare they turn the heads of 5,000 people!

Peter and John were in trouble. They were standing before the most powerful men in the nation of Jews. They had assumed more than a little risk in such a bold proclamation supported by the miraculous healing of a lame man. Jesus had warned them: "... they will arrest you and persecute you; they will hand you over to synagogues and prisons, and you will be brought before kings and governors because of my name" (Luke 21:12).

Forewarned and forearmed, they found themselves in front of the supreme court.

Unflinchingly, Peter confronts his accusers. "Not only is my Lord alive and well, he is in a position of great power even though you plotted to do away with him" he told them. "... the stone that was rejected by you, the builders, [has] become the cornerstone" (Acts 4:11).

The determination of Peter to witness confrontationally ended with the execution of Peter later in Rome. It is not clear whether John died peaceably in Ephesus or was, according to one tradition, killed by the Jews. But, the fact is, proclaiming the name of Jesus can be a risky business. Stephen was stoned at the gate; Polycarp, the bishop of Smyrna, pledged his oath of allegiance to his Savior while the fire licked at the stake; Paul was tormented by his defectors many times before meeting his end in Rome. In our own day, we have witnessed the persecution of Christians in communist states, in the deserts of Africa, and in the humid climes of South America. Not too many years ago, a Protestant bishop in El Salvador sent his family to the United States because of the threats of death squads. A Catholic bishop was shot dead at the altar.

Generally speaking, Christians in the US who invoke the name of Jesus may occasionally have to remove nativity exhibits from courthouse grounds, or, if they are Amish Christians, pay a fine if they refuse to post "slow-moving-vehicle" stickers on their buggies. Once in a while, Christian conscientious objectors on active duty in the military might face a dishonorable discharge if they push the pacifist agenda too aggressively.

The name of Jesus is also a name that can be reaffirmed. Peter and John confront the highly regarded members of the Sanhedrin with their rejection of Jesus, the "cornerstone rejected by the builders." Jesus should have been one embraced by the religious leaders of the Jews, but they dispatched him instead. The implication is clear. Peter and John were giving their accusers an opportunity to open their eyes in the presence of the lame man standing before them. Five thousand in the city might have been moved by the apostolic testimony but the members of the Jewish council stubbornly refused to allow the gospel to soften their hardened hearts. They had their own gospels, their own agendas, and their own status and authority to protect.

We cannot be sure, however. Perhaps some of them began to see the light. In the times of spiritual awakening in our American history, we hear of those who dramatically professed him whom they had rejected. The revival tents, barns, and fields of America were places where many were shaken by the passionate witness of the preachers. A well-known local gambler approached the altar in tears to affirm his faith in Jesus. The preacher instructed him after the meeting to bring his gambling equipment to the next meeting to burn it in the presence of the faithful. The new convert objected. He couldn't do it. "Why not?" asked the preacher. "Well," replied the gambler, "I've truly been converted but suppose I throw all my stuff away and then I backslide. I'd be in a terrible predicament!"

Reject Jesus. Accept Jesus. Reject Jesus again. We Americans have it down to a science. We are in the church. We fall away from the church. We feel remorse so we go church-shopping and start again from scratch. Who knows better than Americans the grace and mercy of the God of second chances?

A pastor visited a family who visited at worship. Nothing happened. The pastor called on the family again a year later. Promises were made but nothing happened. The pastor refused to give up; he reminded the family that people need to address the spiritual needs of their existence. The family finally confessed that they had been kicked out of another congregation because of inactivity. Four years after their visit in church, the pastor made another phone call; he talked about the young sons who would soon be starting confirmation classes; he talked about the opportunities to serve in the community of believers. The wife and mother promised again to return to church. She and her family finally accepted the cornerstone that they had been rejecting in a final way. The two sons faithfully attended confirmation classes for two years. The mother was elected president of the women's club and then she became secretary in the office. Her husband faithfully sat in the balcony at worship and critiqued the pastor's sermons (someone had to do it). The name of Jesus may be placed on the back burner but it can always be reaffirmed.

There is no other name! Peter and John were part of a culture who understood the construct "name" perhaps a little differently than we do today. To mention the name of a god was not something done lightly. The name of the god presented the power and presence of the god and its invocation brought the god too close for comfort. Hence rival factions invoked the names of their gods at the time of battle to bring to bare the fierce power of the gods. We keep the tradition alive when we pray to God or ask that "God bless America!"

There were lots of divine names in the world of the first century. People belonged to mystery cults and placed statues of their favorite gods in their homes. One might say to one's neighbor, "My god is better than your god!"

On one level, however, Peter and John were preaching to the choir. Surely the noble members of the Sanhedrin, regardless of their various parties, confessed the power of the God of Abraham, Isaac, and Moses. But Peter and John understood the God of the Jews in a new and significant way. The teachings of Jesus cast the law in a new light; in fact, he in his person was the fulfillment of the law. God's love and mercy were revealed in a new way. God was, in fact, in Jesus.

An American pastor served a German congregation for half a year. He celebrated holy communion one Sunday for the first time. He was carefully instructed by the other pastors and by the choir director in the nuances of the liturgy. Everything went well until he tried to dismiss the first table of communicants gathered standing in a half circle around the altar. They had received the bread and the wine; he wanted them to return to their seats; he motioned with his hands; they just stood there and stared at him with a blank look. A member of the congregation rushed to his side and whispered, "They won't return to their pews until you recite a Bible verse; there's one up there!" The American looked to his right and saw an eighteenth-century oil portrait depicting Jesus, under whom were the words (in German), "I am the way, the truth, and the life; no one comes to the Father except through me!" (John 14:6). The pastor recited the Bible verse; the communicants smiled and returned to their seats. They had been dislodged by the power of the name of Jesus!

Ignatius, an early church father once said, "Apart from Jesus we have not true life." Jesus has made it possible for us to reclaim our life with God. He is the only way. "But," the enlightened believer may ask, "what about the Hindus, the Muslims, and Buddhists? They seem like good people. Are they going to hell if they don't embrace Jesus?" There are those Christians who might seem a tad liberal if they note that Jesus announced salvation to all people. In ways that we may only understand when we see "face-to-face,"

Jesus is still the only name, the only way to salvation. It remains the business of the believer to proclaim Christ as redeemer to anyone who will listen. It is God's business and the business of the Spirit to take it from there.

It would be strange indeed if a person profoundly loved by someone else had no interest in learning the name of the relative or friend who did the loving. A visitor visited a sheep farm. After lunch, the little girl asked the visitor to go to the pen to see her own little lamb. The guest looked into the pen and saw more than 200 sheep and lambs. The little girl looked into the maze of wool and shouted out, "There he is. There's my lamb!" "How can you tell which one is yours among so many?" asked the city dweller. "Because," answered the little girl, "he's mine. He's my very own and I know him!"

Isaiah once delivered the word of the Lord to the people: "But now thus says the Lord, he who created you, O Jacob, he who formed you, O Israel: Do not fear, for I have redeemed you; I have called you by name, you are mine" (Isaiah 43:1).

At the baptismal font, God has called us by name. Jesus is the good shepherd who knows his sheep; he knows us by name. He who named us is the one whose name we know. Salvation has a name: It is Jesus. Amen.

Easter 5
Acts 8:26-40

Who Am I?

Back in the '60s, a real "hip" kid attended the morning service of worship at an upper-class church. The pastor greeted him at the door. The groovy kid grabbed the minister's hand and said, "Dad, I really dug that sermon!" The staid pastor was taken by surprise and said, "Young man, I don't understand." The beatnik answered, "Dad, I really 'went' for that sermon; it really came down the middle, man, loud and cool; it was like, gone, man."

The minister's dignity was rattled and he decided to confront the young man with some propriety. He said, "Son, I just don't understand what you are trying to say; perhaps you could use some appropriate English." The loose-shirted, blue-jeaned, and sandaled lad tried again. "Dad, what I really mean is, I really went for what you had to say, so much so that I put 100 smackeroos in the collection plate." Suddenly the cast of enlightenment crossed the face of the minister and he said, "Crazy, man, crazy!"

The story is really about identity. The minister presented his identity, staid, professional, dignified, a member of the religious establishment. The hippie wore another identity, an identity assumed, perhaps, for the purpose of broadcasting to the world, "Hey, look at me, pay attention to me, don't ignore me!"

Some years ago, in the '80s, a tour director led some of the older ladies in his group after the evening meal down Kurfuerstendam, the main street of Berlin. The streets were crowded by punkers, one outfit more outrageous than the other. As the leader approached one particular punker, she noticed something furry on his shoulder chained by a pin to his ear. She was startled to discover that it was a rat. A bit of a mean streak seized her and she quickly stepped aside in order to observe the reaction of the lady next in line. The punker also attracted the interest of the tourist. The woman approached him with curiosity, getting closer in order to figure out what he had on his shoulder. When she realized that she was almost within kissing distance of a live rat, she yelled and jumped backward a considerable distance.

The punker, of course, loved it. He delighted in shocking the people walking along Kurfuerstendam. He had found identity and he wanted to flaunt it. In a city that, before the reunification of Germany, was a symbol of lost hopes and futility, the punker found "success" with purple hair, with an outrageous costume, and with a rat pinned to his ear.

How desperate are we to find our identity? At one moment in his life from his prison cell Dietrich Bonhoeffer asked the question, "Who am I? They mock me, these lonely questions of mine."

Once there was an Ethiopian. He was a eunuch and a prestigious minister of the court of Candace, the queen of the Ethiopians. He went on a journey to Jerusalem, perhaps on business for his boss, or perhaps to find his identity. Who knows what kind of identity crisis can occur when one has to become a eunuch in order to rise to a high position in a country so powerful that it was often yoked with the powerful empire of Egypt?

Some historians have observed that the first century in the Middle East was an age of honest doubt and seeking. Many were tired of divine pantheons and loose morals. Many were searching for a religion that offered hope and made sense. The magi came from the east looking for new hope to which a suspicious star pointed. For some, the strict monotheism and values of Judaism offered an answer. Some Gentiles submitted themselves to circumcision and became proselytes. Others went to synagogue worship and read the Jewish scriptures and became God-fearers.

Christians are those who have a strong sense of identity centered in Christ and are those anxious to bestow the mantel of meaningful identity upon others. Before the enlightenment of Peter about inclusion and before Paul was even a believer, there was Philip.

Philip saw the light of an angel. "Get up and go toward the south to the road that goes down from Jerusalem to Gaza." Philip obeyed. On the road to Gaza, he ran into the eunuch, reading aloud some scripture while riding in his chariot (the kind with a seat). Philip wiggled his way into an invitation to join the eunuch in order to interpret a troublesome passage from Isaiah.

"Who's this sheep that was led to the slaughter?" asked the VIP from the south. "Is Isaiah talking about himself or is he talking about someone else?" "Well," replied Philip, "that's a good question. I'm glad you asked. The prophet is announcing the coming of my Lord, Jesus, who died on the cross, like a sheep led to slaughter. He rose from the dead and announced salvation to all who would believe."

"Stop the horses!" commanded the eunuch. "I believe and I want to be baptized, right now!"

Some Christians believe that baptism is something one agrees to when one becomes a believer. Other Christians believe that baptism is a sacrament, that it bestows faith. It doesn't matter. Baptism is a sign of one's faith. The eunuch went back to Ethiopia, cleaned by baptism, in union with Christ, and ready to start a new life. The existence of the Ethiopian Orthodox church today might be a witness to the eunuch's powerful witness. Who knows? The point is this: The Ethiopian eunuch found identity in Christ and probably shared the hope of a meaningful new identity with others.

Back to Bonhoeffer's question. "Who am I?" "Who are we?" Maybe we don't care. But some of us do. Hans Kueng, the German theologian, points out that there are those, however, "who are not content to spend a whole lifetime approaching the fundamental questions of human existence with mere feeling, personal prejudices, and apparently plausible explanations."[1]

Are we the flower children? Are we the punkers? Are we the staid, holier-than-thou Christians who feel soiled in the presence of unorthodox language? What identifies us? Is it our money — our status in the corporate world — our houses, our cars, our profit-sharing plans, our time-shares?

Bonhoeffer answers his own question: "Who am I? They mock me, these lonely questions of mine. Whoever I am, thou knowest, O God, I am thine."

Maybe it's all right to dub the beatnik slouch or the punker outrageousness, or the goody-goody-two-shoes righteous believer. The costume is not the thing. The thing is the lifeline to Christ. The decisive quality is union with Christ. If we know that we belong to Christ, then we can wear practically any outfit we want. Philip and the eunuch became brothers in Christ but Philip wore the sandals of a commoner and the eunuch wore the robes of a high-ranking statesman.

What identifies us is our unity in and with Christ. He called us; we answered; we have returned to him. We are his. What does it mean to belong to him?

A group of American teenagers sat together for evening devotions at the youth hostel in Germany where they were staying. Their leader, an American pastor, introduced a special guest for the evening. Her name was Gertrude Schaefer.

She was born in 1916 in Berlin. Her education included basic schooling in the suburb of Spandau and, later, a basic course in home economics. One day, after the Nazis had come to power, she asked the classmate sitting next to her, a Jewish girl, if she were planning to stay in Berlin. The girl gave no answer. The chair was empty the next day but Gertrude found out that she and her family had successfully flown the country the night before. The Jewish girl and her family were lucky.

Later that year, in 1934, Gertrude met a young man named Paul preparing for the Protestant deaconate at a preparatory school where she got a job in the office. She married him in 1940 and had three days together before he, as a soldier, was sent to the Russian front. Gertrude accompanied him to the train station and bravely held back the tears as she bade him good-bye. She returned to the privacy of her apartment and cried buckets of tears.

In 1941, Gertrude said good-bye again to Paul when she returned to Berlin to gather some of her things from their apartment in Bremen. Paul, on leave, told her by phone not to return to Bremen because a bomb had fallen through their bed. Their home was destroyed. Gertrude and Paul met in Hanover to begin again in a new apartment. Paul went back to the front.

Finally, the war was over. Paul survived. He came home and a new post-war life began in their home, unscathed by the bombs, in Hanover.

The post-war years were the worst. The survivors went to the train station to "appropriate" coal from the open American train cars when the trains stopped to move onto different tracks. The family lived on potato soup and crusty bread soaked in milk and baked in the oven.

Paul continued his work as a Protestant deacon, passed the exams, and was ordained as a pastor in 1964. Gertrude related that, later, one of his sons asked him if he had ever shot another soldier. He replied that he was once ordered to shoot at Russian soldiers approaching his line from a forest. Luckily, his comrades finished off the Russians before Paul could fire. "What if you had refused to fire?" asked the son. Paul replied, "Then I would not be here with you today." The son, sitting beside his mother, could not conceal his emotions.

The young visitors were then invited to ask questions. "How was it living during the war in Hanover?" Gertrude replied that she and her children sometimes had to run four or five times to the bunker to escape the rain of death from the sky. The bunker shuddered violently because some of the bombs fell right upon it.

"Did you know about the concentration camps?" asked another teen. Gertrude said that she suspected that the Nazis were systematically disposing of the Jews but she didn't know for sure until a neighbor with a radio found out about it from an English broadcaster.

By the end of Gertrude's testimony, translated by the American guide, the teenagers were wiping tears from their eyes. Hitler had unleashed a Fascist monster upon the world and his people were also his victims. The widowed lady, age 91, sat before them, one who for many years had been in union with Christ who had called her on her baptism day many years before. In English, she said, "No more war!" The meeting was over. The teens stood and formed a prayer circle around the room. Prayers were spoken. Thanks for the witness of Gertrude. Thanks for her long life. Thanks for the evening. Thanks for him who was in their midst. After the prayers, Gertrude received many hugs from those who were her young brothers and sisters in Christ. It was unlikely that they would ever see her again but they would never forget the aging pastor's widow they had met; with whom they had prayed.

Philip, the Ethiopian eunuch, Bonhoeffer, Hans Kueng, perhaps even a few hippies and punkers, Gertrude Schaefer, young Christians in a youth hostel in the Black Forest; all these have one thing in common. They have an identity forged and perpetuated through baptism into Christ.

"Who are we?" We are those who belong to Christ. Amen.

---

1. Hans Kueng, *On Being A Christian* (Garden City, New York: Doubleday & Company, Inc., 1976), p. 19.

Easter 6
Acts 10:44-48

Enough Spirit To Go Around!

A minister once received a bottle of apricot brandy from one of his parishioners under the condition that the minister thank the donor for his gift in the Sunday bulletin. On the following Sunday, the notice read: "The pastor thanks Mr. Jones for the apricots and the spirit in which they were given."

Some Bible readers look at the words from Acts 10, "While Peter was still speaking, the Holy Spirit fell upon all who heard the word" (v. 44), and conclude, "Aha! A Pentecost story!" Then the words of verse 45 pop out: "The circumcised believers ... were astounded that the gift of the Holy Spirit had been poured out even on the Gentiles." Conclusion? This Easter text is about a *Gentile* Pentecost! We can imagine that the Gentile (uncircumcised) hearers of Peter's words might have said, "We wish to thank Peter for his sermon from which the Spirit was poured out upon us!"

Peter makes it clear that there is *enough Spirit to go around for all interested parties*. He appears to be finally convinced that God's Spirit and the gifts of the Spirit are plentiful enough to be poured out upon the Gentiles, as well. Of course, the few verses that relate the "Gentile" Pentecost hardly seize the imagination of the reader like the account in Acts 2 that led one leading one New Testament scholar to declare that it was an event marked by "a freight-train-sized sound of wind from Heaven, tongues of fire dancing on heads of disciples ... cries of amazement ... and a powerful sermon [resulting] in 3,000 baptisms."[1]

The Gentiles experienced their own day of Pentecost but, alas, it seems that little notice of it is mentioned by the press!

For most of us who are of Gentile lineage, this account should be printed and framed and hung upon a prominent wall in our homes! Or how about a banner for the sanctuaries of our churches? Peter asks, "Can anyone withhold the water for baptizing these people?" Absolutely not! We Gentiles get to be baptized! We Gentiles are included in the kingdom! We Gentiles are candidates for heavy doses of the Spirit!

The history of the early church becomes the story about Gentile converts who take center stage because their Pentecost experience was also a "Day of Grace!"

Paul's missionary story is a story about the presence and power of the Spirit. He went about proclaiming the good news and then he stood back and watched the Spirit take over!

He didn't run for congregational president in any of the churches he founded and he didn't hand out copies of model church constitutions. Paul's model of Spirit-led direction in the church, without concern for ordered church governance, did not prevail. The disciples in Jerusalem, led by James, imposed the traditional Jewish elder system upon the emerging church and churches dominated by Gentiles even themselves wanted churches to be led by bishops and deacons.

The Spirit cannot be discouraged by orderliness and structure! The Spirit that descends upon Jews and Gentiles alike is the Spirit that refuses to be contained nor restrained!

There's enough Spirit to go around to bring unity for all. This lesson for the sixth Sunday after Easter is a lesson about the fulfillment of old prophecies. Division among earth's peoples, contention and war, competition and racial prejudice, and distrust will come to an end. The Spirit of Jesus alive and proclaimed in and among the community is bringing to an end the days of human disunity.

Isaiah saw the deliverer coming "to gather all nations and tongues" (66:18); Jeremiah envisioned the time when all nations will gather at Jerusalem (3:17); Micah announced that many nations will "go up to the mountain of the Lord" (4:2); and Zechariah knew that Gentiles seeking God's favor will cling to the shirttails of the Jews to be dragged to God's presence if they have to (8:20-23).

It took a while for Peter to grasp the concept but he finally got on the bandwagon rolling to the kingdom of the future. In fact, the future was already present on that day when the Gentiles matched the spiritual signs of the Jews. The proof in the pudding was baptism, the great sign of inclusion in the kingdom.

The unity that we believers feel in those precious moments standing at the altar to drink from the same cup of communion and when we pray together the Lord's Prayer is trumped by chaos in the Middle East, rampant genocide and hunger in Africa, and murder and mayhem in our urban ghettos. Early Christians believed that the bread of the Lord's table was gathered from the grain gathered from the fields. As the grain is gathered into one (loaf) so are we gathered into one people. We can envision a world of harmony and unity but we cannot make it happen. Perhaps it is only the vision of the kingdom that is coming that keeps us from absolute despair.

We don't know how biblically literate Peter was (he points out that Jesus is the descendant of the line of David in his Acts 2 Pentecost sermon), but he must have known about the hope foretold by the prophets. It might have taken some time, but he must have caught on at some point and realized that the resurrection and ascension of Jesus was a glimpse into the glory of the future, a future that was somehow embodied in the concept of Jerusalem, the holy city.

A Christian went on a tour with other Christians to the holy land. His was his first trip to Israel. When his group, having just landed at Tel Aviv, was safely settled in at the hotel just outside the old walls of the city, he decided that he couldn't wait until the morning to see the city. As he walked through the ancient gate across the street from his hotel, he felt transported to another time and place. He walked through the dark, narrow streets experiencing the sights and sounds and smells of another world. He heard the voices of another dimension, at the same time parallel and ancient, from behind shuttered windows, in the back rooms of tea cafes and Middle Eastern bazaars. He walked suddenly into the moonlight and saw the Wailing Wall before him. Abraham, Saul, David, Solomon, Isaiah, and Jeremiah whispered to him. He saw the same wall, the same stones gazed upon by Peter, John, Mark,

Paul, and yes, the great carpenter himself, reaching out to him in the soft breezes and shadows of the evening, Jerusalem that night was mysterious, enchanting, other-worldly, and magical. It was a foretaste of the New Jerusalem to come.

And all nations would be gathered there. An American soldier died of his wounds in France in the First World War. His comrades took him to a small church and asked the village priest if they could bury him in the parish graveyard. "Was he a Catholic?" asked the priest. "No, Father, he was not," replied the men. "Then you must bury him outside the fence of the cemetery," answered the priest. The fallen man was buried and his comrades returned the next morning to pay their last respects. They were surprised to see that the fresh grave was within the cemetery's fence. They summoned the priest who said, "My conscience bothered me last evening; I could not sleep so I arose in the night and moved the fence to include your comrade who died for France." Christ died for all people; all people are included within the parameters of the kingdom.

The coming of the Spirit to those seeking salvation (both Jews and non-Jews) is the coming of great power that crosses human boundaries. The "signs" of the Spirit are empowering, life changing.

Once a pastor witnessed the painful odyssey of a middle-aged mother. Her husband met him in his office one day in order to explain that his wife, Sally, had been hopelessly addicted to alcohol for a number of years. Her addiction was ruining their marriage, destroying her relationship with her three teen sons, and perhaps most urgent of all, physically destroying her life. If she did not seek treatment soon, according to the testimony of her physician, she would die of an already heavily damaged liver.

Her husband suggested a plan. He asked the pastor to meet him and Sally's oldest son at their home in order to confront her and persuade her to enter a treatment center immediately.

The minister was not optimistic about the plan; he had recently been involved in a crisis intervention that had failed miserably, although orchestrated by a psychiatrist. But what was there to lose? The three of them surprised Sally in her living room and spoke of their love for her and outlined the continuing consequences of her addiction. They revealed the plan: They would immediately take her to her doctor for a consultation and then whisk her immediately to a treatment center for a six-week detoxification program. Sally broke down in tears. She apologized for all the sorrow she had caused. She thanked them for their love and courageous confrontation.

Three decades later, Sally is still a recovering alcoholic who is one of the finest wives, mothers, grandmothers, and productive Christians the pastor has ever met. Her life took a turn for the better when she realized that she was included within the parameters of God's kingdom. Her "saviors" envisioned a better life for her and, prayerfully Spirit-led, brought to bear the power of God's future into her life. She rediscovered that she in her journey was accompanied by the Lord of the kingdom. She would not fall by the wayside. She would not become a helpless alcoholic tossed aside and forsaken. God picked her up and moved her into the line of countless people heading into the light of God's future.

Peter, likewise, must have been one who saw beyond the dust, the chaos, the treachery, and the hypocrisy of his Jerusalem and shattered lives. He saw the vision of the prophets and savored the promises made to the patriarchs. He was glad to be a citizen of Israel, one included in the world to come. God spoke to him and asked him to take a second look at the words of the prophets. The old Israel was gone; the new Israel was raised from the dust and faded promises of the old Jerusalem. Like the phoenix, Jesus rose from the tomb to raise the heads of those in despair and hopelessness. "Don't look down, my friends," Jesus said. "Look up! See what is before you! See what is coming!" Peter saw a new world coming and he came to know that the new world included all nations.

So Peter went forth. He inspired the Jews who gathered in Jerusalem at Pentecost. He baptized those who wanted to be included. But Peter baptized others. He shared his vision with the Gentiles and marked them with the sign of the kingdom as well. He shared the bountiful riches of the Spirit. Amen.

---

1. Thomas G. Long, *Proclamation 4 Pentecost 1* (Minneapolis: Fortress Press, 1989), p. 5.

The Ascension Of Our Lord
Acts 1:1-11

Ascension Answers

Many folks, especially preachers, don't know what to make of Luke's accounts (Luke 24:50-53; Acts 1:1-11) of the ascension of Jesus. The other three gospels don't mention it and, frankly, the story seems a little too mythical for twenty-first-century readers. Educated people of the western world have discarded the three-tier cosmology. In the understanding of today's universe, it's not possible to know what is up and what is down. People looking up into the skies today might be looking at other beings on other planets looking down at us. That is why the trapdoors high up in European church ceilings are sealed shut. No one would be impressed today by the raising of a figure of Jesus at worship on Ascension Thursday high up through a trapdoor in the ceiling. Perhaps it would be more useful to suggest that Jesus passed from one dimension (earthly) to another (spiritual).

In all fairness to Luke (after all, he is a credible gospel writer), perhaps we ought to try a little harder to understand his point.

In the first place, Luke wanted to answer some questions about Jesus. Luke witnessed to the resurrection of Jesus from the dead and then related some of the appearances of Jesus to his disciples. But there had to be some closure. Without Luke's steps to "tidy things up," there might still be people claiming that they saw Jesus down at the supermarket or on the No. 5 bus to Coney Island. The account of the ascension also, especially in Acts, documents the explanation of the fulfillment of the scriptures by Jesus to all of the disciples following the explanation given to the two disciples on the road to Emmaus (Luke 24:13-35).

Perhaps Luke also wanted to demonstrate the power of the risen Christ. The power of the ascended Jesus is transcendent over all physical and spiritual powers; earth cannot constrain him and the spiritual realms must receive him.

The ascended Jesus also transcends some of the banal and flip popular notions about Jesus. He is more than a rock star or the good-looking guy with long hair who lived a long time ago. He is more than the image on some of the popular "Jesus Junk" items sold at the local Christian bookstore. He is more than the handsome blue-eyed star of a movie in which the lead poetically utters wise and sometimes cryptic sayings to vast audiences leaning forward to catch every pearl of wisdom he verbalizes.

The ascended Jesus is more than the one who walked on water or turned the water into wine. He is more than the teacher who taught great values such as "God helps those who help themselves" (he didn't say it) or "It's easier for a camel to get through the eye of a needle than for a rich man to go to heaven." (He said it, according to Matthew 19:24; Mark 10:25; and Luke 18:25.)

Perhaps Luke also wanted to demonstrate that the crucifixion of Jesus was no tragic accident, a bad ending to a plan conceived by Jesus himself or by God. The interpretations of the resurrection of Jesus by the early "witnesses" serve to make that point but the ascension of Jesus adds one more layer to the persuasion of the early church that the divine plot went according to plan. Jesus was *supposed* to die, defeat the devil, atone for the sins of humankind, and rise up as the victorious one to the right hand of God.

Luke says it his way and the writer to the Ephesians says it his way but the point is the same: Jesus risen to heaven is the absolute, infallible master in our lives, to whom we owe absolute devotion.

During an automobile outing in the mountains of the northern Steiermark, some Austrian friends and their American visitor stopped at a small romantic village. The town was a teutonic wonder caught in time about 200 years ago, complete with cow paths and rustic little lanes curving around colorful gardens and white-washed houses decorated with murals telling the stories of saints and biblical events. The Austrians led the American up to a house to pick up a key. With key in hand, the path continued to lead the party upward to a small stone chapel capping an elevated ridge protruding from the mount. The chapel measured perhaps 20 by 35 feet. Inside was a simple altar framed by the walls of the nave decorated with old, faded frescos from another time and another culture.

One of the frescos depicted the scene of the nativity; another a fortress or a city. The third fresco clearly presented the figure of Christ the King. The visitors took in quick breaths. Imagine — someone came to the top of that mountain 1,200 years before and illustrated their conviction about Christ on that wall. Someone long ago had come over the Alps from the south and proclaimed Jesus as Lord to the mountain folk who as yet did not know him. The Jesus of the artist(s) was the *Kosmocrator* (ruler of the cosmos), the *Pantocrator* (ruler of all things), the ascended one who has all power over all physical and spiritual things. The builders of the chapel said it 1,200 years ago but Luke said it first.

Secondly, Luke wanted to answer some questions about the church. He brings closure to the postresurrection appearances of Jesus by affixing the span of time, forty days (a time of completion), between the resurrection and the ascension.

The blessing of Jesus at the end of Luke's gospel is complemented and paralleled by Jesus' acknowledgement of the call to be witnesses recorded at the beginning of Acts. God's plan has no interruptions: Jesus dies, Jesus is resurrected, Jesus ascends, and the work of the Spirit begins immediately. In a way, the power of Jesus on earth is transmitted to his followers, to the church. The time of Jesus' earthly presence on earth is followed by the age of the church.

Furthermore, Jesus' followers are assured that Jesus, in some fashion, is still with them. The resurrected Jesus didn't just fade away; he didn't head off into the sunset and disappear. He visibly heads up into the clouds, accompanied by angelic beings, thus assuring the disciples that everything is going according to plan. Instinctively, the disciples know that the talk about the Spirit is talk about Jesus' continuing presence with them. They are at ease; they have a plan; they have their mission; their doubts are assuaged.

The disciples are given a sneak preview of the last chapter of God's plan. Knowing about the end of the story, the great consummation, the second coming, encourages the disciples to turn their shoulders into the task. There is no thought about "waiting it out." There is work to be done. The disciples are to be witnesses in Jerusalem, Judea, Samaria, and even "to the ends of the earth" (v. 8).

It's official: As mentioned in the sermon of Lent 1 in this series, the ship of the church is launched; it will now begin its voyage through and around all the storms and obstacles that the world can conjure up. In some ways, sailors understand the task of the church more than others. Seafarers in northern Europe adorn their churches on land with ship models. The ship sails through troubled waters as Christ, the captain, mans the rudder while assisted by the crew, the grunts of the church. The ship sails through all conditions of life but it will safely anchor in the harbor of the kingdom of Christ. The model ship reminds those who see it about the time when Jesus safely delivered those in peril in the storm on the Sea of Galilee. The model ship is also a reminder about the ark of the Old Testament that safely delivered Noah and his family to dry land.

The ship sails in all kinds of weather, on all the seas of the world. It stops at many harbors and its crew invites all to board it for the journey. The crew is always granted shore leave so that it can engage in the worlds of those close to the harbor. The crew members are willing to be identified with the people of the port but they are not "of" the people since their home is the ship. The ship is large; those who sail in it are of every race and color, age, and class.

The liturgical name of the portion of the church where worshipers sit is the "nave," derived from the Latin word for ship whence we get our word, "navy." The ship reminds us that the real crew members belong to a great company of sailors, past, present, and future. The real church embraces all who have ever fought the good fight and won the good race in all ages. Jesus ascended into the heavens; with his foot he launched the ship of the church. Obstacles lie ahead but, in its own good time, the church will reach the kingdom.

Thirdly, Luke's account of the ascension answers some questions about the attitudes of individual believers. Christians are encouraged in their faith because the ascension was an event in straight (or linear) time. God's creation doesn't move historically in a cyclical repetitious fashion nor is it haphazard. The witness of prophets, the birth of Jesus, the death of Jesus, the resurrection, and the ascension, are events moving right along in a linear fashion. In straightforward, respectfully historical fashion, the second coming will conclude and wrap up all things. Maybe the world will be turned upside down but it will not be turned inside out. Don't panic; things, for the time being, will remain what they seem to be. But God's re-creation will go ahead according to the rules; believers can be rest assured that God's historical game plans have not been changed.

The most important earmarks of the believer are joy and anticipation. The first short account of the ascension at the end of the gospel of Luke emphasizes the happiness of the disciples. Luke's version in Acts shows that their joy is founded upon Jesus' power residing in them and the promise that he will come again.

A pastor once met a mother at the bedside of her dying son in the hospital. The mother had separated herself from the church some years before but the pastor went to see her frequently during the weeks of her lonely vigil at the side of her dying son. The pastor noticed how she nursed her son with quiet calmness and showered him with tender maternal love during his painful demise. She did not betray with a single sign how much she herself was consumed by pain and anxiety. One day, the minister spontaneously said to her, "I admire your attitude." She replied, "Attitude, yes, perhaps, but don't look underneath, pastor; I haven't a thing to hold on to."

The impending death of her son was an unintended and unwanted intrusion into the mother's linear view of her life. Mothers are supposed to die before their sons. But the witnesses to the ascension of Jesus saw a heavier line moving through all the fine lines of personal human histories. It was the heavy line moving forward to the event after the ascension, the event of justice and closure, the event that would answer all the questions, disappointments, and doubts of the world.

A glider pilot once gave an enthusiastic speech to an assembly of young people. He talked about the thrill of flying, the silence when gliding thousands of feet above the ground, and the use of air currents to direct the plane to lower or higher altitudes. He explained that he could overcome turbulence by adjusting the glider's altitude and use a current of warmer air to raise the plane to a higher altitude.

In fact, the glider exclaimed that he always preferred to seek the higher altitudes with less turbulence in order to prolong the flight. His listeners understood that his speech was really about choosing direction in life. Afterward, a young man who heard the speech summed up the message by saying, "We've got to get ourselves some altitude, dudes!"

The disciples looked up as Jesus ascended to that place whence he would come again. The disciples began their mission task with joy. When threatened by the loss of that joy, they looked up and they remembered.

Remember the ascension. Remember to look up. Amen.

Easter 7
Acts 1:15-17, 21-26

Be An Apostle! Proclaim Life!

Three young lads once rescued a famous politician from drowning. "I will give you anything you like," happily promised the grateful politician. "Thank you for saving my life!" The first lad said, "I'll take a bicycle." The second hero said, "I'll take a motor bike." The third perplexed rescuer said, "Sir, if it's all the same to you, I'd like a military funeral." "A military funeral! Why?" asked the politician. "Because," the boy said, "when my dad finds out whose life I saved, he'll kill me!"

Life is precious. Perhaps one way to define the goal of civilization is to say that we struggle together in the pursuit of life. Some psychiatrists are agreed that some people, for whatever reasons, are opposed to life and all the positive things it represents. Indeed, our present generation encourages others to "get a life" or "get with the program." Find something in life that is worth doing and refocus one's self from that which is mundane to that which is more essential and meaningful.

Luke's account in Acts 1 describes the process of replacing the apostle Judas so that the full compliment of twelve apostles is again achieved. The loss of Judas (did he commit suicide or did he accidentally die?) is not as important as maintaining the complete number of twelve. The perfection of the number twelve (the number of the tribes of Israel) seems to be important. The focus on structure and a full complement of apostles seems to have diminished after the Day of Pentecost.

The text points to two important apostolic issues.

First of all, there are the *qualifications* necessary to be an apostle. An apostle (according to Luke) had to have been a companion with Jesus, and, secondly, had to have witnessed the resurrection of Jesus. Later, in Luke's Acts account, Paul makes a case for his title as "apostle." In faith, modern apostles (believers; followers of Jesus) are those who have become acquainted with Jesus through word (and for some denominations) and through participation in the sacraments.

Model "apostles" are many in the history of the American colonial church. John Stauch, for example, was a Lutheran born in York County, Pennsylvania, in 1762, who earned a living as a wagonmaker and farmer. Although he felt called to the Christian ministry, his pastor discouraged him, so he married and moved with his family to Aurora, West Virginia. Since there was no pastor in the town, he volunteered to read sermons and lead worship for his fellow settlers. His reputation as a preacher became known to other settlers in the wilderness forest and many turned to him for spiritual counsel, including a barefooted and animal-clad couple who asked him to marry them. Without license and without authority from any ecclesiastical authority to marry, he "solemnized their nuptials," but soon thereafter sought and received authority from the court to marry.

The Treaty of Greenville of 1795 opened up the area west of the Ohio and the Whisky Rebellion brought German-born soldiers west to get a glimpse of unlimited space and farmland there for the taking. Stauch tossed and turned in his bed, unable to shake from his mind the spiritually deprived settlers deep in the Ohio forests, doing their devotions morning and evening kneeling in the dust upon their earthen floors. Stauch visualized them praying for the great shepherd to send them pastors to baptize, confirm, visit them in their afflictions, and bury their dead.

Stauch later wrote in his journal, "I heard their Macedonian call for help." He gathered up his family and moved on into the wilderness of Ohio and organized the Ohio Synod in 1818 at Somerset, Ohio. After many requests on his part to the Pennsylvania Ministerium, Stauch was finally designated a "lay catechist," and then eventually was ordained as a pastor. Stauch was, first of all, a product of a firm witness to him by his parents, family, and friends. He received the apostolic authority, not by virtue of a documented "apostolic succession" but by virtue of the faithful apostolic witness to biblical faith commended to him by the faithful who preceded him.

John Stauch stands side by side with many who likewise heard the Macedonian call for help in colonial America: Heinrich Muhlenberg, Peter Cartwright, Charles Grandison Finney, Francis Asbury, and George Whitefield.

They were all people who were commissioned by God to take the gift of life, hope, and forgiveness to others. They had all, in some sense, walked with Jesus and witnessed his resurrection.

An apostle, therefore, does not need to be theologically trained and ordained. A woman by the name of Inez was an artist in Flint, Michigan. After her devastating divorce, she ended up living at the YMCA in a small room with a narrow bed in which she cried herself to sleep at night. One evening she returned to her home and was on the elevator to the women's floor when another woman said to her, "I want what you have. You look so at peace with the world." Inez couldn't believe that she gave such a "peaceful" impression. Without thinking, all she could say was, "It's because of Jesus."

"Are you serious?" asked the other woman. "Yes," replied Inez, "I cannot lie. What you see has to be the Lord. He's all I have." The other woman softly said, "I want to hear about *your* Jesus." Inez said, "Come to my room and I will tell you what it is I know."

In the footsteps of Peter, Paul, and Mother Teresa, Inez was an apostle, faithfully proclaiming the old, old story.

The stories of John Stauch and Inez, both of whom walked with Jesus and witnessed the power unleashed by his resurrection, also point to the second point Luke makes about apostles. They are those to whom has been given a *task*. They are to proclaim Jesus' death and his glorious resurrection and proclaim repentance and forgiveness.

Luke's account of the election of Matthias makes a point of presenting Peter as the one who convenes the meeting. Luke affirms the persuasion of the early church that Peter was the leader.

He was the first to come to the conclusion that the tomb was empty because Jesus had risen from the dead. (In John's account, Mary Magdalene sees the risen Lord first but Peter was the first to enter the tomb, before John, and find it empty.)

Peter thus comes to faith first and explains it to the rest of the disciples. Peter was also the one instructed to "feed my sheep" and plays the leading role in the postresurrection accounts of John 21.

While acknowledging Peter as the "first among the other disciples," not all Christians find in that fact the basis for a documented, orderly, "apostolic succession" confessed by the Roman Catholics, the Anglicans, and some Lutherans. Whether the church really needs this list of successors working through human offices to visibly represent the legacy of witness is debatable. The reformers taught that only the preaching of the word and the sacraments rightly administered are necessary. But the office of the bishop can be a meaningful, visible sign of the succession of the witness of the apostles. Bishops or no bishops, we have been authorized to witness to the resurrection and proclaim the call to repentance and announce forgiveness in the name of Christ.

There's an old story about an elderly Scotsman confined to his bed. The parson came to call and the elderly man confessed that he lacked the ability to pray; he just didn't know *how* to pray. The parson, an apostolic witness, simply suggested, "John, just imagine that Jesus is sitting on the chair over there and just have a conversation with him. That would be prayer."

Some time later, the daughter of the elderly man came to the parsonage to tell the minister that her father had died peacefully in the night. "But there was something strange I noticed when I entered his bedroom this morning," she said. "What was that?" asked the parson. "The chair was pulled over to the side of his bed and his hand was resting upon it."

The parson kept company with Jesus. He announced repentance and forgiveness. The elderly Scotsman found company with Jesus and discovered forgiveness and acceptance. Life passed from one to the other. The apostolic task was accomplished in Scotland that day. Amen.

Sermons On The First Readings

For Sundays
After Pentecost
(First Third)

Dancing In Holy Places

William J. Carl III

To my sons,
Jeremy and David,
who have endured my sermons
all their lives,
and are still alive to tell about it

Preface

For 22 years I preached week in, week out, to the congregation of First Presbyterian Church, Dallas, Texas, a church committed to both evangelism and social justice ministries. I am thankful for their tutelage, their patience, and their ability to nudge me along in my study of scripture and my growth and development as a pastor. I felt their constant prayers and encouragement. Every pastor needs that kind of support to deal with the "relentless regularity of Sunday morning." Reinhold Niebuhr was right. We learn more from our congregations than we could ever teach them.

But, I also learned a lot from my sons, Jeremy and David, who kept me honest in my preaching and challenged me to give my best every week. I never told them this, but one of my homiletical goals was to preach well enough to keep them awake figuring that everyone else might stay awake, too. Because of that, I dedicate these sermons to them. Another reason is that Jeremy and David seemed to like those wild, swash-buckling Old Testament texts with all those flawed heroes and heroines doing more than they ever imagined at God's command. With one exception, every sermon is from the Hebrew Bible. Surely the great novelists and authors found inspiration for character development and story line from texts like these. Every single one sneaks up and surprises with divine serendipity, especially the one where David dances, which inspired the title for these sermons.

Thanks to my colleagues in ministry at Pittsburgh Theological Seminary — world-class biblical scholars, theologians, historians, practitioners, and mentors who daily remind me that sacred texts interact with contemporary contexts in truly incarnational ways.

Finally, I want to thank Wesley and David Runk for inviting me to write this collection of sermons in the first place, and my wife, Jane, for agreeing that I should. She seems to think I have a few things to say to the church and that I should keep saying them. So here they are.

The Day Of Pentecost
Acts 2:1-21

What A Way To Start A Church!

What a way to start a church! It's certainly not the typical format for new church development. Where is the planning committee, the fund-raising, the arm twisting, the real estate deal acquiring the land, the faithful few who volunteer from other churches to give the whole thing its initial push? Not everyone has the personality to start a church from scratch, but Paul did. "I planted, Apollos watered," says Paul (1 Corinthians 3:6). Some preachers are just good at planting churches and getting them started.

My dad was good at starting churches. I remember when he started a new church development in 1955 in Bartlesville, Oklahoma, with all those services in an elementary school gym until the first building was built and all the enthusiasm as everyone worked together with a common goal. My mind is a newsreel of church picnics, smiling faces, high hopes and hymn sings, of groundbreaking ceremonies and the burning of notes as building after building went up over the years. But there was nothing like this in Acts 2. Just a mighty wind, some tongues of fire, some speaking in tongues, a great disturbance, and lots of excitement. What a way to start a church!

What happened here, anyway? Three things to be exact. The first one was this: God came unexpectedly, which of course is nothing new. God seems to make it a hobby of sneaking up on the human race when no one is looking except those with the faith and the heart to recognize God in their midst. Look at how God comes in the oddest forms — a burning bush, a tongue-tied stutterer named Moses, a child with a slingshot, and a babe in a manger.

Here is this little band of frightened disciples whose leader has gone off and left them; they are stunned, confused, and unable to figure out what to do. They're about to give up, saying things like, "We're never going to get this thing started, never going to get it off the ground. It's never going to grow!" Then along comes God unexpectedly when no one is looking.

That's just the way God is. It's like the story of the little boy by the name of Angelo, who lived in the small town near a South American border, who one day crossed the border and came back with a wheelbarrow full of sand. When the customs inspector got suspicious and asked him what he was smuggling in the sand and the boy replied, "Nothing," the customs officer made him pour out all the sand and sifted through it before he was permitted to go on.

The next day, the same thing happened; then the third day, fourth day, and so on. Weeks, months went by. Every day, the inspector said, "I know you think I'm going to get careless someday, Angelo, and you're going to smuggle something across but as long as you bring sand, I'm going to make you pour it through this screen. So don't ever think you're going to get by me."

Angelo kept coming for five years, each day appearing with his wheelbarrow and each day the customs people poured it out, sifted through it and found nothing. One day Angelo did not show, but everyone heard how that he had prospered, bought a big house, and opened a thriving business. One day, years later, the inspector who'd retired met Angelo on the street and asked him how he had become so prosperous when he had spent so much time hauling sand across the border and there was never anything in it. Angelo smiled and said, "My friend, during those five years, when you were paying so much attention to the sand, I smuggled 1,593 wheelbarrows into this country!"

Surely this little story is apocryphal, but in a way it makes a point that lies at the heart of the Pentecost experience: namely, we grow so accustomed to thinking of God in a certain way and looking for God in a certain form that we're caught completely off guard as to who God really is and where God can actually be found. The disciples had their preconceptions and were no doubt shocked beyond words when the Spirit came upon them when they least expected it. The fact is, the God of Pentecost is the same God who came at Christmas and rose on Easter morn and who keeps appearing unexpectedly in our lives.

This story is not only about starting a church but starting anew in our Christian lives. Perhaps you have been through a difficult time. Someone you love has come and gone the way Jesus did for the disciples. You're confused and disoriented, and along comes God totally out of the blue. Perhaps God has been there all the time smuggling little bits of grace into our lives in ways we never imagined. The Spirit did it.

When I was doing graduate work at the University of Pittsburgh, one of my professors, a galloping atheist and gleeful secularist, didn't despise Christianity, but saw it as wishful thinking for the weak and the old. He had us studying Billy Graham and Adolf Hitler side by side as examples of mass persuasion. He always offered fascinating rhetorical analyses of various movements and famous speakers in history. One day he came into our graduate seminar looking a little awestruck and said, "I can't believe it. Last night Billy Graham spoke in Korea to a gathered audience of two million people. I can't believe it. It's the first time it's ever happened in recorded history. Now I have exhausted all the plausible rhetorical and sociological explanations for this phenomenon from Aristotle to Kenneth Burke and find it is totally unexplainable. Graham himself says it's the power of the Holy Spirit, and I have concluded that he must be right!" Three thousand new members in a single day! Why? Because God came upon them unexpectedly when no one was looking. What a way to start a church! What a way to jumpstart a tired and worn out Christian life.

The second thing that happened was that the church caused a disturbance unexpectedly. Clearly something happened that day. We're not exactly sure what. But it was kind of wild and swashbuckling and hard to explain, a little like a Men's Renewal Conference I attended a few years ago. I've never seen anything like it. It was a male bonding experience where men go out in the woods. It was a combination of beating drums, Rotary Club, a Friday night fraternity party, Moose Lodge, and one of those fly-fishing, "Hey, it doesn't get any better than this!" commercials. Imagine the deafening sound of nearly 500 men from all over Texas, Oklahoma, and Louisiana singing "Be Thou My Vision" at the tops of their voices.

It reminded me of being in the mission fields in Taiwan, China, India, South Africa, and Russia. In Taiwan, the prayers of the people consisted of everyone praying out loud at the same time. I encountered the same thing in Russia with Pentecostal Presbyterians worshiping in a bomb shelter three stories below ground in the Ural Mountains. In China, there was so much noise and disturbance in a huge church in Qingdao that the neighbors complained to the government authorities who told the complainers to go visit the church because it might be good for them. Christians in India can get pretty noisy as well with all their enthusiasm, but it is even noisier in South Africa. I preached in a black township church in Guguletu on the outskirts of Cape Town where the people beat their Bibles with their bare hands to provide percussion and set the rhythm for the hymns. The glow on their faces was overwhelming. Clearly something had happened to them and they just couldn't keep quiet about it any longer.

Think of that first Pentecost. There was a big disturbance with lots of commotion. The world said, "They must be drunk!" But Peter, a real have-sermon-will-travel kind of guy, said, "No, they can't be drunk. It's only 9 o'clock in the morning. But now that I have your attention, let me tell you about Jesus Christ." Now here's an interesting model for evangelism. No revival or crusade with thousands stumbling forward to "Just As I Am," but instead the church does something startling in the community and the world says, "What are you doing over there?" And the church responds, "Let me tell you about Jesus Christ."

When churches make a decision to feed the hungry and help the poor in their communities, it's amazing how many non-church types sit up and take notice. Some of them even sign up to serve stew or help counsel people who are struggling with financial responsibility and interviewing for jobs. I've seen it all over the country. Invariably, these altruistic do-gooders will ask the crucial question: "Now tell me again why you do this?" And like Peter, church members have their opening — "Let me tell you about Jesus Christ." Or if we don't want to be that explicit, we can treat it the way Philip did with Nathanael and simply say, "Come and see. Come to church Sunday morning, or come to this Bible study or check out this class, and see for yourself."

What a way to start a church! First, God came unexpectedly. Second, the church caused a disturbance that made the world sit up and take notice. Third, the people came together in a way they had never done before.

It's always amazing to me how God brings us together — people with different languages, different political persuasions, and different theological ideas. God's goal is to remind us that we have "one Lord, one faith, one baptism, one God and Father of us all." I remember climbing Mount Sinai years ago. I started at the bottom at St. Catherine's Monastery at 3 a.m. with hundreds of pilgrims from all over the world. We made our way to the top in the dark by flashlight. We arrived just in time to watch the sunrise on top of Mount Sinai. Around me I heard at least nine different languages. The Middle East may be the melting pot of the world with enormous political differences, but something broke down the barriers so dramatically that morning that suddenly we could understand each other as we watched the sun rise with huge smiles on our faces. We were listening to each other in a new way for the first time as on that first Pentecost. The Spirit had burned away our differences with tongues of fire.

I saw it again in a class I taught at Princeton Seminary in the early 1980s. It was like a small United Nations all rolled into one. There was the black South African Anglican priest who had come to America to take these courses and knew he would go to prison when he returned because that was what happened to any black who left the country and came back before the fall of Apartheid. There was the French Roman Catholic who was a socialist and a supporter of Mitterrand. There was the Australian with his drawling accent from "down under." There was the Canadian who had spent the first five years of his life in Scotland and could shift in and out of a Scottish accent at will. There was the student who thought he was Robert Schuller. There was the charismatic who *loved Jesus* and none of us loved Jesus quite enough for him. And, finally, there was Jeb Stuart Magruder, former White House aide and Watergate defendant, who had spent his time in prison and was still wrestling with the guilt over whether or not he had the right to stand in a pulpit and preach the gospel of Jesus Christ. Everything was represented there from the seats of power to the depths of poverty.

One day the black South African stood beside our table in the dining hall and visibly shook. "It's okay, David, you can join us," I said, to which he replied, "This is first time I sit to eat with whites." The earth kind of moved beneath us. Every day we got into arguments over theology and politics. Magruder got into it with the French Roman Catholic over the common market and the charismatic got into with all of us because we didn't love Jesus enough, but little by little, day by day we began to come together. Why was it that we could eat together, talk together, and live together? Because everyone was there in the name of Jesus Christ.

What a way to start a church! God appears unexpectedly. The church causes a disturbance and gets the world's attention and finally the people begin to come together in a way they had never done before. What a way to start a church! No wonder it works — it's God's way, not ours. Amen.

The Holy Trinity
Isaiah 6:1-8

The Many Faces Of God

Think of all the faces we show the world every day. We scrub up every morning and put our game face on. We never show our real face except to those who know us best, the ones who see through the game face to the real you and me. But with everyone else we change our faces.

The doorbell rings. You're working on something, so you grimace over the interruption. Watch the contours of your face change, depending on who's at the door. Perhaps it's a door-to-door salesman and now you're stuck listening to his pitch through a cracked door. Or, it's a pesky neighbor who is always coming over to complain about something. Watch your face tighten until she tells you her husband just died and she didn't know who else to turn to. How does your face look now? Or, it's FedEx or UPS and you're perturbed by the inconvenience until you see that the package is from your son or daughter or the love of your life and you can hardly open it fast enough.

Look at the many faces we show the world, the different faces we human beings make depending on our conclusions about things. One Sunday, just before I walked in for worship at a church where I was preaching, I saw two of the greeters wearing "Ask Me" buttons, and I said, "I've got a question for you: What happened to the home team last night?" The husband frowned and said, "Yeah, it's awful, isn't it?" However, his wife broke into a huge smile and said, "Oh, Dr. Carl, I told my husband last night, we won it last year; it's someone else's turn. After all, we ought to share, shouldn't we?" I wish you could have seen the look on her husband's face when she said that! We show different faces to the world depending on what we're thinking or feeling. God does, too, but not anthropomorphically. After all, God is God, and God does what God wants to do. God is never a pale projection of the human condition the way some people think.

If you read the Bible carefully you will see that God shows more than one face to the world, which is in part what the odd doctrine of the Trinity is all about. Same God, people, different faces, different essences, but one. Go figure. Look at God in this Isaiah text and you will see God manifested in at least three faces that roughly approximate Father, Son, Spirit or creator, redeemer, sender — three faces and three ways to look at God.

The first is the hidden face of God, which Isaiah seems to have glimpsed in the temple one morning. The scripture says, "In the year King Uzziah died" (v. 1), which tells us Isaiah may have been attending a funeral. Picture a youthful Isaiah joining a throng of Judeans passing through the palace to gaze upon the body of the deceased monarch lying in state the way they used to lay out Russian leaders. From there Isaiah passes into the temple, where, in a moving and heart-searching spiritual experience, he has a vision of the living king who never dies.

Ever had an experience where you see something so penetrating and moving that everything else seems to vanish into a haze? I remember one morning riding the bus in Pittsburgh and noticing a large, elderly, white woman looking down and seeing her shoe was untied; she strained to tie it but couldn't reach it. Across from her sat a young, black man with wild hair with an iPod playing so loudly the whole bus could hear it and tattoos on his arms. He watched the woman struggling for her shoestring then moved from his seat and knelt before her. I watched him tie her shoes gently in a nice, neat knot then grin at her. She patted him on the head and nodded with a smile. No words were spoken. The scene glowed before me like a bright painting that blocked out everything else happening on the bus. When the spell broke I looked around and saw everyone on the bus beaming with joy. It's a cameo spot I will never forget. What is it for you? Riding through the mist at the bottom of Niagara Falls? The memory of a rescue on a battlefield?

Isaiah couldn't see anything else going on that day except this luminous vision of God. Oh, he saw the smoke from the incense, smoke that gets in your eyes and changes your view of things. I remember worshiping at St. Catherine's Monastery at the foot of Mount Sinai in Egypt, that dark, mysterious place, a gilded hall crisscrossed with shafts of light as bearded Greek Orthodox priests chanted ancient tunes while smoky incense swung back and forth like a pendulum and shrouded the entire room.

The hidden God comes to us in glances and whispers. God is the one who dwells in obscurity. The cloud around this God is thick and any Israelite to who dares to come near will die. We're much too chatty in church. As a result we lose all sense of the holiness of God. Once a pastor wanted to teach some young children about worship and stopped at the door of the sanctuary before entering. He stood silently before them until they quieted down. Speaking in little more than a whisper he said, "We're going into a very special room. You must be completely quiet. I don't want to hear a sound as we walk into that room for God is there." As they walked in and sat down, you could have heard a pin drop. They all sucked air as they glanced at the huge dome high above them. There was a holy hush in the room.

I wonder what Isaiah really saw that day. Scripture tells us he saw seraphim, which means fire-spirits. In Isaiah's day, a seraph was an effigy for a foreign god, something like a Sphinx, part-human, part-animal with six wings. Judah wasn't an independent country, and Uzziah was a practical king. He paid tribute to Assyria by allowing the Assyrians to set up seraphim in the temple courts as a reminder of who was really in charge. Though, with his human eye, Isaiah had often seen these ugly monstrosities, with his eye of devotion he perceived them to be around the throne of God, covering their faces and serving the living God. Imagine our gods today — beautiful cars, houses, stock options, trophies — all crammed up under a cross in your church. See the cross as more important than they are and you'll get a glimpse of what Isaiah saw that day.

The hidden God is also the Savior God and the sender God as we discover on Trinity Sunday, which takes us to the second face, the human face of God. In traditional theology we call the human face of God the Christ. But here we get a glimpse of him in Isaiah's vision. Look how God uses even these human-made forms to bring about redemption. So, God takes on human form and shows the divine face to every one of us. All we have to have is the eyes to see it.

First we have to recognize our own sin, which Isaiah sees by simply being in the presence of the Holy One. Think about being around someone who is as purely good as you can imagine. No one is perfect, of course, but some certainly approach it. You feel guilty just being in that person's presence. "Woe is me" (v. 5), says Isaiah. Buechner says, "You catch sight of your face in the mirror when you are brushing your teeth in the morning or combing your hair, and often you say, in effect, 'Well, there it is again, the same old washed and slept-on thing I saw yesterday and will see again tomorrow — no better, no worse.' "[1] Sometimes you wonder if it's really you and ask, "Am I my face?" The answer is "Yes" and "No" because we are our faces and we are not. That's how confusing it all is. "Beneath the face there are many layers of self and the deepest layers are for the most part hidden from us." There is that inner voice, which knows the game faces we put on at work and at home aren't the real you or me that has sometimes done some pretty awful things.

But, "fathoms down into the mystery of yourself you go," says Buechner, "into the darkness of guilt ... into the darkness of need ... Deeper and deeper you go until at last the darkness begins to be tinged with gold, which as the poem says, is the gold of light. And in that light you begin to see, as in a dream at first, your own true face ... It's the face of love, because it's a face like Christ's."[2] "Woe is me, for I am a man of unclean lips, dwelling in a people of unclean lips." The seraphim fly to him and touch his lips and the sting of forgiveness opens for him the human face of the God who loves and redeems, the God who will never let us go, no matter how bad we have been, the God who will give up everything to save even one of us. Of course, this godly human face is the one we Christians call the Christ.

Which brings us to the final face of God, the heavenly face that oddly enough is only seen, from our perspective, here on earth. We see the heavenly face of God in the faces of those who have caught the contagion that Isaiah is spreading. It's the power of the gospel that, once it gets hold of you, cannot let you go. We see the heavenly face in the hurting world, the hungry, the sick, the naked, and the sad, empty faces of dying children who have no food. The face of the poor is the face of God reaching out to us for help. The next time someone in need is a nuisance to you, remember that you may be looking into the very face of God. "Inasmuch as we do it unto the least of these ..." and all that.

The heavenly face is also the one for whom the gospel has taken hold and the Spirit has inspired. "Whom shall I send?" says the Lord. And Isaiah, who before wouldn't sign up for anything at church, raises his hand and says, "Here am I, send me!" (v. 8). One heads off to seminary. Another one suddenly begins raising money for children who don't have much and need an education. Another one signs up to serve stew at the local soup kitchen. You can tell by the glow on their faces. Light a candle in broad daylight and you hardly see it, but light a candle in a cave and it brightens the whole room. Just as a light is muted in the sunshine, but magnified in the dark, so the heavenly face of God stands out in the world. Who is it that illumines our faces in this way? It is the very Spirit of God, the one who fills us our lives with faith, hope, and love. You can tell with people who have the Spirit. They are "in-spired" (*in* + *spirare* = to breathe into or blow upon, to have an animating effect) and "en-thusiastic" (*en* + *theos*, that is, filled with God's breath and moved to new action).

What am I talking about? I'm talking about people who have the gift of encouragement. Someone once identified three kinds of elders: "yes" elders, "maybe" elders, and "no" elders. The person making the distinction was talking about a man who had just died who was a "yes" elder: agreeable, interested, ready to try things and never slamming the door shut the way "no" elders do. "Yes" elders are encouragers and inspirers. You can tell by the glow on their faces. You've seen that glow. It's the same one people have when they talk about their grandchildren. They say, "Have I told you about my grandchildren?" and the reply is, "Not in the last five minutes. Got any pictures?" "Thought you'd never ask!" I remember talking with a man who was proud of his grandson who played on his college baseball team. "He has the most runs on the team and is just a freshman!" said the grandfather with great excitement. When I asked what his grandson was majoring in, there was a long pause then this response, "I'm not sure. Baseball, I guess. I'll have to find out." But his face was aglow with joy.

That glow on that grandfather's face is what Isaiah must have had that day. It's the heavenly glow of the saints whom we see, not just in stained-glass windows but in real life, the ones through whom the light of Christ shines — like Stephen. They said of him that day that his face shone like the face of an angel.

What about you? I wonder what others see in your face. In worship, we see the hidden face of God, who creates and provides. In Christ, we see the human face of God, who saves and redeems. The only way for the world to see the heavenly face of God is to look at you and at me.

I wonder what the world sees in your face and mine. Amen.

---

1. Frederick Buechner, *The Hungering Dark* (New York: Harper and Row, 1985), p. 19.

2. *Ibid*, p. 22.

Proper 4
Pentecost 2
Ordinary Time 9
1 Samuel 3:1-10 (11-20)

Having Trouble Sleeping Through The Night

Having trouble sleeping through the night? You're not alone. Samuel did, too. Sometimes you hear a haunting phrase that sticks with you years later. I heard one like that from Gardner Taylor, that great African-American preacher who once held forth in the pulpit of Concord Baptist Church in Brooklyn. I don't even remember the sermon, which is all right — we're not supposed to remember sermons anymore than we should remember meals; we're supposed to be fed and challenged by them at the moment. I don't remember what Gardner Taylor was preaching that night. All I remember was this single phrase. I can still see him standing there as he said it: "I am for anything that can help a person get through the night."

Believe it or not, some people have trouble getting through the night. Do you know anyone like that? Perhaps you are one, fidgeting and turning. Have you seen the commercial for one of the sleep aids that shows the husband flicking on the light and saying, "Honey, honey? Are you awake?" And the woman replies, "I am now!" Young Samuel keeps tossing and turning then getting up and running to old Eli saying, "Are you awake?" All Eli can say is, "I am now! Go back to sleep, child, you're hearing things!"

So the preacher stands in the pulpit and says, "I am for anything that can help a person get through the night."

For some people, the problem is dreams. We dream about this and that night after night, sometimes waking up in a cold sweat. Some of the dreams are terrifying. Some are about things you'd never *dream* of actually doing. Other times, you are frustrated because you can't remember all the details — like the cartoon about a minister on a psychiatrist's couch saying, "I have a recurring dream in which I have all the members of my church board pleading for mercy; but when I wake up, I can never remember how!"

Is that what Samuel was doing that night, dreaming? Dreaming about the way things could be because religion in his time had taken a turn for the worse? After all, says the biblical writer, "The word of the Lord was rare in those days" (v. 1). Maybe Samuel was the only one who could dream because visions were not widespread. People had lost their way and their connection with God.

Some say dreams are like visions, and as such become a source of creativity, an answer to present problems and difficulties. Apparently, this was the case for Isaac Merritt Singer who invented the sewing machine. As the story goes, his creditors had given him one or two more weeks to complete his invention or they would pull their financial support. So he went to sleep that night with great anxiety and dreamed of being out in a jungle captured by natives who were cannibals. The boiling pot was ready. His hands were tied. As the natives came toward him with the faces of his creditors, they held up their spears ready to finish him off when suddenly he saw holes in the points of their spears, and just in time awakened with the answer to his problem of how to finish building the sewing machine!

Sometimes dreams are a source of great creativity. That's what the people in the Bible believed. Look at Joseph interpreting dreams in Pharaoh's court and Jacob wrestling with the angel at the Jabbok River and Ezekiel watching the dead, dry bones of Israel spring back to life. What about the carpenter, Joseph, dreaming of the danger of Herod then fleeing to safety in Egypt? Think of Peter, a Jew's Jew, in Acts 10 dreaming of eating Gentile food and then heading for Cornelius' house. Maybe the prophet Joel (2:28) is right about "the old dreaming dreams and the young ones seeing visions." Out of all this dream talk and wrestling in the middle of the night come some of the great theological themes of the Christian faith. Doctrines like sin, justification, and sanctification don't just drop out of the sky. They have emerged from the life-blood experience of the Israelites and the early Christians with their God, often in the middle of the night — out of the visions and dreams of the Israelite people. Some of the best theology comes out of the sleepless nights of restless dreamers. "Woe is me," says Isaiah in his vision, "I am a man of unclean lips."

Sometimes our dreams can be frightening as we come face-to-face with our shadow selves. We toss and turn in the night, groping for God. Sometimes it's like a bad dream that seems all too real. In the 1880s, a seven-year-old boy cried himself to sleep every night terrified of the fact that if he died he might go to hell. His solicitous mother, out of patience that the fearful teachings of the age brought such apparitions to his mind, was trying in vain to comfort him. Fifty years later that boy, Harry Emerson Fosdick, stood as the preacher before the congregation of Riverside Church in New York City. Even great preachers toss and turn in the night.

Samuel woke up in a cold sweat and ran to Eli thinking Eli had called. Precious Samuel was born to Hannah, Hannah's gift to God. If God would just give her a child, when he reached a tender age she would give him up for the Lord's service. Like a scene from Bertolucci's movie, *The Last Emperor*, where the child is taken from his mother's arms to be the new emperor of China, so Hannah in tears gave up her only begotten child to the old priest Eli and his evil sons. Samuel served as a temple gopher, a page of sorts in a time when the word of the Lord was rare in the land. Like another boy child, David, called to take on a different kind of evil in his time, so little Samuel had no idea what he was getting himself into, that is, until he came to this ancient nocturnal bar mitzvah.

"Here I am, Lord," he said running to old Eli who grumbles, "Go back to sleep, child, you're hearing things," which is very much what the church says to all dreamers, isn't it? "Go back to sleep, Moses, you're dreaming. Go back to sleep, Gandhi, you're dreaming. Go back to sleep, Martin Luther King Jr., you're dreaming. Go back to sleep, Mother Teresa, you're hearing things!"

Maybe the dreamers of our world really do hear God speaking to them. Rabbi Burt Visotsky, in the Bill Moyers' PBS discussion on Genesis, at one point says, "You know, I'm actually surprised to be surrounded by people who so readily hear voices. I'm a praying Jew, so I talk to God all the time, but I don't usually hear answers. It's a much more subtle process. God may tell Abraham to get up and go and change everything in his life. But nobody ever says that to me. If I hear God at all, it's somewhere between the lines of a page I've been studying for hours when I am studying the Torah, and what I hear is maybe, 'Burt, turn the page.' "

Young Samuel, waking up in a cold sweat that night says, "Here I am, Lord. Here I am!" But he didn't know who was calling or why because he didn't really know who he was as a child of God. When God first calls us in the middle of the night, the most you can know is who you are as a broken human being, and admitting that to yourself is the first step toward wholeness, health, and peace in your life, in other words, Shalom. Some people toss and turn and finally cry out, "Okay I give up. Here I am, I am in trouble, I am hurting, I am even hurting other people. Yes, I admit it. Here I am." What do you mean when you say, "Here I am" in the middle of the night? People say it in different ways. "Here I am envious of others who have more than I do, who are smarter and faster and get more attention." Some of us are envious, some of us are selfish. Listen to Shel Silverstein's "Prayer of the Selfish Child":

Now I lay me down to sleep
I pray the Lord my soul to keep,
And if I die before I wake,
I pray the Lord my toys to break,
So none of the other kids can use 'em ... Amen.[1]

Here is a mother who can't understand what went wrong with her teenage child. She feels guilt deep down never able to realize that she has done all she can and that most if not all of it was never her fault. But in the middle of the night, she hears her name called and says, "Here I am."

What I am trying to say is that you and I have to face up to ourselves and this self-revelation often occurs in the middle of the night as it did for Samuel. Until we do that we will never really hear God calling our names and leading us into new ministries and new lives. We will never hear God's redeeming and cleansing word of grace. Samuel didn't hear it the first time or the second time or the third. Maybe he was having a hard time hearing it because no one else was hearing it in those days. Eli certainly wasn't because "the Word of the Lord was rare in the land."

Maybe it's hard for us to say "Here I am" that openly because we aren't really ready for God to come into our bedrooms and our dreams peeking into our innermost selves. How ready are you for God to peer into the hidden corners of your life? I know a family that has a rule that if one of them sees someone driving up to the house unannounced that family member is legally bound by the rules of the house to yell "Firedrill!" and everyone jumps in cleaning the house, scurrying around frantically to pick everything up. The rule is everything gets thrown into one room and when that door is closed it gets locked, and no one, not even God, can go into that room! Those are the rules of the house. We all have a room like that in our lives, and when God comes calling we scurry around cleaning up and throwing everything into that one little room, lock the door, and throw away the key. Oh sure, Lord, we scrub up and come to church on Sundays, but don't ever call on us in the middle of the night or in our businesses, our marriages, or our friendships. Please, Lord, we're not ready for that. Here are Adam and Eve hiding in the bushes and trees of the garden. Here we are hiding our secret sins in a room that not even God can enter, or so we think. We say casually, "Here I am, Lord. Speak, Lord, for your servant is listening." But are we really all that ready for God to come in? Not that room, Lord. Any room but that one!

Of course, we lay our lives on the line when we answer God's call the way Samuel did by doing it in community. Notice that Samuel isn't hiding in his room by himself sitting around talking to God. No, he's saying "Here I am," in community because he speaks to Eli every time. He's laying out all his guilt and grief and sin. He's holding nothing back. "Just as I am, without one plea." Here he comes laying himself finally before the altar of God. Ultimately, he opens that one locked door and even lets God in there. Only when he was able to say "Here I am," openly and honestly both in community and by himself and "Speak, Lord, for your servant is listening," did the scripture follow with "... and Samuel grew and the Lord was with him."

Jesus said "Here I am" over and over again. At the temptation, he said, "Here I am, torn with ambition." At the tomb of Lazarus, he said, "Here I am, broken and weeping." At the Mount of Olives, he said, "Here I am, wanting this cup to pass from me." Even his last night, tossing and turning unable to sleep, he prays for God's guidance. Even on the cross during the worst nightmare of all — he was torn, "My God, my God, why hast thou forsaken me?" But at the very end he was at one with the Father, at peace. Picture him there praying the old Jewish prayer that a child would say the last thing before dropping off to sleep, "Into thy hands I commit my spirit." "Here I am, Lord. I am yours completely and fully."

Having trouble sleeping through the night? Quit playing games with yourself, others, and God. Take the first step toward wholeness and peace. Say, "Here I am, Lord. I am yours now and for the rest of my life." Having trouble sleeping through the night? Perhaps God is calling you to new life, but I wouldn't know about a thing like that. Why? Because a thing like that is between you and God. Amen.

---

1. Shel Silverstein, *A Light in the Attic* (New York: Harper and Row, 1981), p. 15.

Proper 5
Pentecost 3
Ordinary Time 10
1 Samuel 8:4-11 (12-15) 16-20 (11:14-15)

God Never Gives Up On Us

Have you noticed that no matter how much of a mess we make of our lives, God never gives up on us? We try to do the right thing, but fail over and over again. Paul talks openly about the fact that he knows the right thing to do, but just keeps doing the wrong thing. He can't seem to help himself. I guess it all started with the first Adam who got to work early one morning and parked on the line between two parking places so that everyone who came after him has parked on the line ever since. What a mess we humans keep making of things. Theologians call it sin and it touches us all.

It's not just you with the stumbles and missteps you've made along the way. It's all of us. We keep making mistakes. Some were on purpose and some just happened. You know the difference. Insurance adjusters with a touch of grace often calm anxious drivers who call in from their wrecked cars, "It's going to be all right. That's why we call them accidents." The problem is we can't take them back anymore than we can put toothpaste back in the tube once it's squirted out in a spurt. What a mess we make of our lives. Some of them we try to cover up, some we just try to live with. Some gnaw at us for years, even decades, later because we can't let them go. The good news is God is always there patiently waiting to help us pick up the pieces. Why? Because God never gives up on us. That's exactly what happened in this story of Samuel and the people's persistent complaining about the need for a king. If you look carefully you will see there are three key themes echoing in this story.

The first one is this: Samuel's sons have made a mess of things and the people don't see any good prospects for the future. If Samuel's sons are the next ones in line to take over, the future is dim at best and the people are demanding something different. What's wrong with Samuel's sons? Well, they are about as different from their respected father as anyone could ever be. Contrary to that wise, old saying, in this case the apples fell a long way from the tree! Like old Eli's sons, Samuel's boys were only out for themselves. Surely Samuel saw the irony. Like some politicians and business leaders even today, they were feathering their own nest and did not care about the people they were supposed to be serving and leading. They made the abuses of Enron and Tyco look like a grade school picnic with all their "bribes and perversion of justice" (v. 3). It's further proof that unethical behavior at the highest levels both corporately and governmentally has been around for a very long time. It didn't just start yesterday. It's also a reminder that CEO really should stand for Chief Ethics Officer since proper ethical behavior needs to begin at the top and be modeled for everyone else.

Apparently, Samuel's sons never figured that out but the people under Samuel's care did and they were going to have nothing of it. They wanted a change and they wanted it now! They certainly weren't timid about expressing their feelings. It reminds me of the young monk who entered a monastery where everyone had to take a vow of silence. The abbot told the young monk that he would only get to say two words every five years. The young monk knew this would be a challenge but agreed grudgingly. At the end of the first five years the abbot asked him, "What are your two words?" The young monk replied, "Bed hard." At the end of the second five years, the abbot asked him what his two words were this time. The young monk replied, "Food bad." At the end of the third five years when the abbot asked him what his two words were, the young monk replied, "Want out!" And the abbot said, "I'm not surprised; you've done nothing but gripe and complain from the moment you got here."

Some people complain just to be complaining, but in Samuel's case it looks as if they had plenty to complain about. They were worried about their future and the future of their children. The old man had been a good leader, but his sons were another story altogether. The people were determined to make some changes, so they asked for a king. After all, other nations had a king and graduating from judges to kings would certainly elevate their status with their neighbors.

Notice carefully now what God does at this crucial moment in biblical history. God could have easily intervened and put a stop to it all. God could have rescued his faithful servant Samuel and saved him a lot of undue stress even though God knows the people could be making a mess of things by insisting on a king. What does God do instead? God simply let things take their own course by letting Samuel and his people sort it all out themselves. Here is another one of those early examples of the doctrine of free will where God gives us human beings room to maneuver. Theologians call it *the permissive will of God.* We get to choose between right and wrong and then suffer the consequences. Sometimes we choose between the lesser of two evils as in political elections. At other times we choose between the better of two goods, which is much more challenging — great characters in classic movies often make choices like these. Whatever the case, God lets us choose. Why? Because God decided from the beginning not to treat us like marionettes on a string dancing about at the whims of some divine puppeteer.

So, in our story, God stands in the shadows to see what we are going to do. Are we going to continue to gripe and complain and push for change even though we have no idea what will come of it? What is poor Samuel going to do with this protest crowd setting up camp at his doorstep every morning? Instead of intervening to save the day or deciding we're not worth it anymore, God never gives up on us.

Which brings us to the second key theme in this passage — Samuel makes a mess of it by taking it all too personally. How easy that is to do. Poor guy. Look how quickly we've jumped from his birth and boyhood to his semi-retirement when he's thinking about hanging it up and passing the baton to someone else. Like the owner of the business who has been thinking all along about turning the family business over to his own children, or at least one of them, Samuel was hoping beyond hope that his no-account sons might shape up just in time to take on the reins, in this case ruling the people as God's servants on earth.

Oh, he knows what they're really like. He's watched them get in trouble all their lives, especially through the teenage years. You know that tear-filled feeling you have as a parent when you drop your firstborn off at some college or university halfway around the country, knowing all the time that this act signals the break up of the family as you've known it? If you're really honest, you have to admit it's a bittersweet moment. You're happy for your child who is moving on with life and getting a good start on their education and career/calling. You have a lump in your throat because you're going to miss the little troublemaker. But, then you realize suddenly that God has given us the teenage years to get us through the grief of having them leave home!

Once a Sunday school class was discussing the story of the sacrifice of Isaac when a young mother who had just left her newborn in the nursery for the first time said with a sound of shock in her voice, "I can't believe this is in the Bible! I can't imagine killing my own child!" And another mother piped up quickly, "You obviously haven't had teenagers yet!" It gave a whole different perspective on the sacrifice of Isaac story. Garrison Keillor once said that we know Isaac was only twelve and not thirteen, fourteen, or fifteen because if he'd been thirteen, fourteen, or fifteen, it wouldn't have been a sacrifice!

We love our children despite their sibling rivalries that are as old as Cain and Abel. But they do have a way of trying our patience at times, and Samuel's sons have really put him in a tight spot. They have made such a mess of things that life was never going to be the same for Samuel or his people. In fact, their mess threatened to change history forever. Because of his no-good sons, the people were not only criticizing his family, they were pushing him out the door adding insult to injury.

So, what did Samuel do? He turned to his old friend for help. Who was his old friend? God — the one waiting in the wings to see what we're going to do. How often we try to fix things ourselves. But Samuel, being a holy and righteous man, knew better than to try solving this one himself. Instead, he took a deep breath and headed off for some time with God, the one who always seemed to have the right answer. Samuel had learned long ago that worrying about something didn't get him anywhere. In fact, worry, which affects one's health by eating at you, is a sure sign that you don't really trust in God to help you handle whatever trouble you are in. Samuel may not have been the sharpest arrow in the quiver, but he definitely had faith and lots of it. Be that as it may, he goes to God in prayer all worked up over the people's seeming affront to him as a leader and their attack on his family.

What does God do? God pats him on the hand to calm him down and says, "Relax, Samuel. This is not about you, it's about me. I've dealt with this before. It's me they're attacking. You need to learn how to self-differentiate." It's so easy to take everything personally when you are leader, especially a church leader. But, guess what — it's not always about you. Sometimes people are just mad at God like after a death. After all, they have to blame someone, and as a representative of God whether clergy or lay, you are often the closest one in sight so you bear the brunt of their anger. That's what happened to Samuel. At least that's what God was trying to help him see. God calms Samuel and reminds him that sometimes you just need to let things go, let them go into God's loving hands. After all, that's what prayer is — a place to let our worries and anxieties go. What we need to say is this: "God, I have tried everything I can to solve this problem by myself. I have exhausted all the plausible possibilities and now find myself turning to you. I'm letting this worry go to you, God. It's all yours now." That's what Samuel finally figured out.

Notice again, God doesn't intervene to change things. God knows as does Samuel that a king won't necessarily solve things. God tells Samuel to warn the people that kings have a way of being selfish and demanding things and messing things up themselves, and that sometimes they may not turn out to be any better than Samuel's rotten sons. "I won't take it personally," says God, "if they still want a king. I'll work with them on this." And that's exactly what God does.

Which brings us to our third key theme — God never gives up on them even though they insist on doing things their way. Samuel warns the people that it's not going to be perfect with a king, but the people insist because of peer pressure, which makes the people sound as adolescent as Samuel's no-good sons. Like a loving parent who gives his/her children room to grow up and make mistakes, God gives them what they ask for knowing that human kings make a mess of things — Saul, David, and so forth down the line. God gives them kings who aren't perfect but do the best they can. What does this show but the great flexibility, grace, and generosity of God? That's the whole point of this text.

As we look from this story through the whole sweep of human history, we see that things haven't really changed that much. But, the good news is that God is always there to help us pick up the pieces no matter what we do. From Samuel on, humanity kept making a mess of things even as we do today, so God does something radical — God gives us a new king, a king for all time. Who is this king? It is the one we call the Christ, the King of kings and the Lord of lords, the one who picks us up when all we seem to be is down, and because of him, we have the blessed assurance that God will always be with us cleaning up the messes we make of our lives. That's why we should never give up on God, for God will never, ever give up on us! Amen.

Proper 6
Pentecost 4
Ordinary Time 11
1 Samuel 15:34—16:13

Samuel Was The Search Committee

I don't know about you but when I was growing up I always loved hearing the story of Cinderella. There was always something magical about it. It was more than Walter Mitty or Lee Iacocca — small-town boy made good. It was more than Prince Charles and Princess Diana in all their regal splendor long before Diana's untimely death.

It was like the triumph of the poor and the oppressed over the powerful and the arrogant — the quintessential example of the first shall be last and the last shall be first. It was the divine reversal in action as if God had actually written the story. It was liberation theology brought to fruition, the triumph of the proletariat over the bourgeoisie set in the context of a monarchial drama, an incredible conflation of political images. It was, in Reinhold Niebuhr's terminology, the transvaluation of values. Of course, when I was six years of age I didn't think all that. I just thought it was a neat story, and I loved everything about it: The poor girl down on her luck, her mean stepsisters and their mean mother, the nice fairy godmother, the pumpkin carriage, the horses, the ball, the fantasy evening that whirled by like a waltz — round and round and round she went — an evening we all dream of that's over before we know it. Then there was the glass slipper that fit only her foot. I loved it when the older sisters got theirs for being so greedy. A tragic story with a happy ending. I loved everything about it.

I loved it as much as I did the story of the young boy who pulled the sword Excalibur from the stone, the one Merlin had been searching for all these years. Others had tried, others who were older and bigger and stronger, but for some reason this young lad was the one who could do it. This little one who Merlin called Wart would be crowned the king of England. Who'd have thought it? Neither the young boy nor Cinderella ever imagined that he or she would be chosen.

In a way, this story of Samuel searching for a new king is a kind of Cinderella story, isn't it? Samuel is the emissary who comes looking for the one whose foot fits the glass slipper. Samuel comes looking for the only one who can pull Excalibur from the stone. Like Merlin lurking through some medieval forest for King Arthur, so Samuel comes looking for the next king of Israel. And like Merlin, Samuel is a little unsure of his task. In both cases, as in the Cinderella story, there are many other forces vying for the prize. Others want the slipper. Others want the sword and the power that goes with it. But only one will be chosen. So off goes Samuel searching for a king. "Fill your horn with oil and go. Go to Jesse who lives down the road in Bethlehem, for I have provided for myself a king among his sons."

"What?" thought Samuel. "No nationwide search? No church information forms to fill out? No denominational approval? No resumes to read? The town and the home, already picked out? I know a few search committees who would like to have heard that! No job description to fill out, no inflated ideas about finding God's gift to Christendom that is thirty years of age with forty years of experience."

No. Samuel was the search committee who went off looking for the next king, and God had made it all easy by narrowing the search down to the little town called Bethlehem, which of course we hear about it later when shepherds and wise men appear searching for another king.

Samuel came to the house of Jesse that day, and Jesse trooped his sons in one by one for interviews with Samuel. The search process always includes the interview. And each search committee does interviews in different ways. Who knows how this one went? One scholar thinks the episode is reminiscent of Saul's election by lottery. Others think it involved interviews with "Yes" and "No" answers. The whole thing reminds me of the former football coach,

Bear Bryant, visiting some Alabama farm looking for his next football star, and Mama and Daddy trooping all their sons by to see which one he wants. So here is Jesse, proud father that he is, trooping his sons one by one — Eliab and Abinadab and Shammah and Nethanel and Raddai and Ozem. And in every case something wasn't quite right. In every case Samuel would say, "No, that's not the one. Next. Next. Next...."

Samuel learned three things about his search process, things that all search committees and congregations need to keep in mind: First, the search takes a lot longer than you think. Second, you look at a lot of candidates who on the surface look pretty good but aren't quite right somehow. They all have good qualifications but there's still something missing. And third, you should never give up because the right one will come along someday. You just know it. Samuel knew it, but he didn't know why. I'll tell you why. It's because God does the choosing. Samuel may be the search committee but God does the choosing. That's always the way it works.

So there is the prince's emissary looking astonished as he fits the glass slipper on the poor girl's foot; there is Merlin looking astonished when the scrawny boy pulls the sword from the stone. There is Samuel amazed when the kid comes in from the field. Why? Because Samuel was the search committee but God did the choosing. Is this not a theological statement about the sovereignty of God over your life and mine, the sovereignty of God over all nature and history? The protagonist in this story isn't Samuel or Jesse. It isn't even David. The protagonist in this story is God.

We think we have God's plan for our lives all figured out, but it's God who does the choosing. We think we have the right person for this position or that, and we work hard for that choice, but it's God who does the choosing. Notice that God often chooses ones we'd least expect.

Why? Because God doesn't look on appearance. God always looks on the heart. Look at David, the youngest son of Jesse. David was so young and insignificant that he couldn't even come to the sacrifice but had to stay and tend his sheep. He was the one chosen because God looks not on appearance; God looks on the heart.

Some people say, "I'm all used up or I'm too handicapped or I'm too old or I'm too young. God will *never* want me." That may be what David thought that day as Samuel, a search committee of one, came around looking for a new king to take Saul's place. The farthest thing from David's mind was that he would even be considered, much less chosen. Chances are it was the farthest thing from Samuel's and Jesse's mind, too. Jesse was just excited to have someone in his family tapped as king; all he could think about was the connections he would have to the seat of real power, so he scrubbed all his sons up and dressed them in their finest, that is, all but the little one he'd left out with the sheep, and paraded them by Samuel one by one thinking surely this was the one. "Well, if not this one, surely that one. They all look so good, don't you think? Mama and I have done our best to raise them right. All the best schools, sports, and music programs. Bringing children up in today's world is no easy thing," says Jesse. "But haven't they turned out great?"

While Jesse is showing Samuel the family trophy case and photographs of their latest achievements, Samuel is checking them out carefully and looking each one right in the eye since the eyes really are the windows of the soul. Initially Samuel is really impressed with Eliab, the tall, dark handsome one, the one with broad shoulders who has a kind of regal air about him. "But no," says the Lord, "that's not the one." Next comes Abinadab who has all the right stuff, "But no," says the Lord, "that's not the one." Then there's Shammah, but he's not the one, either. All seven sons troop by, but, "No, no, no," says the Lord, on every one of them. Samuel and Jesse like any search committee are getting pretty frustrated.

So Samuel says, "Is this all you've got?"

"Well, actually," says Jesse, "there's one more, but he's just a boy out running with the sheep."

"Bring him in here," says Samuel. Everyone kind of giggles, just as the older sisters do in the Cinderella story. "Little David? Samuel will take one look at him and laugh his head off." But that's not what Samuel did at all. As the little red-faced, runny-nosed child stepped through the door, Samuel knew immediately. Call it divine intuition, call it providence, call it whatever you want. But

Samuel knew right then. The biblical writer says it was all in the eyes, for David had beautiful eyes.

I don't know what it was. All I know is that God has an odd way of working because the moment that little boy bounced through the door with "Hey, Dad, what's going on?" his life was changed forever and so was the life of Israel. How could something like this happen? It happens, says the biblical writer, because the Lord sees not as mortals see. The Lord looks not on outward appearance. The Lord looks on the heart. God does not look at your clothes, or your cars, or your houses, or your investments, or even at how much money you give as some TV preachers would have us believe, or how much you do in social justice ministry, or how many jobs you've done around the church, or how many Sunday school classes you've taught, or even how many years you've sung in the choir. No, the Lord doesn't look at how strong or healthy you are or even how much experience you've had. The Lord looks on the heart.

Paul sings the same song in his great peroration on love in 1 Corinthians: "If I speak in the tongues of mortals and of angels, but do not have love, I am a noisy gong or a clanging cymbal. And if I have prophetic powers, and understand all mysteries and all knowledge, and if I have all faith, so as to remove mountains, but do not have love, I am nothing. If I give away all my possessions, and if I hand over my body so that I may boast, but do not have love, I gain nothing" (1 Corinthians 13:1-3). We may put up a great charade among our friends at church, at work, and in our own neighborhoods; we may even be able to fool ourselves for a while. But we can never fool God. Why? Because the Lord looks not on outward appearance or achievement. The Lord looks on the heart. Walk your way through the Bible and you will see. Here is Moses who got tongue-tied every time he had to speak and not even Dale Carnegie could get him over his stage fright; Samuel and Jeremiah were entirely too young, but God still chose them. Why? Because the Lord looks not at age or outward appearance; the Lord looks on the heart.

God chooses the ones we'd never expect. Paul says in 1 Corinthians: "For consider your call, brothers and sisters, not many of you were wise according to human standards, not many were powerful, not many were of noble birth; but God chose what is foolish in the world to shame the wise, God chose what is weak in the world to shame the strong, God chose what is low and despised in the world ..." (1 Corinthians 1:26 ff RSV). Never think that you can't serve because God might choose you before you know it. God chooses the ones we'd never expect — Paul, the murderer; Augustine, the womanizer; Luther, the heavy drinker. "You're a preacher?" says someone to John at the high school reunion. "Weren't you the hot-headed brawler on the basketball team? And Wayne, the tough kid on the block, he's a preacher, too? You guys must have really changed." Or to Susan, the bratty girl in class: "You're a preacher now? Well, you always did like to talk."

God chooses the ones we least expect. Look at a prominent journalist for the finest newspaper in the land whose colleagues say to him, "You go to church?" "What's gotten into you?" God chooses the ones we'd least expect to do God's will and bring in God's kingdom.

God chooses the ones we'd never expect. We think we have God's plan all figured out but we don't. Samuel was the search committee but God does the choosing. God chooses you and me in unexpected ways. If Jesus saw something in IRS types and fishermen and publicans and sinners and even a little scoundrel like Zacchaeus who'd been treed like a cat, imagine what Jesus sees in you and me! Jesus' x-ray vision saw right through the woman at the well and Peter and James and John. Just as with David and you and me, the Lord looks not on outward appearance or achievement; the Lord looks on the heart.

"You've got to have heart to play on this team, boy," says Bear Bryant. "I don't care how big you are." "Is this all your sons?" he asks the Alabama mother. "Well, no" she replies. "There's the little one in the barn. But he's so small." "Bring him in," says the Bear.

I don't know where you come from or how you got where you are. But for some reason God has called you and me in unexpected ways. Why? Because that's the way God works. Thanks be to God! Samuel may be the search committee, but it's God who does the choosing. Amen.

Proper 7
Pentecost 5
Ordinary Time 12
1 Samuel 17:(1a, 4-11, 19-23) 32-49

The Real Underdog!

Every boy I knew growing up in the Midwest loved this story. We acted it out. We imagined ourselves as David, the shepherd boy, with nothing but a sling and a few smooth stones. Goliath represented for us every neighborhood bully who had ever picked on us. Of course, we only had dime-store slingshots. You know the kind where you pulled back the bungee cord-like launcher with the little patch in the middle and tried to nail your target. The idea that David pegged Goliath with nothing but a leather strap and a pouch you swirl in the air made the story all the more dramatic. However, the main reason we loved this tale was that we identified with David as the underdog, and better yet that God seemed to side with the underdog.

No wonder we saw this famous David and Goliath story as the ultimate triumph of the underdog. After all, isn't that the way it was promoted from both the pulpit and popular culture? If you had a creative Sunday school teacher, you'd get to dramatize it in class, which helped you overcome Sunday morning drowsiness. Movies like *Facing the Giants* still trumpet this approach. The beat-up, down-trodden-bunch-of-losers-football-team overcomes all odds and knocks the cocky, arrogant state champs off their high horse. It's the way all those story lines go. In fact, the David character rarely ever loses, and the whole theater cheers! Oh, how we love this little story that could be summarized with this phrase: "The bigger they come ..." well you know the rest.

There's only one problem with this particular interpretation.

It's wrong.

You have no idea how hard it is for me to admit this. You may even want to stop reading because you've decided that this stuffy, seminary professor has ruined everything by being a spoilsport. Believe me, I'm a big fan of underdog stories. And in sports events I often root for the ones who aren't supposed to win. So, you can imagine my own disappointment when I began taking a closer look at this text and realized that this is not a story about God siding with the underdogs of the world taking down the bullies and putting them in their places. No, when you analyze this text carefully, you find that there's a lot more going on.

In fact, in many ways, David isn't the underdog at all here for at least three simple reasons. First of all, he was prepared. He wasn't the scrawny little 98-pound weakling popular culture sometimes makes him out to be. Oh, to be sure, he wouldn't have been playing right guard for some NFL team like his older brothers. He wasn't that big and brawny. But, he still might have played free safety for the high school team. I picture him now as wiry, sinewy, solid as a rock, and fast as a gazelle. When he hit you on a dead run in the open field, he could send you flying. David was one tough, little guy. Like the boxer in the ring who hangs in there with the champ, he had more heart than anyone in the room.

In scripture, he gives us his own resume: "When a lion or bear comes and carries off a sheep from the flock, I go after it and attack it and rescue the victim from its jaws. Then if it turns on me, I seize it by the beard and batter it to death. Lions I have killed and bears, and this uncircumcised Philistine will fare no better than they ..." (1 Samuel 17:34-36). Wow! This is the talk of either a very courageous young man or a real fool. These, as we used to say in Oklahoma, are not the words of some city kid. These are the words of a boy with calloused hands, a courageous heart, and lots of moxie. After all, how many lions' jaws have you pried open lately? How many bears have you battered to death? David is a gutsy guy who threatens to turn Goliath and his whole army into bird food. He's smart enough to identify Goliath's weakness — his arrogance — and witty enough to conceal his own strengths — his faith in God and his measly, little sling. We also know how strong David was when after burying a stone in Goliath's forehead he decided that wasn't enough so he mounted the fallen giant, drew his mighty sword from his scabbard and lopped off his head. Hardly the actions of a gaunt, bony, little underdog. The sword alone must have weighed a ton.

The second reason we know he's not an underdog is that he remains true to himself. When Saul tried to load him down with a heavy tunic, a big, bronze helmet, a coat of mail, and a whopping sword, David knew immediately that he would be lost out there loaded down with this extra weight. The author of Hebrews must have had David in mind when he penned his two famous verses at the beginning of chapter 12: "Let us run with perseverance the race that is before us, laying aside every weight and sin that clings so closely." Another translation, The New English Bible, says "... we must throw off every encumbrance...." David knew he couldn't be in "the zone" if we wore all that armor. What did that extra weight represent — the pretenses of the world; in other words, trying to be someone you're not. David realized he had to be himself. He had to play the way he always had, the game he knew the best, the game that had gotten him to this moment in his life and this competition. Advanced weapons the world tried to give him were not his ticket to victory. He had to trust his own instincts knowing that he was not alone.

That brings us to the third reason David was not an underdog: He had God on his side. God was not on David's side because he was an underdog, but because David trusted in God completely. In fact, he becomes in this story a model of faith and trust for all of us who face obstacles we think we can never overcome, traumas that threaten to take us down, and stresses in life that worry us to death. David felt God's presence in his life from the moment he was born. His boldness stands out amidst a whole field of cowardice when his brothers think he's left his flocks to come gawk at the carnage that is about to happen, and David utters this startling sentence in Saul's presence, "Do not lose heart, sir. I will go and fight this Philistine." He must have struck everyone strangely mute until Saul with almost a laugh and a hint of envy in his voice tells David that Goliath will tear him limb from limb. When David recites his conquests out in the wilds and ends with this phrase, "[Goliath] has defied the armies of the living God. The Lord who saved me from the paw of the lion and from the paw of the bear will save me from the hand of this Philistine," even Saul sees the real reason for David's bravado, and says, "Go, and may the Lord be with you" (1 Samuel 17:36b-37).

I've sometimes wondered whether Saul thought this would be a good way to rid himself of someone who was already becoming too popular. But there is no hint of that in the text at this point. To Saul's credit, he must have recognized the glint in David's eyes as the Lord looking right at him because Saul remembered once what it was like to have the Lord with him.

So, for these three reasons — 1) David was prepared physically, 2) he remained true to himself, and 3) he knew God was with him — David was anything but an underdog here. In fact, have you guessed yet who the real underdog is in this story? Goliath. That's right, Goliath. Why? Because the battle here is not between David and Goliath; the battle is between God and Goliath. Poor little Goliath; he's the real underdog. He's not fighting little David. He's really going up against God and because he's dumb as a post he doesn't even realize it. He's doesn't even know what hits him until it's too late.

Don't you see? David is just a tool of God here. This isn't a story about little David's triumph over the big giant against all odds. It's a theological statement about the power of God over everything that seeks to bring us down. God is the main protagonist on this stage, not David. God is the main actor who drives the story. Goliath represents evil and sin and all the destructive practices of abuse and injustice we fight against every day of our lives. The good news is we aren't fighting them all by ourselves. God is fighting in and through us — that is, if we trust in God enough to join the battle. For some of us Goliath is fear, for others of us Goliath represents worry. Either way, we are immobilized the way Saul's army was when it came face-to-face with the Philistine giant.

Too often we only want to see David and Goliath meeting at high noon at the OK Corral. However, when we forget God is Goliath's real foe, we turn this story into another Manichean version of Star Wars where good and evil are equal, duking it out for who's in charge. This story really is an answer to the question, "Who's in charge here?"

The answer comes back resoundingly, "God is in charge of our world and your life and mine." In the end, evil will not have its way. Oh, sure it thrashes around here and there pushing us off our compass course. It terrifies us and tempts us into more nefarious sins. It threatens to keep us turned in on ourselves. David shows us a better way. David shows us how the Goliath who stands for evil really is the underdog in this story. That's why David won that day, because God was with him all the way.

We see it again in the cross and the resurrection. Evil keeps trying to beat us down, but no matter how hard it tries, Christ is victorious. In the face of Christ, evil doesn't stand a chance. I realize there are times we think we will be overcome by the Goliaths around us — drugs, addictions, envy, greed, malice, and the like — Goliaths in our lives globally, communally, and personally that threaten to strike us down. But when they do, we need to pull this story out and read it again, not because we want to see David, the underdog, conquer the big bully, but because the big bully is really the underdog and his opponent, God, will win every time.

No wonder that simple gospel song spells it out so well. The battle is not David's or yours or mine. No, the "battle belongs to the Lord — no weapon that's fashioned against us will stand, the battle belongs to the Lord." If the battle really does belong to the Lord, and I believe it does, then we can join David with God on our side taking on the injustices around us knowing that the Lord will be with us from this day forth and forevermore. Amen.

which to change. This story really is an answer to the question, "Where in our heart?"

There [illegible] finally, "God is such a gracious [illegible] and [illegible] the [illegible] evil that has its way. Oh, such a [illegible] around here and there [illegible] pushing us off our course [illegible] and tempts us into more [illegible] that [illegible] to keep us [illegible] on our [illegible]. David shows us a better way. David shows us [illegible] God [illegible] stands for evil [illegible] the [illegible] Evil [illegible] that [illegible] God will [illegible] [illegible]

[illegible] Evil keeps trying to [illegible] how hard it tries. This is [illegible] [illegible] will [illegible] [illegible]

[illegible]

[illegible] when they [illegible]

[illegible] because [illegible]

[illegible] really [illegible] and [illegible]

[illegible]

Proper 8
Pentecost 6
Ordinary Time 13
2 Samuel 1:1, 17-27

Getting Through The Grief

Getting through grief may be one of the hardest things we do as human beings. One of the best ways to begin the process is to find it within ourselves to stand up and say something in a public setting that puts into words both the personal and collective feelings of all who have gathered to mourn. History is replete with stunning examples. Pericles' Funeral Oration as recorded by Thucydides in *The Peloponnesian War* is certainly one of them. At the end of the first year of war, the Athenians held, as was their custom, an elaborate funeral for all those killed in the war. The funeral oration over these dead was delivered by the brilliant and charismatic general, Pericles. His famous eulogy demonstrates a classic statement of Athenian ideology when he says, "Such was the end of these men; they were worthy of Athens, and the living need not desire to have a more heroic spirit, although they may pray for a less fatal issue."

Lincoln's Gettysburg address provides another stellar example: "We have come to dedicate a portion of that field, as a final resting place for those who here gave their lives that that nation might live. It is altogether fitting and proper that we should do this. But, in a larger sense, we cannot dedicate — we cannot consecrate — we cannot hallow — this ground. The brave men, living and dead, who struggled here, have consecrated it, far above our poor power to add or detract. The world will little note, nor long remember what we say here, but it can never forget what they did here. It is for us the living, rather, to be dedicated here to the unfinished work which they who fought here have thus far so nobly advanced."

When President Lincoln died in the house across the street from Ford's Theater, his Secretary of War, Edwin Stanton, standing at Lincoln's side, said, "Now he belongs to the ages."

On January 28, 1986, in his television broadcast to the nation on the day of the space shuttle *Challenger* disaster, President Reagan concluded: "We will never forget them this morning as they prepared for their journey and waved good-bye and slipped the surly bonds of earth to touch the face of God."

Charles Earl Spencer said the following about Princess Diana: "Diana was the very essence of compassion, of duty, of style, of beauty. All over the world she was a symbol of selfless humanity. All over the world, a standard bearer for the rights of the truly downtrodden, a very British girl who transcended nationality. Someone with a natural nobility who was classless and who proved in the last year that she needed no royal title to continue to generate her particular brand of magic." Nehru said of Gandhi: "Friends and comrades, the light has gone out of our lives and there is darkness everywhere ... the light has gone out, I said, and yet I was wrong. For the light that shone in this country was no ordinary light. The light that has illumined this country for these many years will illumine this country for many more years, and a thousand years later that light will still be seen in this country, and the world will see it and it will give solace to innumerable hearts."

Getting through grief begins with saying something nice about the ones who have died and most of the time that's pretty easy to do. When people come up to me after a memorial service and say, "That was a beautiful eulogy," I always reply, "Thank you, but the reality is you write your own eulogy with the way you live your life," which is a sobering thought! I can tell by the startled looks I get. I also usually add, "Remember to be nice to your friends and family and also your pastor or priest because they will have the last word!" Not that it matters much once you're deceased, but you'd like to think they could find a few kind words to say about you no matter what kind of life you lived. After all the word eulogy itself comes from two Greek words that, when translated, mean "good word." That's what we say about people in eulogies — good words.

But, what do you do when they weren't so good? It's like the story of the two wealthy brothers who were scoundrels and cheats, and everyone in town knew it. When one of the brothers died, the other one came to his pastor and said, "Preacher, if you will say in my brother's eulogy that my brother was a saint, I will give the church a million dollars for your new million-dollar capital campaign." Now this was a moral dilemma. The pastor thought for a moment and then agreed. The brother called his banker and had the money transferred right there on the spot. On the day of the funeral, the pastor got up and said the following, "Now everyone in town knew that the dear departed was a scoundrel and a cheat ... but compared to his brother, he was a saint!" Sometimes it's hard figuring out nice things to say about some people. Have you ever read or heard a good eulogy for Hitler?

Such was the dilemma David found himself in when Saul and Jonathan died. Saul had been out to get David from the moment he realized David was more popular with the people. David was a constant threat to Saul's authority, not because David intended to be, but because David obviously had the presence of the Lord in his life. Saul knew that God's presence and authority had left him about the time David assassinated Goliath. It was all downhill from there.

Saul was dead, slain in battle, and David had to muster a few good words to say about him. It was no problem saying something nice about Jonathan. Jonathan was his beloved friend. Jonathan was precious to David, one whose love for David surpassed "the love of women" (v. 26). There was an amazing bond between them. You can feel the deep anguish and grief pouring from David's heart as he cries out in this famous lament. It's almost a dirge for the war dead, like a father who has lost his son in battle.

Once, while we were in Angel Fire, New Mexico, my wife and I visited the Vietnam Memorial there and were surprised that it had been built by one single man, Dr. Victor Westphall, and his family in honor and memory of his son, First Lieutenant Victor Westphall III who died in Vietnam. After their son's death, Victor and Jeanne Westphall, assisted by their second son, Walter, determined they would build a memorial to all servicemen who were dying or being maimed in body or spirit in Vietnam. Using Lt. Westphall's SGLI payment as seed money, they engaged a young Santa Fe architect, Ted Luna, to design the Memorial Chapel. When we went into the little theater to watch a documentary film in the museum, I noticed boxes of tissues placed on chairs around the darkened room and wondered what they were for. By the end of the film, I knew and was using them myself.

Imagine the tears falling from David's eyes and all who were gathered there the day he delivered his eulogy. You sense that a deep friendship has suddenly come to an end. It's not hard to say "good words" about someone you loved, but how hard it is to say them about someone who tried to do you in. Yet, David does exactly that when he speaks of Saul. Maybe it was easier to lump them together. A eulogy about Saul alone would have surely taxed David's patience, but throwing him in with Jonathan mollified the whole thing. After all, he wouldn't have wanted to taint his loving tribute to Jonathan with a tirade against Saul. Maybe that's why he contained himself.

Maybe he just decided to let bygones be bygones. Why dredge up all that old stuff? Another reason that some commentators suggest is that David was already a skilled, master politician. He didn't hold a grudge. He understood how the game was played. Someone who might be sticking you in the back today might turn out to be your ally tomorrow. No need for vengeance. I've seen politicians fight tooth and nail in primaries then, when the battle was over and one of them had won, they'd make up and work together. Maybe David was just a good politician who decided to bury the hatchet and knew how to put the public good above any personal animosity he'd had toward Saul. Here we have a foreshadowing of Jesus' "love your enemies and pray for those who persecute you" (Matthew 5:44), and Paul's admonition to "overcome evil with good" (Romans 12:21). Purged of any bitterness or malice, David delivers his eulogy for Saul and Jonathan with what appears as true grief for both of them.

But, I think there is something more going on here. David is more than just a good politician. David is filled with the Spirit of the living God, a God who doesn't hold grudges against us no matter what we have done. David's eulogy is full of grace because he is filled with the grace of God. He understands that the greatest honor one has as a spiritual leader, whether pastor or lay, is to usher someone into the presence of the almighty. My greatest honor as a pastor has always been to pray someone who is near death right into heaven. In many ways, that's what we do when we offer a eulogy. We turn our loved ones and friends over into the loving hands of almighty God. We do so with grace and dignity, and that's what David did that day because he had been ushered into the presence of the almighty when he was a little shepherd boy. God filled his life from beginning to end. God so filled David's life that even when he transgressed God gave him another chance.

The good news is God does the same for us. God takes the long view of our lives and, when we come to the end, erases the sins and welcomes us in because of the one we call the Christ. Contrary to what some might think, God isn't a giant frown in the sky. David's eulogy is a prime example of God's beneficent grace acted out through one of God's flawed servants.

I know a pastor who got a call one day from the sons of one of his predecessors, not his immediate predecessor but one further back. Their father, a former pastor, had been asked to leave the church. The new, younger pastor didn't know why; he had only heard about it from some of the older members. The details were sketchy, but, it was clear his predecessor had left under a cloud. Now, he had died and his sons were wondering timidly if they might come down to the church and have the new, younger pastor say a few words and a prayer for their daddy since they'd grown up in the church and hadn't been there since. "We understand if it's not possible," they said with a lump in their throats. "I'd be honored to say a few words," said the new pastor. So he spoke to a larger crowd than the sons ever expected. Despite his indiscretions and flaws, the former pastor had obviously touched a lot of people's lives. The healing that occurred that day for those sons was palpable. Why? Because God always makes something good out of the bad, no matter how bad it is.

At Mickey Mantle's memorial service, sports broadcaster, Bob Costas, said, "In a cartoon from this morning's *Dallas Morning News*, Saint Peter has his arm around Mickey, 'We know some of what went on in your life. Sorry, we can't let you in, but before you go, God wants to know if you'd sign these six dozen baseballs.' " Costas went on to say, "I just hope God has a place for him where he can run again, where he can play practical jokes on his teammates, and smile that boyish smile, 'cause God knows, no one's perfect. And God knows there's something special about heroes. So long, Mick. Thanks."

If God can welcome Saul through David's magnanimous eulogy after all Saul had done to David, imagine what God will do with your life and mine.

To God be the glory! Amen.

Proper 9
Pentecost 7
Ordinary Time 14
2 Samuel 5:1-5, 9-10

Finding Our Roots In God And Country

It's a scary thing to go back and explore your roots. You never know what you might find — some errant ancestor who was a brigand or a pirate. Maybe one of them spent a fortnight in the stocks or was strung up on the gallows. Nevertheless, Alex Haley and genealogists around the world encourage us to book a ticket and take our chances traveling back in time.

In a way, that's exactly what we do every Sunday when we open the Bible and step carefully like Alice into a biblical wonderland or the children making their way through the wardrobe into the magical world of Narnia. We go back in time and see not only our spiritual ancestors but, says the French phenomenologist, Paul Ricoeur, we see ourselves reflected in the mirror of the text. It's what we do every Fourth of July, isn't it, when we reexamine our theological and political roots here in this great land.

Of course, no matter how scary it is to explore one's roots, it also creates the sense of coming home. David must have felt that as he made his way into Jerusalem just before his coronation, as he made his way into the great city of Zion, which some day would be named the city of David. In a way he was finally coming home to his true purpose and goal for life.

I certainly had that feeling a few years ago as I preached and lectured in Cambridge and Oxford in England. The church in which I preached in Cambridge, St. Columba's United Reformed Church, had, I discovered only after arriving, the names of two women whose works I had studied for years written all over the church's history. Agnes Lewis and Margaret Gibson, two eccentric sisters who became famous nineteenth-century Cambridge professors, experts in Greek and Hebrew, traveled to St. Catherine's Monastery at the foot of Mount Sinai in Egypt to examine ancient manuscripts just as I had done a few years ago. I was stunned to learn that these same women, these two "Ladies of Castlebrae" as they were called, had founded and endowed Westminster College at the University of Cambridge late in the nineteenth century. In fact, St. Columba's Church has a Lewis Hall and a Gibson Hall named after these two sisters who were generous benefactors of that church throughout their lives. Preaching there and meeting with students at Wolfson College Cambridge was an amazing experience. It felt like coming home.

Of course, there are roots everywhere you turn in a place like Cambridge: our musical roots, our architectural roots, our theological roots and yes, especially our academic roots. After I had preached in the morning service, I went to lunch with the pastor of the church and one of the Cambridge dons, a biology professor, who was quite keen on showing me Emmanuel College where he had attended and taught before retirement. He showed me around campus pointing to the room where he lived when he was a student, the room where he taught when he was a tutor, and another one when he was a fellow.

He was very proud of Emmanuel College. Most of all, he seemed very insistent on showing me one particular plaque. "Ah, yes, here it is," he said, opening a side door where we entered what appeared to me to be nothing more than a broom closet with mops and ladders at the bottom of a back staircase. My eyes adjusted to the darkened space as thin shafts of light crisscrossed the room. "Yes, this is it," he said with great delight. There on the wall in the broom closet was a simple plaque that read, "John Harvard, who attended Emmanuel College then moved to Massachusetts and started a college there." It was almost a "That's what you get for having the American Revolution," the plaque of one of your most famous Americans relegated to a broom closet! Still, I felt very much at home.

What's fascinating about exploring your roots in God and country is that you begin to see how much you have in common. The elders of Israel made that point with David when they wanted to anoint him king over Israel. "We are your bone and your flesh. We have a kinship with you. Thus you must become our king." In other words, we have a lot in common. One does not have to scratch very far to see how much we have in common with our Christian brothers and sisters in England. Our liturgies, our liturgical vestments, our hymnody, and even the architecture of our sanctuaries are similar. The worship spaces around North America reminded me so much of the churches in which I preached in Cambridge, Oxford, and even in the Methodist church in Keswick up in the lake district that I felt very much at home. So many professors and students walk or ride bicycles through town dressed in their black robes that walking through Oxford one Sunday morning in mine didn't look out of place at all.

Everywhere you turn in Oxford you see our common roots and our common history. You see John Wesley, a Fellow at Christ Church College, Oxford, whose 300th anniversary they were celebrating while I was there. Then you stroll down the street to Magdalene College where C. S. Lewis was cornered by God one day and converted. He wrote to a friend, "I have just passed on from believing in God to definitely believing in Christ ... My long night talk with Tolkien had a great deal to do with it." Tolkien later admitted that without Lewis' encouragement he would not have finished writing *The Lord of the Rings*, sections of which he read aloud at weekly meetings with Lewis, Charles Williams, and Owen Barfield, who would also read from the works they were writing at the time. The very air you breathe is filled with history. Even the Chapel at New College, which looks more like a small cathedral, where I preached and listened every night to the soaring sounds of the New College choir, those little boys and those men who filled that place with shimmering beauty — New College was named New College because it was new when it was founded in 1379!

Everything was old around there. One of the professors told me about a man from Texas visiting York Minster, that great cathedral in York. At one point, the man from Texas asked, "Now, is York Minster pre-war?" Instead of asking him which war he meant, since York Minster is 1,000 years old, the guide simply replied, "Sir, it is pre-America!" How brief and short our American history is and yet we find our roots in England and Scotland, in Ireland and Wales.

Like David, we have a lot in common in both adversity and unity. God knows that our two countries have experienced our share of adversity: their civil war, our civil war. David certainly did before coming to this point in his life. David had come a long way from his early sheepherding days, through his appointment by Samuel, his bout with Goliath, problems, delays, and civil war that thwarted his plans to reorganize a fractured nation that had been torn apart at the seams. David experienced all of that — he had spent many years as an outlaw amidst internal conflicts and external strife. God knows England and America understand about conflict and strife with the civil wars that our countries have suffered and there are still differences with all the denominations and all the differing theological and social opinions about the way things should be done.

I even saw this at lunch one day eating with the Oxford Dons. My host, the dean of the chapel, sitting next to me said, "Do you see that man three seats over from you?" "Yes," I replied. "That's Richard Dawkins, world-renowned geneticist and atheist who wrote in *The Times* that religion was the cause of 9/11, and I wrote a counter article disagreeing with him in the same paper, and he hasn't spoken to me much since." She said, "He doesn't like clergy-types very much. Steer clear of him." We find our common roots in the ways we deal with adversity knowing that what does not kill you can actually make your stronger — something that David surely discovered.

We also find our common roots in unity, not overcoming adversity, but overcoming our differences. When I preached at the Methodist church in Keswick up in the lake district, I mentioned that I felt right at home since my Grandmother Correy was a lifelong Methodist and that my mother grew up a Methodist. After the kind compliments about the sermon after the service, the pastor said in front of a group of parishioners, "We can forgive you for the American Revolution, but I'm not sure we can ever forgive you for leaving the Methodist church to become a Presbyterian!" Yes, we have our differences, but when we look at our roots we find that we have so much more in common.

We have a lot in common in adversity, but so much more in overcoming adversity, which leads to true unity. David demonstrated that as the elders anointed him king of Israel. By virtue of his office and by virtue of his own person, being anointed as king meant that he brought people of Israel and the people of Judah together into one, and brought them together in great union. Since he was already King of Judah, he now created a union between the two nations by virtue of his new office.

Thankfully, we see these kinds of unions occurring around the world — in India with the Church of South India, in Canada and in England with the United Reformed Church, which combines the Presbyterian Church of England, the Congregational Church of England and Wales, the Reformed Churches of Christ in England and the Congregational Union of Scotland. Fortunately, the northern and southern wings of the Presbyterian church here in the United States finally came together in 1983 to form the PCUSA. So, as we look at our roots we see that we have a lot in common in both adversity and in unity as did David of old. That coming together was never more evident than when in both Cambridge and Oxford I shared in the leadership of the Lord's Supper as we broke bread and shared the cup together, all in the name of the Lord Jesus Christ.

We also shared a common simplicity and honesty about the task before us. David was anointed king in a very humble service. The Hebrew here is very simple. If you read carefully you will see. It's sparse and bare. No inaugural fanfare with pomp and circumstance. Why? Because David was ready to get to work. He went to work with a great sense of enthusiasm as he shared the word of God and helped the poor. We are also anointed to share the gospel and help the poor with enthusiasm. I saw that in England, especially in the little Methodist church in Keswick in the lake district, Southey Street Methodist Church, named after the poet, Robert Southey. But, I also saw this enthusiasm for the gospel in other places.

One of the bishops told us about Ian Paisley, that great Presbyterian evangelist in Belfast who preached regularly to huge crowds. One night, as he was just getting started, he said, "Tonight there will be wailing and gnashing of teeth." A woman jumped up from the front row and yelled, "But I got no teeth!" and Paisley yelled back, "Teeth will be provided!" There is an enthusiasm for the gospel and a care for the poor.

At the conclusion of the service in Oxford, I was privileged to participate in a laying on of hands of elders being ordained. I noticed that one of them had read the scripture because that was the honor provided for those being ordained. He stammered a little as he read, but there was a huge glow on his face as he knelt before us and we laid our hands on his head and prayed for him. Afterward, I asked the pastor about him, "Oh yes, he came to us homeless, a street person, with nothing. We helped him get established, helped him get a job, and now he is an elder in our church, and he feels more pride for that than anything else in his life."

David understood that. He knew how to share the good news of God with great enthusiasm. Keats, in one of his letters uses a vivid expression to describe the literature of Shakespearean England. He speaks of the "indescribable gusto of the Elizabethan voice." Think of the indescribable gusto with which David took on his new responsibilities, just as the earliest apostles took on the work of sharing the gospel and helping the poor. Why? Because they knew God was with them. That's what David knew as he moved into the future God had planned for him. He knew God was with him; and so do we. We know God is with us to the end of the age. Amen.

Proper 10
Pentecost 8
Ordinary Time 15
2 Samuel 6:1-5, 12b-19

Dancing In Holy Places

Dancing in holy places — that's the theme of this text. I don't know about you, but sometimes in parish life you just don't feel much like dancing, especially when as a pastor you have to deal with several deaths in one week, and still have to get up and preach with a smile on your face. In a reversal of that British movie, *Four Weddings and a Funeral*, I remember one week when I was in the parish when we had "Four Funerals and a Wedding," and it was a bittersweet time for all of us.

With two expected deaths (seemingly expected, that is, because when is death ever really expected?) and two tragic deaths, one a car accident and the other a plane crash, the only dance some of us seemed to be doing that week was the dance of death. Maybe that's not all bad. Sometimes when parishioners come on Sunday mornings you can tell by the looks on their faces that the only dance they care anything about is the dance of death. So if they are going to dance at all they come to church dancing the blues because, as with Job, life has been hard. Sometimes life is like that. Sometimes it's just so hard. No matter how much we try to put the bright face on it, no matter how many wise theologians we listen to, no matter how many times we read Rabbi Kushner's fine book, *When Bad Things Happen to Good People*, the hurt just doesn't go away. Worst of all, the "Why?" question never gets answered, maybe because there isn't an answer to it this side of heaven.

So dancing in holy places has to start first of all with this sad and mournful dance of death like those long, slow marches to the cemetery in New Orleans with the band playing the blues and the dance steps measured and slow because everyone feels the pain — a dull, dark ache that just won't go away.

In a fascinating twist, some scholars see Michal at the window in this light. Oh, you can read your way through all the speculations about her and the reason she wasn't down there dancing with David. One is that the woman at the window is a literary motif in Hebrew literature and a sculptural motif in ivory plaques in several Middle Eastern countries. One is associated with the cult of the goddess Kililu — known as the queen of the windows because her name means "the one who leans out windows," or the Cypriote goddess called Aphrodite Parakyptousa, which in Greek means literally, "Aphrodite Peeping-Out-The-Window," which referred to love poetry where the bride stands waiting in her chamber for her lover's entrance, something that reminds us of a wedding.

Another meaning I'd never noticed before goes like this — Michal at the window represents the anxious or grieving bride or mother waiting often in vain for a young man who has disappeared or perished. Think about it. David is returning from an important expedition that involved at least two battles. He could have been killed. Michal is the woman at the window awaiting her husband's return after war.

I asked a young widow, whose husband was killed in a plane crash, how she first heard the news and she said that one of her husband's closest friends and colleagues drove up her driveway with a somber look on his face, the kind of look military officers and chaplains display when they approach certain marked houses knowing that the loved ones are peeking at them through the curtains as they bring the somber news of soldiers who have fallen in battle. As the body count increases daily in Iraq, I can't get this scene out of my mind. David's wife, Michal, is the woman at the window wondering if she is going to be doing the dance of death, waiting there at the window for a husband who might never come home like mothers and fathers waiting at the window for sons and daughters they will never see again.

The first dance is the dance of death. You'd think that would be the one David would be dancing. After all, David was still mourning the death of Saul and the death of Jonathan. Later, it would be the passing of his first child by Bathsheba, and later than that, and even more traumatic, it would be the death of his beloved Absalom. "O my son Absalom, my son, my son Absalom! Would I had died instead of you, O Absalom, my son, my son!" (2 Samuel 18:33). David knows how to dance the dance of death. The scripture says that he went up to the gateway and wept and wept. He covered his face and wept like families who have lost loved ones. The widow I talked to said she cried so much that her eyes had nearly swollen shut. The first dance is the dance of death, the one you'd think David would be dancing.

However, instead of the dance of death he was doing what might be called the "dangerous dance." The "dangerous dance" was the bold and political dance that testified to a new relationship with God and a new way of living, a way that would no longer kowtow to the old ways of doing things, a way that said, "The world is not about death and murder, but about new relationships where we love God and love neighbor as ourselves." Of course, in his time this was a radical message. It was a message that said death will not dictate or rule our lives or beat us down so far we'd never be able to get up again. It was a daring and bold move that David took that day, a dangerous dance to be sure.

David knew he needed something, some old symbol that everyone could rally around, something that no one would question, even the oldest and most traditional among them. Suddenly he remembered the Ark of the Covenant that had lain dormant for nearly twenty years. It had been shelved in Kiriath-jerim on a hill in the house of Abinadab. Because the Israelites feared it and looked upon it as a hazardous, unpredictable object representing the very presence of God, they were stunned to see David entering Jerusalem dancing around it with a dance of joy and celebration. It was a brilliant, strategic, and political move on David's part, a dangerous dance at best, to celebrate his victory over the Philistines and bring the Ark home to its rightful place all in one bold and stirring act like a huge Fourth of July fireworks celebration. It was like pulling the American flag out after its having been packed away for twenty years or more and waving it before the people.

Since the Ark stood for the old ideology of Israelite jihad or "holy war" and pointed to the dangerous and raw presence of God, thus embodying the unity of Israel's various clans and tribes, in this one bold and dangerous dance, David brought the old conservatives over to his side as he pointed to a new era for the people of God that meant a new way of living and relating to one's neighbor. He thus pulled an enormous coup by putting the old traditionalists into a tight spot. They had to make a choice. Because of his popularity and the fact that he had the Ark, they had to go along. They had nowhere else to go. So, instead of doing the dance of death, David is doing the dangerous dance with joy and celebration.

Why? This must have been what Michal was wondering. It must have been what the older brother was wondering when the prodigal came home and the father threw him a party, and all he could hear as he came in from the field was singing and dancing. "What is going on with David?" they must have been asking themselves. Has he completely lost it? Does he know something we don't know? Does the prodigal's father know something we don't know? Perhaps so — perhaps he sees deeper into the heart and purpose of God than anyone else could see.

I visited with a mother whose sixteen-year-old daughter, Meredith, had been killed in a car accident, the second child this mother had lost that way. And I visited with the widow whose husband went down in that plane. I was stunned to see the deep faith, hope, and love each woman had. In the presence of so much tragedy, tears, and pain, both, with scared and yet brave faces kept saying, "We want uplifting songs at the memorial service. We want emphasis on resurrection, hope, and joy. We want to celebrate their lives." Like David dancing that day, it made me want to ask, "Do they know something we don't?"

That must have been what David's wife, Michal, kept asking him as she watched him dancing with so much joy. It wasn't just that he didn't have much on, a symbol of the fact that he'd stripped away all the pretense of religion, all the trappings and protocol of proper worship and was focusing on his spontaneous devotion to the living God. "Does he know something I don't know?" It must have been what the older brother kept asking as he watched with shock and dismay all the partying and celebration. It must be what some people ask when African Americans and charismatics show so much joy and frivolity, dancing as David did long ago, not just the dance of death not the dangerous dance, which demonstrated a new theo-political reality. No, it was more like "destiny's dance," the "dance of the divine." What was this "divine destiny dance"? It means a singing and a dancing that testifies to God's presence with us no matter what happens to us or our loved ones. It means believing in God and praising God even in the midst of our sufferings, even in the darkest nights of our souls. It means dancing with an unfettered, unashamed extravagance.

The divine destiny dance means letting go and sharing our joy as we share our goods and ourselves with others even as David gave people bread and raisins and fruitcakes for their spiritual journey as a symbol of our giving with each other and especially with the poor. It means not just tapping our toes on the sideline but getting into the dance. It means knowing that there are times when we just need to let go and realize we won't have a heart attack if we show a little bit of enthusiasm, God forbid! Vic Pentz, pastor of Peachtree Presbyterian Church in Atlanta, in a sermon at the Presbyterian General Assembly, wondered what had happened to the full-hearted awe that Scottish Presbyterians brought to America. Pentz noted that Scottish Presbyterians who came to this country were rough-hewn rednecks, the inventors of the log cabin, people who said "critter" instead of creature and "widder" instead of widow, who were always "fixin' to do something" and whose "young'uns growed up." As people with strong passions for what they believed and quick tempers when someone challenged them, Pentz noted that they were easy to provoke into a fight, a part of our heritage we haven't lost. But, said Pentz, "the next time you tune into a country music station, that's Merle Haggard channeling your Presbyterian heritage." So the greatest legacy these old Scots left to us was their enthusiastic, awestruck worship of God, the sense that something is happening here that makes a difference to us and to our loved ones, especially those who have gone on to be with God.

Thus David's divine destiny dance, full of joy and hope, is our dance, too, one that we do no matter how hard life has been because our Lord Christ danced on Easter morn and we can, too. I don't know about you but that's the only thing that gets me through a week with lots of deaths in a church.

Don't you see? All of life is a dance and we spend our lives learning the steps. God spends all that time trying to get on our dance cards; trying to show us that no matter what happens to us we never have to dance alone and we really should "dance with the one who brung us." I think the sixteen-year-old girl named Meredith whom I buried years ago understood all that. At a wedding reception not long after her funeral, I felt a tap on my arm and looked down and saw one of the little girls in our church asking me to dance, and suddenly imagined sweet Meredith, dancer that she was, tapping Saint Peter on the arm and taking a turn on heaven's dance floor.

Dancing in holy places — that, my friends, is what life is all about. Amen.

Proper 11
Pentecost 9
Ordinary Time 16
2 Samuel 7:1-14a

Finding The Right House For God

Have you ever noticed how some families move a lot? Some are corporate moves, some are military, and some are United Methodist pastors. Whatever the case, every time they move they have to find new lodging. In the military, quarters are often provided. The same may be true for clergy if churches own a manse or a parsonage. But, sometimes you have to look for a new home, which means spending some time with real estate agents traveling here and there to find the perfect house. Of course, no house is ever perfect. When you own a home, no matter where you sit you see something that needs fixing. But when you're looking, you hope to find something that's just right with a minimum of fix-up. Every family searching for a new home has its own requirements — so many bedrooms, bathrooms, and a certain style garage. Finding the right house means there will be no rest for the weary. Some decide to give up looking and build the perfect dream house, and if that doesn't cause you to lose your religion, nothing else will!

One day, David got the bright idea that God needed a house, and David even volunteered to help. Never mind that God hadn't needed a house so far — that is, for eternity. God had gotten along just fine without one. But, when a king like David gets something in his head, there is no stopping him. Yet, unlike other leaders who simply announce something and expect it to be done with the snap of a finger, David decided it might be a good idea to consult his chief religious counselor, the prophet Nathan, who would later nail David with "Thou art the man!" But, for now Nathan has just come to listen to see what his king has on his mind.

The room gets very quiet and David makes his announcement, "Here I am living in the lap of luxury in this house of cedar and God is housed in nothing but curtains. It's just not right." The hidden and understood message was, "I want to build a house for the Lord." Who is Nathan to question something like that? After all, David gets it. He understands that God is more important that he is, right? David doesn't want his God to be slumming it down in the ghetto while he's living it up in the high-rent district. What a nice idea, Nathan must have thought. Now here's a king who has his priorities straight. What a great boss I have! Not some atheistic ingrate, you know the kind — a self-made man who worships his maker. No, David knows he's a servant of the Lord.

It's almost as if David and Nathan have peeked into the future and know that later the prophet Haggai will give the people a hard time for allowing God's house to fall apart while they were building mansions for themselves. "In the second year of the King Darius on the first day of the sixth month, the word of the Lord came through the prophet Haggai to Zerubbabel son of Shealtiel, governor of Judah, and to Joshua son of Jehozadak, the high priest: These are the words of the Lord of hosts: This nation says to itself that it is not yet time for the house of the Lord to be rebuilt. Then this word came through Haggai the prophet: Is it a time for you to live in your own well-roofed houses, while this house lies in ruins?" (Haggai 1:1-4). Haggai goes on to pronounce a curse on the people's land for not rebuilding God's house. That really got everyone's attention, especially good old Zarubbabel who put everybody to work renovating the house of the Lord.

So David's instinct is right. We shouldn't live uptown in nice digs while God is nearly homeless. It all makes sense. No wonder Nathan said, "Sounds like a great plan!" He said it in part because he knew that God had always been with David and "assumed" that meant that God was giving David all sorts of good ideas. Later in the story, when David comes on to Bathsheba, Nathan will realize that some of David's bright ideas came from his own sinfulness and had nothing to do with the Lord. But, that one was easy. It was outright murder and adultery. This one's harder to figure out. It has to do with the fact that all our decisions and choices in life are tainted in self-interest in some way or another, even our seemingly altruistic ones. Like why do some people help build Habitat for Humanity houses or serve stew in soup kitchens? Is it to be seen doing volunteer work in hopes of getting the volunteer of the year award in their hometowns? Or impressing future clients or business partners? There is no way we can ever know all the ulterior motives we have for doing good in our communities. That is the universal and radical nature of sin. It touches all of us and infects every part of our personalities. As Augustine once noted, "There is evil in every good person and good in every evil one."

So, how was Nathan to know that David had anything nefarious in mind? Of course, Nathan blurted his affirmative response out before consulting with God. Big mistake. What was he thinking? It's not the first time clergy-types have given elected officials bad advice, and I'm sure it won't be the last. David must have been excited to hear his chief counselor agree with him. As Nathan went off to pray just to make sure the Lord agreed with him, David went to bed thinking which architects and builders were going to get the contract. You've got to admit David seems to be trying to do the right thing. He wants to do something good for God.

Well, imagine Nathan's surprise when he knelt down to pray that night. "It's me again, Lord, Nathan, your humble servant checking in. The most amazing thing happened today. David, your beloved one, wants to build a house for you! How about that?" And Yahweh replies, "You think you're telling me something I don't already know? I know your every thought and his. And guess what? Both of you are wrong about this. I don't want a house. Don't need one. When are you guys going to learn that I'm in charge around here? If a house is going to be built for me, I'm the one who's going to suggest it, not you, and certainly not David. Who does he think he is anyway? You go back and tell him to put his building tools away and keep doing his job. I'll build a house when I'm good and ready, and he won't be the one who's helping build it anyway. You tell him that!"

Scripture doesn't tell us whether or not Nathan was quaking by the end of this prayer but I would have been. God really set him and David straight. I wonder why? I think there are several reasons. First of all, David and Nathan are both anthropomorphizing God in thinking that God needs a house like human beings. Stephen made it clear in his famous speech when he quotes the prophet saying, "Heaven is my throne and the earth is my footstool. What kind of house will you build for me, says the Lord, or what is the place of my rest? Did not my hand make all these things?" (Acts 7:49-50).

Second, anthropomorphizing God is a way of putting God in a box, which we're guilty of doing all the time. Let's reduce God to something we can know and control. J. B. Phillips is right — our God is too small. That's why God offers this gentle rebuke. David's plan for a house is seen as a threat to God's freedom in an effort to control God's presence.

Third, David's own self-interest pokes through in his desire to elevate his own status as a king by building a temple for God, something that will sanction his own reign as king. Tents represent a nomadic culture, the bottom rung of the social ladder. David wants to build something that will last as a way of saying that his kingdom will have more of a sense of permanence about it.

God sees right through David's ruse, and seems to be saying, "I don't need a temple now. I'm doing just fine without one. Temples are not for me; they're for human beings anyway. Besides, I'm more interested in obedience than sacrifice." What God is helping both Nathan and David understand is that the "place" of God is not as important as the "presence" of God. God's "presence" was with Saul for a time and then it left him and went with David. God's "presence" is the crucial thing.

Throughout the history of the Judeo-Christian tradition, we have seen two types of architecture that represent different theologies — holy place and holy people. One is seen in the temple with its special holy of holies where only the high priests can go. Holy place theology is also seen in Romanesque and Gothic architecture during the medieval period and the Counter-Reformation. By contrast, holy people theology is seen in the synagogue, the catacombs, the early house churches, the Puritan plain-style churches, and more theater-in-the-round churches in modern times. In holy people theology, there is no one sacred place, but a gathering of God's people where God's "presence" is felt in every heart. God's essence is celestial, not confined to this building or that in material existence.

God is not telling David that there will never be a "place" to worship. God is telling David that it's just not so important that he has to build it now. In fact, it will be David's son who will build it someday, Solomon. In many ways, God's house is wherever the people of God are. Families that move around a lot know that "home" is wherever they are, not the particular houses in which they have lived through the years. God's house is wherever the poor are being fed, the downtrodden are being lifted up, and wherever justice is being done.

There's more, and this is the surprising part of the story. God doesn't just turn down David's offer. God gives David an even greater one. "I will build a house for you." What's cool about this is that there is a play on words here. The Hebrew word for "house" — *beth* or *bayit* — has multiple meanings. It can mean a simple dwelling, a physical structure in which a family lives. It can mean a palace or a temple. But, it can also refer to a tribal group and even a dynasty. It's this latter meaning that God has in mind when God promises to build a house for David. I wonder if David actually got the amazing offer God was laying before him.

So often we go to God with an idea — something that will be good for the community and perhaps even for us. It's a prayer, a wish. And without any hesitation, God says, "No." At first we are disappointed thinking that God must not love us. Then, if we listen carefully we will see that God has something even greater in mind. As Luther once noted, "We pray for silver when all along God wants to give us gold." That's what happens for David. God says, "I will make you a great name among the great ones of the earth. I will assign a place for my people Israel; there I will plant them and they shall dwell in their own land ... I will give you peace from all your enemies. The Lord has told you that he would build up your royal house." There, that's it — the "royal house." This is the House of David that will be forever. Now, isn't that better than a little old temple, especially one that will get sacked during the Babylonian exile? David can't see that far ahead, but has enough sense that he's getting gold when all he asked for was silver.

There's one final point. God mentions how David's son will build the house for the Lord. I think there's something hidden here. God is not just referring to Solomon who will build the temple. God is foreshadowing David's greater son, the one we Christians call the Christ, the one who is of "the house and lineage of David." He will be the fulfillment of God's promise to David.

So, you see, finding and building the right house for the Lord is not as easy as we might have originally thought. Why? Because we aren't the ones doing the building. God is the chief builder all along. But who is really surprised to hear that? Amen.

Sermons On The First Readings

For Sundays After Pentecost (Middle Third)

Being Two People At Once

Donna E. Schaper

Proper 12
Pentecost 10
Ordinary Time 17
2 Samuel 11:1-15

Being Two People At Once

David gets in trouble the way many other men get in trouble. Some women do also but often in a less adulterous way. Women get "twitterpated" by beauty but often think of themselves as the one who should become beautiful. I think of the movie, *The Devil Wears Prada*, which is the story of fascination with fashion — the women are all hooked deeply on how they look, so deeply that they think a size six is too fat. David's issue is different but also connected: He takes the problem of his lust for Bathsheba into a conniving and deceitful way. He arranges to have the husband of his lover killed. Whether passive or active, taken upon the self or taken upon others, becoming lustful over the matter of beauty appears to be a universal matter.

What we know about David later as a man and as a king and as a leader is that he is a man of God. What we know about him from this one story is that he is a man of lust and violence. How can the same man be both men? Those of us who know ourselves know exactly how this can be. We understand. We also have a double nature. We may be very kind outside of our homes and very unkind inside. We may be lazy at work and full of energy at home. We may have a secret habit and hope that no one ever finds out. We may pose as a man of God but also have lust and also use violence. There are a great number of ways to be both good and bad at the same time — and most of us are both.

We are people whom God both loves and chastens. We are often harder on ourselves than God is on us. I remember receiving a long letter from a writer friend of mine. He wrote the letter beautifully and said that he was no longer able to write! Unlike David, it was not his sin that clouded his vision but his virtue. Bob died a while ago at a young age. He never understood the full extent of his gifts. He ended the letter about not being able to write anymore with these lines from T. S. Eliot. He wanted to write like Eliot! He, too, had become lustful toward beauty.

I said to my soul, be still and wait without hope ... for
hope.
... and wait without love ... for love
There is yet faith but the faith and the hope and the love
are all in the waiting....

Do not think for you are not ready for thought.
So the darkness shall be the light
And the stillness the dancing.[1]

Like David seeing Bathsheba from the roof, Bob saw Eliot's writing and wanted it to be his. Anything less was not good enough.

I am often surprised at how close our virtue and our sins are. The very thing that makes us good also makes us want to be better. The very appreciation of beauty that we do have makes us think our words are ugly or that we are not pretty enough. It is so hard to get things right! Once we are successful at just about anything, we are condemned to repeat our success. I know a young man who won the chess contest in his region: guess what? He lost nationally. It nearly killed him. He still played a beautiful game of chess — but no longer knew it.

Our relationship to beauty can be, like David's, fraught with difficulties brought on by the very beauty we love! Zen Buddhists have a theory about some of this paradox. They say that praise and criticism are both sides of the same coin. In other words, we let things outside of us, things other than the grace of the Tao or God, determine what is good for us. We become averse to criticism and addicted to praise. We *must* be beautiful. We *must* win the chess contest. We *must* write like T. S. Eliot. We *must* have Bathsheba.

In a world where even something as good as religion is comfort to some and poison to others, we do come, eventually, to understand our double nature. We understand the link between virtue and vanity, the link between lust and loveliness, the strange connection between praise and criticism. We join David in *having* to *have* what we want — rather than living by the grace of learning to want what we have. Violence is never far away.

How do we resolve this tremendous need we have for balance and self-control? By learning to want what we have, I think. Most of us want the Bathshebas or Eliots; we want what we don't have. To learn to want what we have is maturity. Maturity, however, can be very dull; when the excitement of lust is gone in a life, we are talking gray, not colorful.

Often what we need once we know how to want what we have is a method of constant reinvigoration. "Sometimes when you look up from your lot in life, you can tell it needs to be completely plowed up and replanted." Serial renovators of the world unite! Many of us are in need of constant plowing up and replanting.

We need focus if we are people spread too thin. And we may need to spread ourselves more thinly if we have become too much of a rut kind of person. Balance is the key — as well as constantly being willing to plow up and replant. That way we don't get stuck in wanting toxic things. Joseph Campbell said it well: We have to give up the life we know if we are to receive the life being offered. New life is always being offered to us — including how to live without Bathsheba or how to live as an ordinary chess player rather than a champion.

Consider the butterfly. These insects know a lot about becoming new and remaining colorful without descending into lust and violence.

In *An Obsession With Butterflies: Our Long Love Affair With A Singular Insect*, Sharman Apt Russell, says this about butterflies: "A bag of goo crawls on a leaf, obsessed with eating. It hangs upside down. It becomes something else. A butterfly is born, a bit of blue heaven, a jazzy design. It is a gesture of beauty almost too casual."

Becoming new is a gesture of beauty almost too casual. It is a set of incremental steps in learning to want what we have rather than becoming the prisoner of our own desires. Do we really need a full sabbatical to do it? Do we really need a long vacation to become new or can we put in place very quiet simple rituals that allow us to be who we are slowly? This casual way is about style but not just style. It is not about how old we are or how young we are. We are the right age for renewal, no matter our age.

Can you imagine who David might have been had he not *had* to have Bathsheba? Might he have slowly become a man of great cool and collectedness? Might he not have become a better king, one acquainted with lust and desire and even violence but who knew how to forswear it? God was offering David another chance even as he made the choice to take Uriah out. David missed it. The good news is that he didn't miss all his chances. He managed to serve God and find his way to casual consistent beauty. He was forgiven a terrible crime, a hideous lust. He was forgiven the way he loved beauty too much. First he had to pay the price in the death of the son he bore by Bathsheba whom he took as his wife, after murdering Uriah. But one day at a time, one story at a time.

We can receive the same power, the same forgiveness, and the same casual beauty. What is our best hope? To learn to want what we do have and stop staring at other people's roofs! The grass will always be greener on the other side of the yard. That we know. Someone will always have a more beautiful wife than we do or write better or play chess better. Those are the facts of life. Learning to love a wife because we love her, to play chess because we enjoy the game, to write the way we write (not the way Eliot writes) is a way to tame both lust and life. The very taming will release power to us. If we are not able to tame our lusts, we will be forgiven. God is much too large and God's love is much too large. However, as Saint Paul would quickly say, "Should we continue to sin in order that grace may abound?" (Romans 6:1). No — we are to tame our lusts, to love beauty in a way that makes us more collected and beautiful. We are to tame our lusts and turn the taming into beauty. Amen.

---

1. T. S. Eliot, *Four Quartets* (San Diego, California: Harvest Books, 1968), p. 16.

Proper 13
Pentecost 11
Ordinary Time 18
2 Samuel 11:26—12:13a

Small Sin, Large Grace

This pericope is in two parts. First there is the testimony of Nathan against David. A little trap is laid about another man who has stolen a lamb. David answers without self-consciousness. Nathan has to tell David, "You are the man who has stolen the sheep." "You are the one who should be punished." We are reminded of that wonderful part of the Lord's Prayer, "Forgive us our sins — debts — trespasses — as we forgive those who sin against us." David indeed has stolen the wife of Uriah from him. David has not tamed his lust toward Bathsheba.

The second part is the divine judgment against David. He does take Bathsheba as his stolen wife. She does bear a son. The son dies. First, David receives the judgment of his dear friend Nathan. Then he receives the judgment of his God. In that judgment he loses the coveted son of the beautiful woman for whom he has been willing to commit murder. While I find it impossible to imagine that every child that dies early is a kind of punishment from a cruel God, this particular punishment seems quite well connected. It does seem that it would be way too cruel to Uriah if his wife were to bear David a son.

Is there any hope for David? After his sin and his retribution? Of course — we will see the hope and see how it unfolds as these stories continue. But for now, we must stay close to the punishment. There is no way around it but through it. We may try to go for the "big" picture and think of this act of murder and adultery as too small for God's attention. We will be wrong. But that won't prevent us from trying.

Sometimes when I rise to preach, I think I will rise to say one word — galaxy. Then I will sit down. I might add another — cosmos. Then I will sit down again. My awe — as in awesome — in the size and grandeur of the world in which my small soul seems to be awake is so large that I can't imagine trying to convince you that *anyone* is really important. David was, after all, a little man in a big world. Why would a universe this large and fertile and big bang ongoing *need* protoplasmic or genetic repetition? Why would it care about what we do to each other? We live. We die. The universe continues. David just can't be *that* big a deal.

The very problem that causes me to want takes a premature seat — that the world in which we are awake is awesome and awe filled — keeps me standing. Why would a world this grand *not* create a myth of resurrection and ongoing life? Why would a world this grand not really care about a man as small as David, a life as little as Uriah's, a beauty as inconsequential as Bathsheba's? Is such a myth more amazing than an orchid or a bumblebee? Is it more amazing than a Long Island woman with three facelifts and a whole lot of *bling bling*? Is it more amazing than a man who loved the heck out of crystal meth but manages to get unaddicted to it? Why would a world so fab not also create doubly fab myths about itself? Why would a world so large not enlarge human being and doing as well? Why would a cosmic world not worry about a small man? The greatness is large enough to include both — a transcendent and an immanent God, a God far away and a God close by, a God who cares about what David did to Uriah and a God who cares about far-off stars.

By myth of resurrection and caring about both large and small life, I do not mean untruth. I mean something so true that it keeps repeating itself. Myth, to me, is fact plus. It is fact plus interpretation. Facts are myth "lite." Myth is not something untrue so much as it is something truer than true — it is the density or DNA of the fact. Myth is something so true that it keeps repeating itself, as do the resurrection stories. Christians are not the only ones to come up with cockamamie ideas about human significance and rebirth, as you know. So let's admit that the preacher could be seated after breathy repetitions of the words "cosmos" or "galaxy," but that instead she will remain risen, as an act of praise to the human spirit.

You see, David comes back from this horror. He manages a new and useful life after his double insult and injury. He manages to have new life. He is a living example of resurrection before Jesus ever went to the cross.

I went to St. Mark in the Bowery's Good Friday Blues Service. A man sang with a voice as robust as Paul Robeson's, "Jesus just left Chicago for New Orleans," and it brought me straight to tears. Why? I have no real idea. I just know that songs don't die and New Orleans doesn't die and Chicago doesn't die and that the blues aren't dead yet. If the blues aren't dead, I can stay standing here telling you about the blues not being dead yet. I can also claim some hope for the likes of David and the likes of you and me. That is important news.

Even more important is the news about David. He gets a second chance. He rises from the grave of his lust. We, too, can have a second chance, no matter where our lust or foolishness has left us.

Last year, after I left the Miami church I loved, I entered a period of what I can only call "a fertile void." Thank God a friend of mine gave me that expression. Maybe it will help you, too. I said to her jokingly that I was suffering from status anxiety and applause deprivation. I was suffering from a sense that maybe I was professionally dead. She said the Buddhists have a phrase for our transitional periods — the fertile void. It is when we empty to fill. It is when we pour and spill and let go in order to create an openness to something new. I was hit one day that the fertile void is what the tomb is. It was empty. My own personal Easter observance could stop and start right there. I don't need Jesus walking next to me telling me I am going to live forever. I do need to believe that good can come from bad and full can follow empty. I do need the testimony that the "heavens opened" (*schizo* in the Greek) and that the curtain of the temple ripped (*schizo* again). These rents of the veil strike me as the way in which we rise. We have veils covering, protecting, distorting. When we rise from whatever death we have, we pull aside the veil. We open the tomb. David had to dive into a tomb, a tomb of judgment from Nathan and a loss of an infant son. He died, and then he rose.

Muslim women "slip scarf" when they want to both hide and reveal. When the tomb opens, we hide and reveal simultaneously important things to ourselves. David will have to forget and remember what he did to Uriah. He will never be the same.

I believe that sin like David's is very real. He was a man of great sorrow, great lust — and great triumph. All of this, way before Jesus, mimics the life of Jesus. No, Jesus did not commit adultery or murder. But yes, Jesus was a man acquainted with sorrow. I used to add to the Eucharistic prayer a sentence, "Thou whom even nuclear holocaust cannot destroy." I believe that the cosmos will withstand both large and small human sin.

The stone on our own tomb is rolled away. We think the curtain between earth and heaven is permanent. It is not. We live as though the stones were real and they are not. I'll never forget my bike rides at an old zoo in Miami. They had taken all the bars off the cages. I laughed every time I saw those empty tombs. I was sure many animals would stay in those cages as though they couldn't get out! David had to go through more hell before he got to more heaven. Surely, Bathsheba was not happy once she had lost a child. Surely, she, too, was a part of the sin — although it is hard to know what her choices really were. Could she have said, "No," to David? Probably not. Could she be a true lover to David afterward? Could she be a true wife? The sin, once committed, reached its long tentacles into the future.

So did the hope. There is hope for the renewal of broken relationships, just as there is hope for the renewal of David and Nathan's relationship, David and God's relationship, and even David and Bathsheba's relationship. The hard line is drawn for Uriah. Sin is not cosmic or too big to notice; sin is real. Real people lose real lives when we commit violence of any kind.

Nevertheless, and even so, God has a cosmic grandness, which allows resurrection to be as real as the myths that drive our lives. Even before Jesus' time on the cross, the universe was marked by a cosmic resurrection. David went on to enjoy it. That is good news for David and for us. Amen.

Proper 14
Pentecost 12
Ordinary Time 19
2 Samuel 18:5-9, 15, 31-33

When Necks Break

What is the point of war? Even wars of old? The horrible story of Absalom's neck breaking as he rides his horse as part of an ancient army is very hard to take — and still many of us teach it in Sunday school! One picture that I remember from my own heavily Sunday-schooled youth is of Absalom, beautiful, long, black hair, riding along on a white horse, with a branch straight at his throat. Chapter 18 of the second book of Samuel tells quite a story of violence and death. We get nothing but a slight favoritistic demur from David: Please protect Absalom if you can. Please take care of my son — as he sends three units out to war. The three units also have great casualties — but Absalom is gone. "Oh, Absalom, Absalom, Absalom...." But David's cry might have been for every woman's son, every man's daughter sacrificed to war.

How are we to resolve human conflicts if we do not go to war? How are we to be people who understand the casualties of war, with David's agony in tow? Can we do something about conflict before our sons have their heads chopped off? I think we can.

Conflict is omnipresent, at family dinner tables, family reunions, the United Nations, and in most countries. No activist or virtuous person will be far from conflict for long. In our urge to make a difference in the world, we will run smack dab into human pessimism, cynicism, and grief over failed attempts at goodness. The majority of people will not want a good person to succeed at anything. They won't know why; they will simply know how important it is for them to sneer at decent objectives.

Conflict is normal, inevitable, ordinary, and expected. The cultural messages are omnipresent: You can choose your pleasure or the world's service, your time or time dedicated to others. "You have to take care of number one." "Life is relationships and taking care of others." There are different versions of these two diametrically opposed cultural instructions (presumably) and many people just fall off the high wire, drop to the ground, and sit there in a muddle. Those who want to walk the wire and not fall will have to realize early and often that conflict will be present in every single setting. For breakfast should they go to the park and sit alone with a high-priced coffee? Or should they sit with the child or husband who has become dull or demanding? Or should they attend a breakfast meeting, the real bane of existence for most activists and high-flying professionals? Why would *anyone* attend a breakfast meeting, knowing that the quiet moment in the park is the alternative? Conflicts like how to have breakfast are normal. They will join conflicts about gym or more email, a walk after dinner or returning a few phone calls, lunch at the river or reading a professional article at our desk, styrofoam take-out not far away. We live our lives in ordinary conflict — ordinary conflicts, unresolved, lead to the horror of war.

Those who want to avoid the fate of Absalom will befriend conflict. We will make it our own. We will become experts at it. We will enjoy it. We will predict it, anticipate it, tame it, laugh at it, and revel in it. Of course, we will say, there are always two plus choices for every moment. I am a choice maker. I make choices. I am aware of the scripted life of the double bind and I unbind myself from it. I choose X sometimes and Y other times and I suffer the loss of the one I don't choose. I am not afraid to suffer. I sometimes choose X and Y at the same time. But I only choose a small pile of X twigs and a small pile of Y twigs. I go slowly. I am rarely the captive of what I don't have and more the captive of what I do have.

I sometimes call this conflict-loving, choice-making capacity that of the tough dove. There is nothing soft about making choices all the time. There is actually something very hard about it. We turn down people who want us. We say real "Nos." We get negative feedback. The people to whom we say no will not like it. The people to whom we say yes will rarely reward us, either. Tough doves live beyond both praise and criticism in an inner world they have created for themselves. They are highly strategic, highly directed, and highly focused at any given moment. Tough doves make tough choices. Do the tough choices that tough doves make avoid war over time? Are they any help to American Absalom or Iraqi or Korean Absaloms? I think yes. They are of help in that they practice the peacemaking muscles. Once we have confidence in our capacity with small conflicts, we are able to consider more. We are able to imagine a world of peace.

Simultaneously, tough doves get buried under and snowed over. Tough doves often fail. They also lose their way in the snow and fog of human interaction. They can feel like they are constantly digging out from a snowstorm. The desk that looked clear on Monday can be buried by Wednesday. I often feel that my life is a constant climbing out of a desk stress hole. The people to whom I should write, the people whom I should thank, join the people at whom I should yell, and the ever-present letters I should, as a Democratic citizen, be sending to my representatives — all combine to turn me into something as small and inconsequential as a dove. We go from tough to dove and back in minutes. We fail at making peace as well as succeed at making peace.

This personal embrace of the inevitability of (actually non-paradoxical) conflict leads to social behaviors that are different from the norm. We are not allergic to conflicts in meetings or families or social interactions. We know that conflict arrives to make something happen. We know that when conflict comes something is about to be birthed. Tensions are being resolved, opposites are attracting, and energy is being created. The points on the battery are inserted in life correctly and we have energy. There is no energy when positive and negative are placed incorrectly in the flashlight. Get the nodes right and stuff happens. We may have to train our stomachs and our vocabularies to be the tough dove that we are in meetings and fights. Training is good. It begins, for me, in humming an old hymn, "Drop thy still dews of quietness, 'til all our conflicts cease...." I call it my Bob Newhart tactic. Newhart is one of my favorite comics and the reason is his timing. It is absolutely brilliant, also a beat behind the trouble. Newhart waits. He listens. He uses his eyes and face to help others see what is happening so he doesn't have to tell them.

When it comes to conflict, we can have tragic results or comic results. By my hymn (spiritual training) and my waiting, I am able to at least hope for comic endings to conflicts. Tough doves work for the comedy, the happy ending. Tough people work to win; winning ends in tragedy. Peacemakers keep our sons from having their heads chopped off by trees.

Once we understand that conflict is inevitable, and it is, we find ourselves in need of concrete strategies to resolve it. How we use our tongues, how we use our mouths, and how we use our speech is the best strategic first step. It is not an accident that parents intervene in children's squabbles to say, "Use your words, not your fists." Neither is it an accident that parents find themselves saying, "Watch your mouth."

Using our words well can contribute to peace in the kitchen and peace in the world. Living well involves finding our tongue's way to praise. We appreciate in a world of severe appreciation deficit. Simply: find something to appreciate even in a situation or person you adamantly dislike. Let what you say take the form of praise and appreciation. We truly can shape our tongues so that they speak the truth in love. Small actions like this result in large matters like peace. Small actions keep our sons and daughters alive. It was too late for David to save his son once the war had started. The point is to stop the wars in the first place. The picture I would really like to see in Sunday schools is a picture of Absalom riding free out of the war on his horse, having accumulated a large amount of small actions, which can be taught to all children about how to make peace. Amen.

Proper 15
Pentecost 13
Ordinary Time 20
1 Kings 2:10-12; 3:3-14

Wise Leadership

Solomon asks for the right thing: He asks for wisdom. He asks for it from a very humble place, the place of knowing that he is but a child and still he has been put in charge of large things. Leadership is a treacherous thing. How can we possibly know so when we are but children? That is what Solomon knew. He knew, even as a child, just how much help he was going to need to be a leader. He already had some of the wisdom he seeks. Ironically, he was wise beyond his years. God rewards him with wisdom for already being wise.

Sometimes we get involved with very circular matters. We need wisdom to know we need wisdom! We need love to be able to love. We need to be appreciated in order to be able to appreciate. Jesus makes it clear in gospel after gospel that we are able to have what we can give away. The irony and the circularity of life is some of the wisdom we need.

One of the large issues that leaders face is being criticized and being unappreciated. I just heard a presidential candidate conclude a speech with that wisdom: "I will now take your questions and comments and any insults you have to throw at me." He was a wise leader. He knew what to expect. Many pastors simply wither on the vine; they just can't take the constant criticism. One pastor I know put out a letter to her whole congregation. In it she said, "If you must criticize my sermon, at least wait until Monday to call me. I am tired of having my Sunday afternoons ruined."

Now here follows immediately *another* irony. If we are wise enough to put out a letter asking for delayed criticism, or wise enough to know that in the Q and A, we may get insulted, still and nevertheless, we have to appreciate the very people who criticize us. We need to appreciate them without manipulating them. We need to give what we may or may not get. Nor may we boast about what we are doing. We can't even be too preachy about it. While we work to reverse the appreciation deficit disorder, we can't boast about what and how we are doing it. That is both manipulative and a sneaky way to pat ourselves on the back. Leadership, such as that to which Solomon was called, keeps the boasts transcendent and the details immanent. We may boast about God, the cosmos, and the largeness in which we all reside. We may ask God for wisdom but not boast about it when God gives it to us.

What changes the world back to its creation is a combination of boasting in the greatness of God and hauling the world back to its root. The wisdom of a leader is to stay in the positive, even when the negatives are hurled at us. Instead of constantly whining about how bad things are, we talk about how good things are in our godly gifted way. Instead of declaring environmental doom, we speak of environmental enchantment. We mean the words, "How great thou art."

We also know the second verse, "How small we are." Our souls connect the two in speech and in action. We make our mantra that, as the world social forum tells us, "Another world is possible."

We pray for the wisdom to boast in God's great possibility. And then we go to work as skillfully as we can. As leaders we expect conflict and we expect to be able to handle it.

The capacity to be an intercessor, like Solomon was to God, is a strong approach in conflict. One night, our dinner guests' children were swimming in our pool. The neighbor children threw rocks at them. They were jealous at hospitality to others and not to them. Our guests were frightened and huddled with their children inside. One of us went out and talked to the neighbor children. Did they want to come in for a swim? Did they want to apologize to the children they had "bombed" before doing so? The answer to both questions was, "Yes."

Our guests had a great time talking about their own parents as the evening progressed. One said, "My parents would have beaten the tar out of me if I had thrown rocks." Another said, "My parents would have never let me play with children who were my enemies." Wise leaders intervene with strength in situations of conflict. They are wise and hopeful in their interventions. Wise leaders know that fight and flight are the normative responses — and then intercede in a different way.

Whether it is genetic engineering, abortion, pulling the plug, making peace, raising the minimum wage, keeping children from blowing up their schools, or something simpler like organizing a family reunion, we humans find a lot of difficulty strewn on our soiled red carpet. We get weak. Our middle name is "thwarted." The good that we would do, we can't. The evil that we would not do, we do. We want to be tough doves — serious proponents of peace — but often we look like dead birds, legs akimbo on the soiled red carpet of our lives. Leaders have to be more than wise! They also need luck to manage the human condition.

Leadership may not always be up front or totally visible. Lyndon Johnson said to Martin Luther King Jr.: "Martin, you go on out there now and make it possible for me to do the right thing." Many of us are more blockers than quarterbacks in the great war for peace and justice. We help others do things. Football fans know that no offense manages without good blockers. We can be a part of things too wonderful to know by understanding that even in dumb meetings and sideline conversations, we can be blockers. So if you think you are a leader, still ask God for wisdom! There is plenty for you to do even if you are not Solomon.

I think of fights of an intimate nature. Families need wise leadership, too. Often we just shift the burden back and forth. Your fault, his fault, and not my fault is the language of love at war. Leaders are prepared to assume the burden and the responsibility (not fault but responsibility) for what they may have done "wrong." We don't avoid burdens, we assume them.

In public and in private we know the difference between fault and responsibility, the difference between being a child and being wise. Wise people know that even huge things, like racism, are not our fault, but they are our responsibility. We bear the burden. We pay from our extravagant budget line called love. We go further than we can. We have a need to use what little wisdom we have every day.

We can speak up when hate enters the conversation. We can refuse to nominate known neurotics to positions of power in our churches. We can question authorities at school, home, bank, and stadium. When small people refuse to give a pass to trouble, leaders get the wisdom they need. When you feel like speaking up, speak up. Open your mouth. If you didn't speak out of fear, write a letter and say what you should have said when you didn't say it. Repent silence.

Jesus never missed a chance to show and say love. Good leaders also opportunize each moment, the way Solomon did when he went straight to God, while still a child, and asked for wisdom. Amen.

Proper 16
Pentecost 14
Ordinary Time 21
1 Kings 8:(1, 6, 10-11) 22-30, 41-43

Dedicating Temples

So much is happening in chapter 8 of 1 Kings that we almost want to get dressed up for an amazing celebration! The Ark of the Covenant is moved into the new temple, the temple is dedicated, a cloud of glory arrives, people have a mystical experience, and Solomon explicitly takes on the mantle of his father David. Then he begins to "preach" a kind of wisdom that is just amazing. While I am tempted to stay with the spectacle of the service of dedication, the sights and sounds and smells, I am compelled to go to the part of the sermon that Solomon gives and to bring it into a modern context.

This is a dress up day. It is a big day. The temple (that will one day be destroyed) is just now being dedicated. It is a moment of consolidation for the Jewish people, consolidation of leadership, of architecture and of nationhood. It is a good time, like the 800 years in France that achieved the great French cathedral at Chartres or the period after the American Revolution when America was war free for a time. Things were able to come together. People had time to think. Solomon's attention turned from wisdom to the generation of principles by which to guide people. His first principle was that of fatherhood: he wanted to make his father proud. He wanted to fulfill his father's promises to their now common people. Solomon was showing what many leaders do when they move in next to the town statue. They position themselves as the one whom tradition favors. Think of the musical *The Music Man*. New guy comes to town and sings his first song in literally the same posture as the statue at the center of the town common. Many leaders know the folk wisdom, "You can do anything for which you can declare a precedent." Say that "we have always done it this way" and in most organizations you are home free. Solomon dedicates the temple, has a mystical experience while doing so — even nature cooperates — and then goes on to deliver a very consolidated sermon. That is what compels me to this text.

He says many good things but then he says one surprising thing, "Likewise when a foreigner, who is not of your people Israel comes from a distant land because of your name — for they shall hear of your great name, your mighty hand, and your outstretched arm — when a foreigner comes and prays towards this house, then hear in heaven your dwelling place, and do according to all that the foreigner calls to you, so that all the peoples of the earth may know your name and fear you, as do your people Israel, and so that they may know that your name has been invoked on this house that I have built" (vv. 43-44).

Solomon is taking the very consolidation of his leadership and his temple and his moment and spreading the goodness around. He could go "tribal" here. He could go local. He could refuse to stretch his people and tell them they are great just the way they are. That is not what good leaders do. Good leaders push their people. Good leaders expect a lot from their people. Good leaders see that to make a great country you must give it away to the "aliens," the newcomers, and the foreigners. Good leaders see that the foreigners have something to offer.

Surely those who are working on the magnificent movements of immigrants to our country listen in on this passage. Surely the two-year-old girl who died crossing the desert, buried with a rosary around her neck, in Tucson, Arizona, would have welcomed Solomon as her leader. Surely the families of people who are deported because they have broken the American law and are here in our great country "illegally" would have welcomed Solomon as a leader.

Strangely, and especially strange to the stranger and the newcomer, periods of consolidation of nation and tribe result in openness to the new, the different, and the strange. These are periods when the locals feel afraid. These are periods when aliens are in danger. I think of the great line by *New York Times* columnist, Thomas Friedman, that "the price of oil and the pace of freedom seem to go in opposite directions." We need safety in order to have adventures. We need safety in order to be open to the stranger. Solomon was giving people that safety — he was spending down his legacy, spending down the money in his bank. He was taking a risk precisely because he was so secure.

We might actually argue that the great social gains of the '60s were the direct result of the security of the '50s. Women's lives completely changed. Now they haven't fully changed but they surely did change. The post-war security allowed America to consolidate its energy and spend its budget.

How many women have been president of the United States? How many women pitch for the New York Yankees? Check out, sometime, how many op-eds are written by men and how many by women. In the *Times* the number is about 80/20 in any given month. For years, I kept a tab on my refrigerator of how many women were on the front page of the *New York Times*. It wasn't pretty compared to the number of men. But so much change has happened!

Once I broke down in tears while driving on Route 91 into Hartford. Why? There were two women on the side of a large building in basketball uniforms. The UConn women's team had won big and the Hartford skyscraper had decided to write them forty floors high. Why was I crying? I played basketball in high school and college for a team that had to push its bus up a South Carolina hill while being passed by the working bus the men had. They laughed as they passed by. We were often late for games. We wore the same uniforms years in a row. The men did not.

I am simultaneously amazed at how far women have come in terms of social equality and how far we have to go. We need a period of consolidation and security before we are going to be able to go any further. Women shall be aliens until that great leader and great time.

Carol Gilligan, a remarkable scholar of girls, tells us that her research shows that things are actually not better, internally, for women. She sums up her research as follows: An eleven-year-old girl goes to a pizza shop and orders pepperoni. A twelve-year-old girl with the same group of friends, in the same pizza shop, orders, "I don't know." She can't decide what she wants. Even if she knows what she wants, she is not sure she wants the boys to know that she knows. A fourteen-year-old girl with the same friends, in the same pizza shop, may say, "I'll have whatever you have." This summary of the experience of girls is Mary Magdalene's story, a story that is remarkably important in an age of stasis regarding the social equality of women and girls. We go from a strong woman bearing religious truth to weak women afraid to speak. The fact that Magdalene got written out of the big book is very important. Girls don't know how to order pizza because Magdalene was written out.

Why does the situation of aliens matter? Because Solomon was right as a leader; he saw that to have good power you had to spend it on behalf of the outsider. We consolidate precisely in order to grow. We secure precisely in order to be free. Solomon's sermon had one line that made all the difference: "because of your name" the aliens come. It is the very success of a great country that pushes it to be greater and even freer. It is not a bad America that struggles in an ongoing way with the rights of immigrants or women! It is a great nation leaning and urging itself to be greater.

Solomon showed us the way: In the name of our fathers and our past, in the name of the very temple we have dedicated, new and better things are on their way. Amen.

Proper 17
Pentecost 15
Ordinary Time 22
Song Of Solomon 2:8-13

Joy Is For Leaping

This ode to spring and to love is almost always used at Passover. It is part of the most ancient of Passover liturgy. The language dances, like the lover, over the mountains. Imagine a human leaping upon mountains. Imagine a human like a gazelle or a young stag. I saw two men just yesterday on Broadway. I was about to pass out from the heat — they were racing each other to the hot dog stand. I couldn't decide if I was happy or not and finally decided to choose happiness. What joy to see young men leaping in 100-degree heat, like gazelles. Broadway can be as formidable as any mountain. There was joy in their dance down the street.

The next part of the passage, after the gazelles leap, is that the gazelles stop at the window and stare in through the lattice. The image is so descriptive and so full of longing. After we dance, often we want to sit quietly and not dance. We want to *gaze*. From gazelle to gaze — we know the passage. Then after the dancing and the gazing, the loved one beckons to us to arise and come away. Such great preparation! I think the next time my husband asks me out to dinner, I am going to recommend first a leap down Broadway or over a mountain, then a gaze at each other through a window, then the date. "Arise and come away": these are beautiful words, whether between lovers or in courtship, or even in a more subdued and less lively context.

When vacation time comes, as it does, we are beckoned to arise and come away. The vacating part of vacation is different than going out to dinner. Dinner dates are filling, both spiritually and actually; vacations are emptying. We are beckoned by those who love us and by common justice to arise annually and go away. Why does this Solomon script invitation come? It comes not as an August vacation at all but instead as the winter passes and the spring comes. What an evocation of spring we have here: The winter is past, the rain is over and done, and the flowers come. Human singing joins nature. The time of singing has come and in the background, singing with us, we hear the voice of turtledoves. Smack dab in the middle of this springtime symphony, the fruit comes to the fig tree. As the melody of spring increases, we are to "arise and come away."

Why is vacation so important to people? Or is it just an idea whose time no longer comes? Why is spring so important to people? Do we still know just how deep the cycle of nature is? Or have we forgotten to note the ripeness of figs, given the packages we can get any time of year in just about any store?

Are the cycles of spring and vacation still important to people? Or have we grown beyond the sensuality of these cycles? A conversation helped me understand that we are most definitely *not* beyond these cycles. We were with a group of people making the old joke about faculty meetings. "The fights are so hard because the stakes are so small." Surely you have heard this joke. My academic husband differed: He said the stakes about the truth are large. What gets taught is huge. What makes it into the canon and curriculum is what forms and shapes truth. I found myself agreeing with him. The deeper and longer the cycle, the longer the ideas held within, the more important it is. We dare not be fooled by packages of figs in the store.

Natural cycles matter no matter how postmodern or industrial we have become. Liturgy joins cycles to show us how important trampling out the vintage where the grapes of wrath are stored, in Julia Ward Howe's famous words in her hymn, "Battle Hymn Of The Republic." Our language and hymnody is filled with natural images. We lose them and we lose the meaning of much of our tradition.

Many think Christianity is the least sensual of religions. Nothing could be further from the truth and you have only to read the book of Solomon to know just how sensual it is. We are not, however, the only sensual religion. Consider the description of Hinduism in the *Life Of Pi.*

> *I am a Hindu because of sculptured cones of red kumkum powder and baskets of yellow turmeric nuggets, because of garlands of flowers and pieces of broken coconut, because of the clanging of bells to announce one's arrival to God, because of the whine of the reedy nadaswaram and the beating of drums, because of the patter of bare feet against stone floors down dark corridors pierced by shafts of sun light, because of the fragrance of incense, because of flames of arati lamps circling in the darkness, because of bhajans being sweetly sung, because of elephants standing around to bless, because of colorful murals telling colorful stories, because of foreheads carrying, variously signified, the same word — faith.*[1]

I once made a Christmas garden, which also became an Easter garden, too. We had 55 poinsettias left over from the Christmas service. No one wanted to take them home as they had dried out and were drooping. In southern Florida, we have almost no dirt, only sand and coral rock. I was always composting and buying dirt and fertilizer just to grow a few gnarled tomatoes. I took the entire group of poinsettias home, turned them on their bottoms and watched my new garden appear every day. I added the Easter lilies, too. I upended them, too — and sure enough the next spring, they shot little shoots up out of the ground. "Arise," they said to me, "arise." I loved my Easter/Christmas anti-waste garden. And I took all the pots back to the garden store. They were very happy to have them rather than to see them end up in the trash. These plants had a good life while blooming; they may as well have a good life as dirt. Most of us hope for the same for our bodies. When they say ashes to ashes and dust to dust over us, we hope our bottoms will turn up good soil. When I think of resurrection, I will be able to think of this soil I built, gleaned from the old flowers. When I think of resurrection, I think of springtime and I hear the voice of God saying to me, "Arise, my loved one, and come away, the voice of the turtledove is heard in the land."

Let me tell you something about the Spanish colonialists, which you may not know. They tried to stop the cycle of spring. They destroyed the seed corn when they came in. They didn't just plop churches on top of everything. They institutionalized waste. That's what we do when we ignore the power of the seasonal cycles. We institutionalize waste. Fortunately, the same people who put cayenne on grapefruit on corners in Mexico today also hid the seed from the Spaniards. They knew how not to waste, how to stay in relationship. They knew how to be sensual about food and spring, flowers and figs.

Some people find the Song of Solomon a little much, a little too sexy as a book of scripture. I think just the opposite. I remember when a church I served was having a big fight about homosexuality. The entire congregation had come out to vote one way or the other. People were being brought in from nursing homes in vans. The entire confirmation class showed up on a Tuesday night. I was amazed and I said so to one of the children I knew well. "So why is everybody here tonight for this discussion?" She responded without blinking, "Because you are finally talking about something important." What an amazing statement. A fifteen-year-old girl showed up at church because we were finally talking about something that interested her. I wish I had shown her Solomon before. I wish I had shown her how deeply human sexuality fits into the cycles, the seasons, the great and awesome reproductivity of earth and spring, of fig tree and gazelles, of dinner dates and gazing at each other through lattice.

The church is always talking about something important: life and death, birth and fecundity. We have a lot to say about the subject. Most of it is terribly important. No wonder there are so many good fights about it.

Spring is important. How we think about is important. Spring is connected to important matters like sensuality, seed corn, sexuality, and vacation. Solomon knew it all early. Amen.

---

1. Yann Martel, *Life Of Pi* (Orlando, Florida: Harvest Books, 2003), p. 47.

Proper 18
Pentecost 16
Ordinary Time 23
Proverbs 22:1-2, 8-9, 22-23

The Place Beyond Punishment

You can tell a lot about a family by finding out what happens if a child spills something. In some families, spilling your milk is a capital offense. A child can get in a lot of trouble if the milk is spilled. In other kinds of families, spilling your milk is understood as an accident, a thing that happened, and a form of chance or luck. In these families, there is no additional pain or punishment on top of the original pain of spilling.

If you are in a poor family, you may not get anymore milk. There may not be any. If you are in a more secure family, and you are not being punished for your spill, you will get more milk, the mess will be cleaned up, and life will go on.

So what is the difference? One family has one point of view on pain, the pain of the spill; the other family has another point of view. One knows only punishment, the other knows the place beyond punishment, where ruined things are prepared. The milk doesn't "unspill." The floor doesn't automatically get cleaned up. But unlike the milk, we are not ruined.

Today, I want to talk about the issue of pain and punishment. You and I know that there are at least three perspectives on the passion story, the one that spills the wine of Jesus for some reason or another. One is the atonement, now widely theogically discredited, which comes from the family that punishes the spill. God wanted Jesus to suffer to save the world. We'll go into that story more in a minute. The other is the inevitability of love being connected to pain — when we love something, we open ourselves to hurt. This is the relationship or I/thou interpretation. The third is the mystery approach: Who knows why we suffer, who knows how the milk gets spilled, let's get on with it while appreciating the fact that the floor is a mess.

Listen first to the *Life Of Pi* interpretation of Jesus. You will recall that this is a great interfaith book about a young man who manages to befriend Hinduism, Islam, and Christianity, much to the horror of his very secular parents. Pi both loves each religion and hates each religion. Listen to his interpretation of the death of Jesus and remember that his father is really a zookeeper:

> *And what a story ... humanity sins but God pays the price? What? I tried to imagine father saying to me, "Piscine, a lion slipped into the llama pen today and killed two llamas. Yesterday another one killed a black buck. Last week two of them ate the camel. The week before it was painted storks and grey herons. And who's to say for sure who snacked on our golden agouti? The situation has become intolerable. Something must be done. I have decided that the only way the lions can atone for their sins is if I feed you to them."*
>
> *"Yes, father, that would be the right and logical thing to do. Give me a moment to wash up."*
>
> *"Hallelujah, my son."*
>
> *"Hallelujah, my father."*[1]

As you can tell, Pi is not a big fan of the atonement theory. You will find, however, that the people of Mexico are. In fact, they join Bach in the *St. Matthew Passion* in almost finding suffering beautiful. If you know that part of the music, you will know that there is a phenomenal piece where the girls are asking to behold the pain. Daughters, give ear to the suffering.

When I was in Mexico, I had a lot of time to observe a culture drenched in Catholicism, with a church on every corner. Our tour guide, by the way, at Monte Alban, a Zapotec ruin, was more than a little sarcastic about the churches. He said fortunately the Spanish didn't plop a church on top of the ruins! But believe me they didn't need to. There were plenty of churches everywhere, with dozens and dozens of women and children sitting out in front of each one, weaving palm fronds into crucifixes. I asked one woman why a very unusual conception — one I didn't see elsewhere — was so joyful. *(Here I hold up the crucifix, with Jesus' arms waved high from the cross.)* She said, "*El Dolor de Jesus* (the suffering of Jesus) *es muy hermoso, bonito, bueno,* (beautiful, pretty, good) *y tambien* (and also) *El Dolor me ayuda* (his pain helps me)." I already knew I was going to preach against the atonement, with Pi, today. But at some point I have to understand what this woman with the "*allegria*" (happy, joyous) Jesus on the cross means. Is she some kind of new right figure? The kind who love punishment? We know them much too well.

> *The religious right is interested in protecting pain not life. They believe pain is fundamental to justice ... especially when justice is conceived as nothing more than a system of punishment and rewards. The essence of punishment is pain. Whoever owns pain owns power.*
>
> *Like the religious right, I believe in moral absolutes. At the very least I believe in two that were articulated some years ago by the theologian Paul Tallish, those being the "absolute concreteness of every situation in which a moral decision is required," and "the commandment not to treat a person as a thing." In other words, if a child spills milk or a society spills and wastes Jesus, we don't go out of relationship with them and punish. We stay in relationship.*
>
> *In contrast, the right consists of knowing to take its absolutes just far enough, which is to say, never so far as to relinquish the prerogatives of wealth and power. The achievement amounts to an ethical sleight of hand. You work the trick by shifting the domain of moral absolutes to those areas where they least apply. You treat the grey of human existence as though they were black and white, the better to disguise one's self-interested smudging of black and white to gray. You erect castles of rectitude on the frontiers of mortality in the hopes that the murder and raping taking place in the town squares can go on undisturbed. You accept the death of a six-year-old child by aerial bombardment or economic*

sanction and defend the life of a six-week-old fetus. Think of it as taking the high road in Lilliput.[2]

Note also how important it is to punish sexuality. It is not just about death. Of course we are to suffer for a long time before we die, in this theory of life.

> *Enter Turbo Slut, meticulously scheduling her abortions between manicures and sex in the city. To slander their moral courage (of the poor) in defense of moral dogmatism is one of the shabbier tactics of the right.*
>
> *What we have here is the desire of the old and the rich to avoid death at any cost, especially if the cost can be passed on to another generation or another continent.*[3]

What he finally concludes is that the right is "so blithe about illuminating its Gethsemane's with artificial light."

From this punishment-loving world, we end up with deaths less merciful than we allow to dogs. If indeed the defining characteristic of the religious right and the punitive family is to punish spills, what is the defining characteristic of a more progressive view of pain and punishment? I think it is to name life as relationship. That is what Jesus was doing in going to Jerusalem: He was there to create a relationship with it. That will help my Mexican friend as well as help people who need to die, who are ready to die, and who only face suffering as their future. Instead of punishing people for pain, instead of almost liking it, as I said both Bach and my Mexican friend do, there is a way to say that pain is somehow inevitable and that we may dare, by the grace of God, to have a relationship to it. Because we love, we expect pain. We don't like it or appreciate it but we do expect it.

I happened to simply love Mexico, Catholicism and all. The ex-pats are a lot of fun. Women sell grapefruits, sliced and peeled, with cayenne pepper on every street corner. They are delicious. Lime is squeezed on peanuts. Male and female police are the team that defends the city: What a concept in a supposedly sexist society! There is a sensuality about pleasure in a society that also loves pain. Very few have heard in Mexico about the atonement being passé theologically. Simultaneously, there is a level of thought that makes our understandings of post-colonialism very minor.

Consider *Mexico Profundo*, the name Guillermo Bonfil Batalla gives to freedom he claims, "One world where many worlds are possible." The people of pain and punishment want one theory for just about everything. They love universalism. What we may do instead is love relationship — and that means a lot of different ways of dealing with Jerusalem. What Batalla advises is "to look at Mexico not from the West, but to look at Mexico from Mexico." This means, of course, that if a woman wants to create a crucifix with allegria that is her choice, not mine. It is odd, at least to me, that the atonement has produced plain palms, all orthodox — the same, same, same.

Pi wants another kind of God, a different God than I want or the Mexican woman wants.

> *This is God as God should be. With shine and power and might. Such as can rescue and save and put down evil. [Speaking of Rama.]*
>
> *This Son on the other hand who goes hungry, who suffers from thirst, who gets tired, who is anxious, heckled, and harassed, who has to put up with followers who don't get it and opponents who don't respect Him — what kind of God is that? It is a God on a too-human scale, that's what. There are miracles, yes, mostly of a medical nature, a few to satisfy hungry stomachs, at best a storm is tempered, water is briefly walked upon. If that is magic, it is minor magic, on the order of card tricks any Hindi God can do a hundred times better.*[4]

Let me tell you how Farm Share, a project in Florida, handles imperfect vegetables. Farm Share offers the vegetables and us salvation.

While Patricia Robbins was waiting one day outside an office in Homestead, Florida, she watched farm workers dump hundreds of crooked yellow crook neck squash into a dumpster. After the funny looking squash came an equally large number of funny looking tomatoes.

She wanted to know what was going on. Her friend told her that he couldn't send anything that is not quite perfect to market and that he has to pay to have the imperfect vegetables hauled away.

Patricia figured out what her new job was that day. She didn't know how she was going to get paid for rescuing the vegetables, but she knew she was going to do it. Today, Farm Share serves over 650 agencies (homeless shelters, soup kitchens, churches, food banks, and the like) that distribute food to over two million families in Florida each year, Founded in 1992 with one volunteer and one phone, it has distributed over 100 million pounds of food since its inception, most of which is fresh food.

Like the squash, many of us are too crooked to go to market. Many of us are the snarled zucchini or the bruised tomato — ugly and used up — but Jesus went to Jerusalem for us. Whether we are disabled or hurt by crime or whatever else makes us imperfect, we can go to Jesus to help us deal with the waste and the pain. Like Farm Share, Jesus is peace beyond punishment.

Consider Habitat for Humanity's jail project. It trains prisoners to build houses. A flatbed truck wheels the house into the jail where time and life is being wasted. It teaches electrical work as well as building a house. When the house is done, the truck takes the house to its location. The crucifix hates waste. The crucifix uses used-up people.

That is another thing relationship does. It gleans future glory. It sees in the past a future. It sees in the old something new. It sees in the useless something useful. When wine is spilled and pain happens, we become people who clean up the mess and go on.

Can I tell my Mexican *amiga* that she should think differently about the pain of Jesus? No. Can she tell me that I should think differently about the atonement? No. Can we have a relationship? Yes. Can that relationship prevent waste and create life out of death? Should a child be punished for spilling milk? No.

Can a garden come from death? Is there a place for crooked squash and bruised vegetables not good enough for market? Is there room for a dozen different kinds of crucifixes? Yes. Is there a way to not be ruined by the pain? Yes. There is a place beyond punishment. Amen.

1. Yann Martel, *Life Of Pi* (Orlando, Florida: Harvest Books, 2003).

2. Garret Keizer, *Life Everlasting: The Religious Right And The Right To Die* (New York: Harper's Essay), February 2005.

3. *Ibid.*

4. *Op cit*, Yann Martel.

Proper 19
Pentecost 17
Ordinary Time 24
Proverbs 1:20-33

Having A Good Name

Proverbs is right: Having a good name is a terribly important thing. It is important in business, it is important in society, it is important at home, in a family. When we lose our good name, we have lost our trustworthiness. Sometimes it cannot be replaced.

How do we know if we have a good name? What is the measurement? Is it the absence of gossip? Or the presence of trust? Is a good name something that we start out with only to find it comes up missing once we have done one or two things wrong? Or does a good name only begin to be threatened after three things? Again, how do we know? Indeed, do we know?

Having a good name is not just having a good name. It is a matter of the inner matching the outer — and it is also a matter of grooming and training our inner to be good. Very few of us take the time to train. We bop along. Instead of self-definition, the inner work of outer self-presentation, we fuzz along.

Two problems plague most people I know, including me. One is short term. It is the inability to get destiny or destination in place and to act from and toward it. The other is fuzzy goals. Because I don't know exactly what I want from today or tomorrow or you or me or us or them, I often behave non-strategically. I bop along. I buzz along in a fuzzy framework of creeds, stories, scripts, theories, and ideologies. Some days end with me wondering why I moved that whole pile of paper from one side of my desk to another: What kept me from acting on at least two or three pieces of my "preposterous," the name my daughter gave at age nine to my kitchen counter. She had just learned the word and was looking for a perfect way to use it. She found it on the counter. All she could describe was the paper: She didn't see all the hidden scripted messages that were also there.

Both of these problems have positive nuances. What happens as I fuzz and buzz along is often quite beautiful. Sometimes wonderful things find me. Serendipity, what you find that you are not looking for, is a magnificent experience. I remember very well the day I met a woman who has become a dear friend. On the day I met her at a business lunch, I had vowed not to make any new friends until I took better care of the ones I had. I had just received an angry letter from a friend about why I had not responded to her phone calls. As she revealed herself to me during the lunch, I just started to laugh. I was breaking my own promise within hours of making it.

While serendipity and aimlessness are magnificent things, they also get in the way of purpose. They get in the way of art, too, the play we should be writing, the song we should be singing, the change we should be making, and the church we should be becoming. Aimlessness can make the issue of what name we have and whether it is good or not a real problem.

Strategy is good — and to behave strategically, we need to give ourselves over to something like a name, something like a creed.

A name is something with content, something that says who we are. A name is something that goes with what we believe in. We are known by our beliefs, our commitments to those beliefs. Keeping a good name means having a good creed.

A creed is a statement of belief, within or outside of a religious context. It is the choice to commit to this rather than that. We name ourselves by X, not Y. What is good about creeds, according to Jaroslav Pelican, the best scholar on the subject, is that they save us from short term being. They link us to long pasts. They are a stay against individualism, which is different than individuality. Names are often individual parts of group goals. We name ourselves by who we belong to. This loss of individuality is as much a problem as too much individuality!

Creeds are also not so good, according to Pelican, because they tend to romanticize their own history. In his book surveying creeds from 1873 to the present, he found 200 revisitings of the Nicene Creed, most of which came straight out of their year and their nation. Creeds are patently not universal — while often pretending so to be. Even Nicea, which came from the first global meeting of the Christian church, the Council of Nicea in 325, took 56 years to be solidified later at the Council of Constantinople. It was often sung or chanted and thereby memorized by a transnational people who called themselves Christians. The Nicene Creed replaced the Apostles' Creed, which was used primarily at baptisms before 325. The Apostles' Creed was an answer to one historical movement, gnosticism, which denied that Jesus was fully human. The Nicene Creed responded to the so-called heresy of Aryanism, which denied that Jesus was fully divine. We already see that these creeds, which pretend to be universal and objective, are patently not. They are rich in context. Pelican loves creeds because they connect us to fat and long pasts. I like (don't love) creeds because I think they are a kind of shade — a comfort food — a way to get above the preposterous fray and fuzz of the day and connect to my cultural and religious forebears. Creeds give us a good name. From them, we define ourselves and know what we are protecting when we take care of our good name.

I love the way the Massai people in East Nigeria rewrote the "Gem Na" creed in 1960 at their own council, called the Congregation of the Holy Ghost.

> *We believe in One High God, who out of love created the beautiful world. We believe that God made good his promise by sending his Son, Jesus Christ, a man in the flesh, a Jew by tribe, born poor in a little village, who left His home and was always on safari doing good, curing people by the power of God, teaching about God and man, and showing that the meaning of religion is love. He was rejected by his own people, tortured and nailed hands and feet to a cross, and died. He was buried in the grave, but the Hyenas did not touch him, and on the third day he rose from the Grave.*[1]

I have said that I like (don't love) creeds because they give a shade, a collective comfort, to the issue of being born Christian and being part of this living room as opposed to a Buddhist or Islamic one. I have a rug on my floor, as well. Creeds keep me somewhat protected and shaded from the hot sun of my 100 years on the globe (if I am lucky) and the resulting short term it is. They also propel me intro strategic behavior while allowing me openness to serendipity. Creeds name me.

Stephen Jay Gould who sang with the Haydn and Handel societies in Boston for many years and who was a nonbeliever, a man whose creed was science not religion, said that if we had only one thing to put in a time capsule to tell those who follow us who we are and who we have been, he would put in the Bach B minor mass, "Credo in Unum Deum." I would not go that far in praising the accomplishments of Christianity. But again I note the clarity such a mass gives. It gives us ethnic, national, and "birth" Christians a stay against individualism. It gives us an invitation to that place that exists between a welcome pluralism and a disturbing relativity. It gives us a good name to protect.

It is very important to stop every now and then and just think about who we are and what we stand for.

Why do I think it important to step back and think? Because knowing what we believe and why we believe it is important to how we behave, whether we matter, whether we live in the world we make or the world others make for us. Absent creedal thinking, which I mean in the broadest and most strategic of senses, others will be happy to do our thinking for us. They will move their couch and their lamp into our living room and we will sit on it. Let me redefine what I mean by creed: It is our name and its measurement, our epistemology, our theory, our ideology, our script, our screen, and our filter. It is not all these things at the same time but can be any of them at any given moment. While I don't want to go all the way to a fully measured or strategic or directed life, I do want to avoid fuzz. I am too aware of the power of ideology to control me.

Dorothy Bass argues that the way most Americans measure our lives is by whether or not we are authentic, whatever that is. Whether or not we had free choice, whatever that is. Whether or not we made our own choices about who we are. I fear these versions of authenticity drip with individualism. Just drip with it. We are "self-made," like my favorite all-American character, straight from the work of Robert Bellah, the sociologist, who tells us "I am a self-made man" only to discover that he inherited the car dealership from his father! We are the victims of other people's creeds if we don't have our own. We are victims of what other people name us instead of choosing our own names.

Americans think we are self-made. We are not. We are made by each other. In Thomas Friedman's new theory, one I happen to buy, the price of oil and the pace of freedom move in opposite directions. We are made by the price of oil as well as what we had for breakfast and what we learned in school and whether we were born Christian or not.

Surely some people — I think of many foundations and most school testing — take the notion of measurement way too far; contrarily, many of us take it not far enough. How would we measure if our church were a successful congregation for the next chapter? How would we know? If we felt good? If we made our own choices? Or if we had a driving vocation that matters to someone else besides ourselves? The creed matters here: Jesus mattered to someone besides himself. How would we know if our own lives, however long or short, measured up to goals we had set for ourselves? One goal could be to maximize serendipity. Another would be to leave a legacy of beauty or excellence or good jokes. A third would be to be a good parent or good school board member. Knowing our destination is a matter of creed. It is a matter of shade: under which tree do we stand and think and sift and strategize? It is also a matter of what furniture is already in our living room and whether the room in which we live is cluttered with old stuff, like our parents' or our teachers' or the oppressive voices, which inhabit most of our minds. Interior decoration is not a small matter: It is often the act and art of aesthetic strategy applied to our own lives and spaces. A good name is a good thing.

I was compelled by what Jaroslav Pelican said about creeds and their use. I was not surprised to be reminded by him that Saint Augustine concluded his creedal book of thousands of pages with the words, "We have said this not in order to say something, but in order not to remain altogether silent."

Mystery remains long after measurement collapses in the issue *du jour*. I also found my way to a book by Walter Moseley, *Life Out Of Context*. This book is a long essay about Moseley's redecoration of his own African-American living room. Moseley's previous book was *Working On The Chain Gang: Shaking Off The Dead Hand Of History*. In that book, Moseley argued that economic globalism was pushing our lives all the time. Not free choice. Not personal authenticity. Just plain old capitalism slotting us into which couch and which colors to buy.

The new book *Life Out Of Context* is a direct challenge to the creeds and theories, that bind us. He questions the way "America" stands front and center in all our lives, black and white. Why not Africa? Why not the global South? Why is the only story we tell and know is the one where the American team wins? Why not think of:

- Cameroon and HIV/Aids?
- Ghanian's project on Grasscutter Production for Environmental Conservation?
- Kenya's Kibwezi's Goat and Honey Project?
- Mozambique's Introduction of Draft Power?
- South Africa's Khulani Tsoto Goat Project?
- Tanzanian's Fish Farming Development Project?
- Zambian's Chikupi Women's Goat Project Phase?
- Zambian's Water Supply for Sustainable Livelihoods?
- China's Goose and Duck Project Phase II in Jiangsu?
- India's Capacity Building of Marginalized Rural Communities?
- Indonesia's Micro Credit programs?
- Nepalese Itahari Women's Livestock Raising?
- Vietnam's Youth Project in the Mekong Delta?
- Albania and Armenia's Azerbaijan Bull Calves Project?

I have only gone through one quarter of the globe. Why are these places so far from us? Is our name just American or is it global? How do we protect a good global name?

I shiver to think how much my contexts are at war with my creeds — and that I don't take the time to sort them through or to stand in their shade long enough to redecorate my living room — to know what I believe, what I think, who I think it with, and what I am going to do about it. I shudder to think that I am not thinking or seeing or knowing. I shudder to think that I have been duped by something as small as America rather than by something as large as Nicea. Both, of course, are contextual. One context is simply better — global not national, universal not individual, and these matters matter to what I do today in my living room. How I get past my lack of strategy is by taking the time to creed, to think, to sift, to sit under the shade tree and think. There I protect my good name. Amen.

---

1. This was taken from a worship contest in 1960.

Proper 20
Pentecost 18
Ordinary Time 25
Proverbs 31:10-31

Finding The Good Woman Part In Us All

A good woman is a superwoman, or so it appears to me as I read the list of things she can do. In this famous passage from Proverbs, we read that a good woman is precious and that her husband trusts her. A good woman is a good marketer and bargainer, buying fields, trading wool and flax, finding good food from far away. She makes her arms strong! There is certainly no picture of twenty-first-century "typical" femininity here. She is not just precious to her husband or a good businesswoman: she also opens her hands to the poor and needy. She protects both her own and those not her own. Because of her, her husband is known in the city gates. He takes his seat among the elders of the land — "Strength and Dignity are her clothing" (v. 25).

We often hear this passage read at funerals of fine women. They often make the rest of us tremble. How can we be all those things? One way to go is to observe carefully what happened with the book and the movie *The DaVinci Code*.

In case some of you missed it, *The DaVinci Code* was a best-seller. How many have not read it? Are there those who do not know its story? *The DaVinci Code* is a story about a hidden woman, a woman hidden aggressively by the church so that she would not have religious power. Dan Brown, an unlikely agent of the Holy Spirit, but an agent nevertheless, has told Mary Magdalene's story in such a way that the poor woman has been on the cover of *Time* and *Newsweek*, is the subject of a movie, and I could go on. Despite the happy ending of Brown's book, women remain hidden. For years, I kept a tab on my refrigerator of how many women were on the front page of the *New York Times*. It wasn't pretty compared to the number of men.

The good woman in Proverbs is a striking contrast to all these roles. She is not hidden. She is valued and appreciated and public in her community. She is not a virgin but instead makes the clothes of all her household to be clothed in "crimson." Now she is a sexually complex woman: She is truly and deeply valued by her husband who benefits from the strength of her love for him.

I think many women want to be like the proverbial good woman. We often don't think we have the choices. We often work by a holy hidden thread or grail and feel like we are anything but valued or free in our communities. The time I knew the da Vinci dame the best was when Sigma Alpha Epsilon, a fraternity at my college, raped a waitress at the local diner. That night, some of us women took out our thread on the grail and organized a sit in on campus. Why? Because we were tired of being raped. Why? Because we were the ones locked up at 10:30 on weeknights and 11:30 on weekends. Why? Because we were women. We were Magdalenes. God only knew what we would do if we stayed out later. Our first demonstration at this particular college in 1968 was a combination of anti-rape and pro-freedom for women. Mary Magdalene would understand. The proverbial woman might not: She would not know what it meant not to be valued and free and useful and public in her community. What we then proposed is that the college let us free and lock the men up. That would keep the local waitresses safer. By the way, the other thing the men in this particular fraternity did regularly was uproot the tulips in Dwight Eisenhower's office, next door to the Gettysburg Campus. Our argument was lock tight: If women were out and men were in, we doubted the women would uproot the tulips as entertainment. Nor did we think women would rape the cooks or waitresses at the local restaurant.

Some of you are thinking, *What's with her?* Everybody knows things are better for women. Just a short while ago, the Sigma Alpha Epsilon fraternity at Gettysburg College gang raped another local waitress. Sorry: Things *are* better. Title 9 is better. Women no longer have hours on college campuses while men go free and pull up tulips. There is even a woman running for president, which may or may not be a good thing. And more importantly to my message today, the Holy Grail of Mary Magdalene's blood (yes, it is about her blood) beats in my heart and yours today. It flows as strong as any river or any set of healthy veins. Sometimes if you lay still at night, you can just feel the blood flowing through your body. It is her, or so I think. You see, at Gettysburg, whenever the house-mother locked the front door, so as to keep her girls safe, we slipped out the windows. That's how Mary Magdalene survived, too. She survived by trickery. She survived by being hidden in plain sight.

What a relief it is to hear about a full and generative woman as far back as the book of Proverbs, long before Mary Magdalene was hidden.

An old joke about Mother's Day tells the same story: "Mother's Day Special: Free Glass of Wine — Whatever wine is open, so as not to be a bother."

One of the sickest jokes about clergy goes like this: Clergy are out of their place when they get involved in politics. (By the way, male clergy are often insulted as effeminate.) Go back to the stands with the women and children and there observe the real game being played on the real field by the only valid players, real men. Unpacking this joke would take me too long but it is actually what women and girls are told all the time. Stay off the real field where the real game is being played by the real people. Magdalene is the force that tramples out the vintage where the grapes of wrath are stored. Magdalene is about the new wine that women choose. We choose it in plain sight. We choose it by not believing the lies or following orders. We stay on the field. We don't move. We begin to be a bother. We begin to bother. Again the proverbial woman did not have to bother. She was on the field. She bought and sold fields!

Many men have helped many women get on to the field. Think of Ruth and Naomi. Ruth and Naomi get to Bethlehem. Naomi goes to her distant relative, Boaz. He is the third hero in this story. He permits the two women to glean his fields. When someone more justified in being in the fields objects and asks a great question, "To whom do these women belong?" Boaz says they are his. Not only does he protect and feed them, he goes one step further with

Ruth. In chapter 2, verse 9 in the NRSV, Boaz tells Ruth, "I have directed my men not to bother you." In the New Jerusalem Bible, that verse reads, "not to molest you." In the King James Version, the verse is "not to touch you." The verb matters less than the protection being offered to women who were dangerously alone.

Magdalene traveled with Ruth and Naomi all the way. She was the blood stirring in the veins of women who ordered the wine their own way. I think the proverbial woman was traveling with them, too.

These issues of who gets to play on what court or what field are hardly over. I recently read the following article in the *New York Times*. "Critic of No Child Left Behind was Disinvited from Meeting — Patricia Polacco, a popular author of children's books, was disinvited from her $5,000 gig at the International Reading Association annual meeting in Chicago because she would not agree in advance to stay away from her views on testing in her talks. McGraw-Hill canceled her contract, saying it only sought to stop an author whose political agenda might interfere with her book exhibit." Fascinating. I wonder what Mary Magdalene would think about the power of ideas. I wonder what Boaz would have done — side with the men in his field and let them bother Ruth and Naomi? Is it possible that we have come to a world where a leading publishing house is suppressing free and artistic speech?

I am grateful for the strong and free picture of the proverbial woman. She is alive today. Amen.

Proper 21
Pentecost 19
Ordinary Time 26
Esther 7:1-6, 9-10; 9:20-22

The Place Beyond Revenge

A custom is begun! Because of the vengeance that the king took against Haman for Esther, the Jews are to remember their salvation. On the fourteenth and fifteenth day of the month they are to send gifts of food to one another and presents to the poor.

Oh, God, help me to understand violence! Help me to understand vengeance. I am pretty good at the other sins, like lust and greed, pride and gossip, but violence I just don't understand. I also don't really understand the tribalism that is beyond it. Is that because I am an immigrant myself and know that I have lived among many tribes and don't really belong to any one? Is that because I am a coward and don't know how to be truly faithful to anything? Surely there are reasons for me not to enjoy Esther's victory and Haman's use of violence to get behind it. Is the war really set up for war and then for reparations? Can two days for the poor ever justify destroying their villages or their airports or their homes? What is the point of violence? Isn't it finally just too expensive? Does it ever have lasting victories? I think of India and Pakistan and the Mombai train bombing, or South and North Korea and the utter starvation of the North Koreans. I think of Beruit now being destroyed by Israel because some of Beruit houses the Hezbolah. What about Iraq or Vietnam? I could go on. Violence doesn't make sense to me. Not Esther's, not Haman's, not anyone's.

So where do I go from here? In this year of the eighth anniversary of 9/11, perhaps I am best off reflecting on that violence against my country.

The twin towers of the World Trade Center fell on September 11, 2001, leaving nearly 3,000 people dead. As catastrophes go, the death toll is small — but the lingering international and personal effects are not. The intentional and precise violence of the acts, combined as they were with secondary attacks on Washington DC sites, caused an international ripple of fear and installed a new word in everyday vocabularies. The word is "terrorism." On top of these facts there is a thick overlay of religious hostility. The people who bombed American buildings were Muslim. On top of the religious layer to the physical violence, there is the ongoing war in Iraq. This war has killed more people than 9/11 attacks did.

Another number matters: one million people per day visit the exhibit in St. Paul's Chapel in lower Manhattan to see a simple display of what happened that day. They also stare at the hole in the ground across the street and surely have what can only be called a spiritual experience, one of awe, fear, and trembling. Where great power stood, great emptiness prevails.

Linda Hannick, on the communications and marketing staff of the Trinity Wall Street Church, remembers watching a piece of the building fly past her office on 9/11. She joined thousands of others in leaving her office and going to the street to see a life-draining horror. Part of her neighborhood was crashing down around her. Linda put together the exhibit at neighboring St. Paul's. How has she changed in eight years? Not much. The horror remains close and precise. The exhibit gives her a frame for the chaos of the experience. She compares herself to the one elderly woman on the last Staten Island Ferry to leave the city on the original day. "We were all there in stunned silence, with orange life jackets on us. Helicopters flew overhead and you could hear us all think, *Finally, the government has come to help and protect us from whatever is going to happen next.* Then one elderly woman raised her hands to the sky and spoke for the entire boat. In anguish, she said, 'God,' and broke down and wept." Linda's ongoing exhibit is that framed cry of anguish that breaks the silence.

Linda's story takes us back to one clear day in September whose effects linger and linger. Not only do the effects linger internationally in war, they also have uncanny forms of personal reminders.

At airports, we take our belts and shoes off, we open our computers, and we get stripped of our fingernail clippers. It is hard to remember a time when we did not perform these social rituals. Likewise, parents argue that teenagers must have cell phones in school, just "in case" something happens.

We will not know the full effect of 9/11 until the wars stop, the artists and singers start, or until the poets work their way to meaning. For now, on this eighth anniversary, we can begin to see what might have changed in our ministries.

The Reverend Rochelle Stackhouse, pastor-elect of the Church of the Redeemer in New Haven, Connecticut, and a UCC minister, speaks of the fear. "It's like we are in permanent duck and cover mode, like we were when I hid as a child in nuclear fallout shelters. My preaching is almost all about fear."

That theme continues in the memories and current behavior of Rabbi Michael Feinstein, whose work places him still very close to the site of Ground Zero. He reports a new appreciation of evil, a nearly constant below the surface fear. When the attack actually happened, Rabbi Feinstein found himself in a deep darkness. He recalls how when he finally starting running north away from the center that women's shoes were everywhere. They had been abandoned so that the people could move faster. Sometimes he "sees those shoes and almost smiles at the near comic effect of them." He remembers "the darkness" and "the smell" that descended over lower Manhattan. He could not go to work for three months in his same office. When he went back, he knew his ministry had forever changed. Henceforth, he would be "simultaneously aware of evil and fragility and the preciousness of ordinary life." How often does he think about 9/11 today? "Daily," he responds.

The Reverend Jim Smucker, retired conference minister in the UCC, says that 9/11 drove him to a similar sense of preciousness and fragility. He says what is different about him is not just age and living in a retirement village. What is different is that he is profoundly aware of small stuff. He has a sense that terror could again fall from the sky and so he is best off paying attention to what is close by. He names,

The love Onieta and I have shared for over sixty years.
The love and caring the Convalescent Center staff shows toward my helpless wife and many others in the same condition.
The power of music and art to lift our sights beyond ourselves and point to something we are only beginning to understand.

The thrill of wild dancing to a pounding beat.
The wonder and beauty of the constantly renewing creation.
Our oneness with each other and all of life.
The courage and powerful beauty of people who put their life on the line in the interest of peace and justice.

Barbara Cawthorne Crafton is an Episcopal priest who worked at Ground Zero at the time of the attack. She spent hours and days with recovery workers, keeping them strong to do recovery work. Her reminiscence of this time says,

> *We are not the only ones whose hearts are broken by what has happened. God's heart is broken, too.*
>
> *And so is my heart. I show it in odd ways. Can't sleep, of course, and cry several times a day, of course. But I also have lost, quite abruptly, a one-a-day-and-sometimes-two-a-day murder mystery habit that goes back years. I have lost — quite abruptly — lost it without even thinking about it. I just noticed, sometime in mid-October, that I hadn't read a murder mystery in weeks, and I hadn't finished the one I had been reading on the train the morning of September 11, and wasn't remotely curious about how it ended. That I had no desire to read another one. I had always found them relaxing, those page turners, relaxing in direct and strange proportion to their goriness and perversity, as if fictional evil were somehow talismanic against the encroachment of real evil into the world. But no more — I don't want to read*

about people deliberately hurting and killing other people anymore. That I used to like these things seems to me now to be monstrous. The Hell humanity really creates is more than enough Hell for anyone.[1]

I caught Amy Blackmarr, author of *Going To Grand: Simple Life On A Georgia Road, 1998*, on her way to seminary in New Haven. When I asked her if her life had changed since 9/11, she practically exploded. "Changed? You bet it changed ... I am going to seminary." Many studies have shown that an extraordinary number of people have shifted careers in the years since 9/11, trying to go into more meaningful professions. Would they have shifted anyway without 9/11? We can never know. However, Amy Blackmarr represents the more spiritual ribbon of American life that we have all had to notice since 9/11.

James Olson, Associate Dean at Boston University's Marsh Chapel, speaks of being in Vermont and having a parishioner call him and tell him "something happened." Like many clergy, he immediately went to work, engaging members of his congregation in caretaking of others.

> *September 11 may genuinely have been the end of American civilization as we knew it. Not because a few Islamic radicals attacked us; rather, it is the response of some of my fellow Americans, particularly those who lead the government, that may ultimately bring America to its knees and give the radicals the victory they ultimately desired.*
>
> *My own preaching now has become more pointedly against the government's response to the threat to our nation.*

While Olson's preaching about the futility of revenge is one response, so is Stackhouse's pastoral preaching against fear. Between these two related poles, most clergy seem to live.

Pat Marrin is an editor and widely engaged in Roman Catholic ministries.

> *My ministry is an editor of a liturgical resource (*Celebration*) published by the National Catholic Reporter. As the impact of 9/11 sank in, I found myself processing the event through my liturgical lens. More than just an act pf violent destruction, the attacks on the World Trade center, the Pentagon and, presumably, the White House were brilliantly conceived assaults on American identity and the illusion of pre-eminence in the world. The most visible symbols ... were struck, not just on the surface but at that deeper root level. We were dealing ... with masters of metaphor and metaphysics. The perpetrators of 9/11 had executed a flawless, surgical and liturgical blow at the central nervous system of our nation.*
>
> *Our response ... is the problem ... Before 9/11 we worshiped with less insight, in more insular comfort zones. Now every worship service begins with soul-searching and contrition ... we pray better and more deeply.*[2]

Both Rabbi Feinstein and Pat Marrin note a silver lining in the cloud. They see that we have been forced to go deep.

Dr. Martin Marty's ministry is writing and speaking to town-and-gown and professional church leadership, where since 9/11, he has been guided by two texts. One is Jose Ortega y Gasset: "Decisive historical changes do not come from great wars, terribly cataclysms, or ingenious inventions: it is enough that the heart of man incline its sensitive crown to one side or the other of the horizon, toward optimism or toward pessimism, toward heroism or toward utility, toward combat or toward peace." Ministry is less about dealing with world affairs than with the sensitive crown of the human heart.

His second guide is Reinhold Niebuhr who said (paraphrased) in early Cold War Days, that the US is a gadget-filled paradise suspended in a hell of international security, and on 9/11 the cord was cut and we've been dropped into the scene the world has always known: Insecurity ... so we have joined the rest of the human race. Insecurity is the big word, exploitable by politicians and others who play on fear to mess things up. So we ask, what is the nature of the "security" with which people in the nation and of faith might believe?

Clearly, it is too soon to know very much at all. What we have are glimpses. We do have themes, big ones at that. The themes are fear, fragility, revenge, insecurity, a strange joining of the majority of the world, finding ourselves in places from which we thought Americans were exempt.

Woody Guthrie might well have the last word. When he sings of "Songs of generations singing in my veins," we know that remarkable unity that we now have, with the rest of the world but also with each other. We were the people who became one because of an external attack. For a brief period of time there was a nearly splendid national unity. That unity has gone the way of all flesh — into fear, revenge seeking, war.

Ministries may not have yet changed toward something different and better — but they could. Our revenge stands in the long line of revenges, not even begun by Esther and Haman, but going from way before that. We can and should do better.

Prayer for 9/11
Eighth Anniversary

Eight years and yet 9/11 feels like yesterday! Give us the power to forget and remember the horror — both, not either. Let us remember our incredulity and fear, our impotence, and our morbid curiosity. Let us remember the love we have for loved ones lost, even those we only know by newspaper name, even those long forgotten by the numbness that has become our protection and armor. Let us remember firemen and police, mayors and presidents, and all whose spiritual budgets, and lungs, remain stressed.

Let us soon forget the urgency for revenge and the blood now spilled because of the World Trade Center towers toppling. Let us move beyond blood for blood, eye for eye, insult for insult, and bomb for bomb. Let the wars cease and the healing begin. Turn the twin towers to ploughshares, and our revenge and rage into world community. When 9/11 is repented and the cloud's silver linings emerge, let us remember the truth under the rubble of resentment:

bad can come to good. Terror can turn to truth about the world's peoples. We can learn from horror. Weeping endures for the night but joy comes in the morning. Let Allah join Jesus and Yahweh and Buddha and the entire great Pantheon, in a common prayer that peace topple war and friendship replace violence among all God's people. Amen.

---

1. Barbara Cawthorne Crafton, *Mass In Time Of War* (Lanham, Maryland: Cowley Publications, 2003), p. 14.

2. Pat Marrin, editor, *Celebrations* magazine (Kansas City, Missouri: National Catholic Reporter Publishing Company), Summer 2004.

Proper 22
Pentecost 20
Ordinary Time 27
Job 1:1; 2:1-10

Job Is For Real

We find Job on the edge of town, his money gone, his children dead, picking at his innumerable sores and scabs. In the Joni Mitchell version of his sorrow, Job speaks of how the children of the wicked frisk like deer while his are dead and gone. In her version, we are also told that Job sees the diggers waiting, leaning on their spades, at the site of his grave. Job's three friends, Eliphas, Bildad, and Zophar show up to comfort him but they do so in a way that only pours iodine on his wounds. God is just, they say, therefore, Job must have done something wrong. Therefore, Job is the sire of his own sorrow, again in Joni Mitchell's words. Job festers even more because of his friends. They bring a conventional wisdom. Job refuses it to suffer more deeply.

This orthodox wisdom sounds true because it is said so often. Many still think that suffering is their own fault. Everything in the book of Job contradicts that, only to go on to say something much more damning. We suffer precisely because we live the illusion that somehow what we do matters. What we do matters much less than we would like to think. We are small in a large world. Get that straight and new behaviors become possible. One new behavior is humility; another is joy in participation in the cosmos.

What Bill McKibben pointed out in his book, *The Comforting Whirlwind: God, Job, And The Scale Of Creation*,[1] is that often it is the conventional wisdom that hurts us the most. Not only with regard to Job and his exquisite dilemma but also with things that transcend Job, the individual. The same conventional wisdom is spouted regarding the environment. It is not about suffering and guilt so much as accepted truth like "We must have more." Every individual should have a car and a private home. Growth is our orthodoxy in the same way that individual guilt's siring of suffering was Job's orthodoxy. We also nurture Job's orthodoxy, but we nurture the social/political frame even more. Growth is good. Therefore, if we grow we will not suffer. Just the opposite, unfortunately is true. The more we grow, the more the earth will suffer and the more we will suffer.

What is great about Job, according to both McKibben and Stephen Mitchell, the poet who does the translation of Job many use today, is his refusal to accept the conventional wisdom. Job refuses to accept his guilt. He says to the end that he is innocent. The first way that Job is right is that he refuses the conventional wisdom even when it comes from his closest peers. Job has a conversation with God that is transforming but it is on Job's terms, not those of convention.

Job had a terrible experience. He was a good man and things happened to him that should never have happened. The earth is having a terrible experience: things are happening to it that should never have happened. Bill McKibben's important book on God in the whirlwind shows how Job's experience reframes the environmental debates of the day. He argues that Job is absolutely right in his rant at God. He also argues that Job will get nowhere ranting at God. We might say the same of environmentalists.

McKibben's argument is that until we get rid of the conventional wisdom on matters of the earth and on matters of suffering, we won't get it right. The conventional wisdom, according to McKibben, is the *problem*. Job faces a new fact with courage. We are also facing a new fact today, the size of the Copernican surprise. We are experiencing what McKibben calls the *de-creation*. Our very climate is changing, increasing temperatures, with an average of ten species of ten chains of being dying every day. We are eroding the very ozone the trees and we need in order to live. We are voting citizens of the richest country in the world, which has as official policy a decision not to sign Kyoto, as if these new facts were somehow irrelevant to the next 25 years of our lives.

If we are lucky enough to live another 25 years, and many of us will be, in fact the great majority, will be, we will see part of the island on which we now live float away. We will sit at the edge of the city and see our money gone, our children threatened, and pick at innumerable scabs and scores. There we will wonder why we did not wake up sooner to global warming. We will wonder why we accepted the conventional wisdom in the face of unconventional facts. We will have to ask ourselves why we assumed, with our culture and our government that "something" would happen to reverse the trend. A new technology perhaps? A bit of good luck like some catastrophe wiping out half the population so we could have enough air to breathe? A new kind of car? While environmentalists are often described as radical and wide-eyed, romantic kooks, who have doom written on their eyeballs and in their words, the real radicals are those who today reject science. Scientific agreement on global warming is widespread. Only fools stick with the conventional wisdom that nothing big is happening and if it is, those who don't sign Kyoto and those who make no plans to avoid islands slipping away will manage it.

Job is a kind of visit to the frame shop. Like the reframing that happened for many when space ships pictured earth suspended, all of it, before our very eyes, we are in need of a reframing, that is Copernican in size and Hubble-ian in method. The Hubble telescope is so much like God's message to Job that it is not funny. When Job complains of his suffering to God, God responds Hubble-esque. The Hubble is widely known to have shown us a universe of such size that we cannot begin to comprehend it. We are not the only world. There are constellations and galaxies beyond us that we are only beginning to understand. One scientist described the change in our point of view made by the Hubble (now an old tool) like this. We used to think of the universe as about as big as the sand on Jones Beach. Now we see the universe as comprising the sand on all the beaches up and down the coast of Florida, Georgia, North Carolina, and South Carolina. Precisely this sea change (forgive the metaphor) is needed as we look at the climate crisis that our generation faces. We need to reframe the issue.

God reframed Job's suffering for him, using words that deserve repeating.

> *Where were you when I planned the earth? Tell me if you are so wise, do you know who took its dimensions, measuring its length with a cord? What were its pillars built on? Who laid down the cornerstone? ... Have you ever commanded morning or guided dawn to its place to hold the corners of the sky and shake off the last few stars?* — Job 38:4-6, 12-13[2]

Let's just say that the almighty needs a little work on his bedside matter. You are upset, Job? Well, who cares?

> *Who cuts a path for the thunderstorm and carves a road for the rain — to water the desolate wasteland, the land where no man lives to make the wilderness blossom and cover the desert with grass?*
>
> — Job 38:25-27[3]

There are many scriptures that take exactly this point of view. Psalm 104 is my favorite: It uses the same voice from the whirlwind as It confronts Job.

> *You cause the grass to grow for the cattle, and plants for people to use, to bring forth food from the earth, and wine to gladden the human heart oil to make his face shine, and bread to strengthen the human hearts.*
>
> — Psalm 104:14-15

> *Yonder is the sea, great and wide, creeping things are innumerable there, living things both small and great. There go the ships, and Leviathan that you formed to sport in it.* — Psalm 104:25-26

Like the story of the whale who stupidly took off up the Thames, only to lose his life to human activity being enchanted by him, Psalm 104 tries to tell us of great and beautiful things, which we are to enjoy, not destroy.

During the conversation that Job and God have, Job is consistently diminished, made to look small and hung out to dry. God continues.

> *Did you deck the ostrich with wings, with elegant plumes and feathers? She lays her eggs in the dirt and lets them hatch on the ground, forgetting that a foot may crush them or sharp teeth crack them open. She treats her children cruelly, as if they were not her own. For God deprived her of wisdom and left her with little sense. And yet when she spreads her wings to run, she laughs at the horse and the rider. Or did you give the horse his strength? ... Who unties the wild ass and lets him wander at will?* — Job 39:13-19, 5-6a

I think of one of the most powerful moments I have ever had in years of dealing with people with sickness. Jim Crawford, the retired pastor of Old South Church in Boston, told the following to someone I later visited. I went to see a man who was terribly ill with emphysema. Every breath was painful. He wanted to die but somehow his body wouldn't let him go. I was stumbling around trying to make sense of his suffering with him. With Job, I stood on the edge of the city picking away at scabs. He found a way to wheeze to me what Jim had said to him, "When this first came up on me, I kept asking, 'Why me? Why me?' Crawford said to me, 'Why not you?' " And that of course is God's response to Job.

So is Job right? I think so. He was innocent and still and nonetheless he suffered. Why did he suffer? Who knows? Why him? Who knows? May we care anyway? Yes indeed. We may care. But we care about the cosmos more than about our little place in it. That is the turn McKibben wants us to make toward the environment. He reads Job's saga in the whirlwind as advising two things — great humility, and even greater joy.

> *The challenge before us is to figure out how to link these two callings, these two imperatives from the voice in the whirlwind — the call to humility and the call to joy. Each on its own is insufficient. Humility by itself is an*

> *arid negativism: a gleeful communion with the earth around us can turn quickly into some New Age irresponsibility, where we come to identify the cosmos with us and not vice versa. But together they are reinforcing, powerful — powerful enough, perhaps to start changing the deep-seated behaviors that are driving our environmental destruction, our galloping poverty, and our cultural despair.*[4]

We have an old painting. It is a painting of the earth. I don't know how you see it. Maybe with the first shot from Apollo where the earth is suspended so terribly lonely, so far away, so unified. Or maybe it is with the artist who did *Scarface*. Do any of you know this painting? It is by Elizabeth Williams and I have only seen it once. But I will never forget it. She is asked to paint a woman who has been enormously disfigured by an abusive husband. Her face is cockeyed, one eye is half shut, and the lips are bruised and engorged. The nose on the woman's face is sideways. Her skin is pockmarked. First, we see the photo. Then we see William's rendition of *Scarface*. In William's rendition she is beautiful. Like a model. Her skin is firm, her face is not distorted. She is gorgeous. Williams tells us that when she looks at this woman, this is who she sees. The Garrison Institute, 37 miles from here on the Hudson, is doing a monthly series on rethinking environmentalism in our region. How? By inserting religious and artistic perspectives of joy into the doom language of most environmentalists. By speaking of earth as our power not our problem. By reframing the language of pessimism regarding the environment.

The call of Job is a call to reframe. It is to see with the perspective of the Hubbell and the perspective of Apollo. It is to see just how beautiful this old scarface planet still is. It is to see just how small we are — and then from within that consciousness to experience awe and joy.

We live in a world that is straining to catch its breath, losing oxygen and water, and heavy with people. That's where we live and still it is a beautiful wonderful place. It is our home.

The first time Gotham historians think that someone looked at the city, as a whole was in 1853 in an electrotyped woodcut, "Bird's

Eye View of the City of New York" from Frank Leslie's *Illustrated News* encompassed the town as a whole. These new panoramic views of the city changed the way the city saw itself. We need a panoramic view of our city, our planet, and ourselves.

Was Job right in being furious? I think so. From that fury much can be born. We can whirl with the wind. We can escape the prison of our own self-consciousness. We can be pro-nature in a pro-urban way. We can treasure the largeness of it all and not be afraid of it.

We can't fix it. Nor is it meant to be fixed. The earth is created. In fixing it, we often join the de-creation. Instead, with humility and in joy, we transform the size of our footstep on earth. We think outside of the box of ourselves being the center of it all. We who commit mass murder by complacency can stop. We can stop the complacency. We can see the whole earth, not as a catalogue, but the whole earth and ourselves as planted within it. That is the reframe that can begin the saving of the air and water and our island home.

I find going to PETCO helps me. There I am surrounded by a lot of little nutty dogs and their owners who are desperately trying to make contact with nature. Imagine doing that through a chihuahua. Or me through a golden retriever? People sit in leather chairs reading books about how to "tame" a dog. Little do they know that the dog will soon tame them! What is the difference between a cat and a dog? A dog thinks you are the center of the universe and a cat thinks it is the center of the universe. God tried to teach Job to think less like a cat and more like a dog. Not that there is anything wrong with cats or dogs — or Job — or you or me. It's just that none of us is the center of the universe. Amen.

---

1. Bill McKibben, *The Comforting Whirlwind: God, Job, And The Scale Of Creation* (Cambridge, Massachusetts: Cowley Publications, 2005).

2. Stephen Mitchell, *The Book Of Job* (New York: HarperCollins, 1987).

3. *Ibid.*

4. *Op cit*, McKibben.

Sermons On The First Readings

For Sundays
After Pentecost
(Last Third)

From Emptiness
To Fullness

Robert A. Hausman

Proper 23
Pentecost 21
Ordinary Time 28
Job 23:1-9, 16-17

Oh, That I Knew Where I Might Find Him

Then Job answered, "Today also is my complaint bitter." With those words, we go from the patience of Job to the bitterness of Job, from a docile Job to a defiant Job. Last week, Job was the model of submission. To him we owe the powerful proverbs: "Naked I came from my mother's womb, and naked shall I return there; the Lord gave, and the Lord has taken away" (Job 1:21).

Last week, we left Job sitting in his ash heap, scraping away at his sores, and asking rhetorically, "Shall we receive the good at the hand of the God, and not receive the bad?" There, in the story, he demonstrates his stability, his steadfastness, or what the text calls his "integrity." He gives us a map of a moral world, which is so clear, so coherent, and so simple that it is impossible to get lost. All the paths lead to virtue.

However, Job's wife poses the question that challenges such a moral universe. "Do you still persist in your integrity? Why not curse God and die?" She offers the nihilistic option. Life is at best a burden and at worst an obscene joke. Certainly non-being is better than being. Just curse God and die!

Job, of course, does not choose that option. It says, "In all this Job did not sin with his lips" (2:10). The picture we have is one of the universe still intact through the heroic faith of a pious Job. He did not curse God with his lips; but the text says nothing about Job's heart.

Do you remember that, in the first presentation of Job, it said that he regularly made sacrifices on behalf of his children? Now, they had been presented as prosperous and content, so we assume that they were pious like Job. But Job offers sacrifices for them just in case they had "sinned and cursed God in their hearts" (1:5). It may be that here, where it says Job does not curse God "with his lips," the narrative leaves just a little crack in Job's piety — for example, what about his heart? Whether through the efforts of the storyteller who decides to complicate things, or, more likely, an editor who thinks there is more to say, suddenly Job becomes the desperate, defiant Job of our text. Into that crack in the story gets inserted 39 chapters of debate.

First, although Job does not curse God, he does curse the day he was born. "Let the day perish in which I was born, and the night that said, 'A man-child is conceived' " (3:3). In a deep and powerful expression of pain, Job spews curses left and right (3:3-10). Then he cries out the eternal question: Why? (Job 3:11, 12, 16, 20, 23).

Having gotten that off his chest, Job becomes the defender of his innocence. He will not buy the orthodox answers that his comforters give to the problem of suffering in the universe: perhaps it is only discipline? Happy is the one whom God reproves (5:17). Or maybe a warning not to presume on God's grace! But if it is punishment, bear it honestly. After all, "Can mortals be righteous before God? Can human beings be pure before their Maker?" (4:17). So bear it patiently, with the confidence that God will get it right in the end.

The Job of the narrative itself might accept these answers. The Job of the poetry will have none of it. No matter how much I groan, his hand is heavy upon me and I am tired of it (v. 2). I want to argue with him, I want to lay my case before him, I want to hear what he has to say. Job wants his day in court! We all know the burden of feeling that we have been judged unjustly. Whether it be a spat with a spouse, an argument over a traffic ticket, a debate over a course grade, a challenge to the IRS — all we want is a hearing before a reasonable judge and, of course, we will be proven righteous.

Here, in Job's complaint, the legal language is everywhere. Job wants to plead his case (v. 4), fill his mouth with arguments, and contend with God. There it would be, in God's courtroom, that "an upright person could reason with him, and I should be acquitted for ever by my judge" (v. 7).

The problem with Job's wish is not that he might be proven wrong in God's courtroom nor that the verdict might go against him. The problem is that the trial cannot even begin because God won't show up in the courtroom; God can't be pinned down like that. "Oh, that I knew where I might find him, that I might come even to his dwelling!" (v. 3). But, "if I go forward, he is not there; or backward, I cannot perceive him; on the left he hides, and I cannot behold him; I turn to the right, but I cannot see him" (vv. 8-9). In Hebrew, the four directions that one can go — forward, backward, left, and right — are the same words used for the four directions of the compass (north, south, east, and west). So, we could say, nowhere in the world is God to be found.

Such an inaccessible God seems strange for us who have been nourished on the idea of the availability of God. God is very near to us, Paul says, for in him we live and move and have our being (Acts 17:28). People have always claimed to find God present in the created world (natural theology), in the common ordering of societies (natural law), or in the hidden recesses of the soul. In America, we are particularly fond of the image of God as our buddy, who, "though it makes him sad to see the way we live, he always says, 'I forgive.' "

Our text makes it clear, however, that things are not that simple. God is not at our beck and call. God does not show up in court just because Job wants to defend himself. In his wishful thinking, Job imagines that all would be made right if God would just explain himself. "I would learn what he would answer me, and understand what he would say to me" (v. 5). (Job assumes that God would be a font of wisdom which would make sense of the world once again, if only he could learn from God.) Job is not afraid of a divine power play. "He would not batter me down in the greatness of his power. No! But he would just give heed to me so that we could get things straight" (v. 6 cf).

Just when we get used to a confident, rather defiant Job, suddenly he seems a desperate man who lives in dread. "God has made my heart faint; the Almighty has terrified me" (v. 16). Certainly that is an important observation about a God who lives in unapproachable light. The Old Testament is full of stories testifying to a dread of the almighty. One cannot look on the almighty and live! Whether it is Moses on the mountain, Elijah hiding in a cave, or Isaiah confronting God in a vision, clearly a God who is "wholly other," a God of majesty and might, ought to strike dread in our hearts. This is Martin Buber's *Mysterium Tremendum.*

Where does that leave Job? The last verse of our text is ambiguous. Job's situation is characterized as one of deep darkness; but is he overcome by it? The NRSV reads, "If only I could vanish in darkness, and thick darkness could cover my face!" It is a statement of despair, a death wish. The NIV, however, translates it, "Yet I am not silenced by the darkness, by the thick darkness that covers my face."

Continued defiance or despair? Those seem to be the two places we have to stand if we pose the issue in terms of human perceptions of justice. As humans, it is natural for us to perceive reality as controlled by some principle of retributive justice. We heard the psalmist this morning crying out for a balance: "Make us glad as many days as you have afflicted us, and as many years as we have seen evil" (Psalm 90:15). Ultimately, there must be a right and a wrong, and the wrong must be punished and the right rewarded. If not, what sense is there? The Old Testament wisdom literature is full of that challenge. The psalms of lament cry out, "How long, oh Lord, how long?" However, once we put God in the dock and seek to make God conform to our reality, we have a problem. In our modern age, Archibald MacLeish has framed it in a limerick: "If God is god, he is not good; if God is good, he is not God. Take the even, take the odd."[1]

There will be no answer to this conundrum as long as the categories proposed by human reason are justice/injustice. The book of Job cannot answer the question that way, nor can the church. (Theodicy — the eternal attempt to justify the ways of God to man — seldom works.) Our other lessons for this morning ask different questions and point us in different directions. First, the gospel offers a difficult challenge. Jesus says, "It is easier for a camel to go through the eye of a needle than for someone who is rich to enter the kingdom of God" (Mark 10:25). "Then who can be saved?" the disciples ask. Jesus looked at them and said, "For mortals it is impossible, but not for God; for God all things are possible!" (Mark 10:27).

It is a reminder of the total objectivity of grace. It comes to us, not as a reward for our piety, not as a "not-guilty verdict" in our legal case, not as an answer to our questions. Whether our goodness be imagined or real, it is beside the point. All is grace.

When Peter calls attention to the fact that the disciples have left everything to follow Jesus, Jesus promises that they will get it all back; but in a paradoxical way. We are reminded of the tale of Job, where, as we shall see, he gets it all back in a more simplistic way; an abundance of flocks, children, and servants. But the gospel complicates things. Jesus says, you will get "houses, brothers and sisters, mothers and children, and fields," but he means that you get the church. The church will be your new family, your divine community. Yet, even then, he complicates it more: "with persecutions!"

So there is no justice, as we like to say. There is only faith in a God for whom all things are possible, the reality of the church, support in persecutions and, finally, the hope to come. You will get everything, with persecutions, "and in the age to come, eternal life." So, we might say, the resolution is only in God and in God's future. For now, we are left with the gift of grace, the incarnation, death, and resurrection of our Lord.

In the second lesson, Hebrews says: "Since, then, we have a great high priest who has passed through the heavens, Jesus, the Son of God, let us hold fast to our confession. For we do not have a high priest who is unable to sympathize with our weaknesses, but we have one who in every respect has been tested as we are, yet without sin. Let us therefore approach the throne of grace with boldness, so that we may receive mercy and find grace to help in time of need" (Hebrews 4:14-16). Amen.

---

1. Archibald MacLeish, *JB* (Boston: Houghton Mifflin, 1956), p. 14.

Proper 24
Pentecost 22
Ordinary Time 29
Job 38:1-7 (34-41)

An Answer Out Of The Whirlwind

What does it mean to be great? That is the question our texts raise today. "Great" is a wide-ranging word: You can have a great king, great skill, a great storm, a great number, great joy, or great fear. You can use it in its Greek form, *mega* — as in megachurch; or in its Latin form, *magna* — as in magnify. It can refer to physical form, size, or height. Pull yourself up, stand tall, like the cedars of Lebanon! Be great!

Oh, just to touch on greatness! To shake the hand of an all-star, to have an audience with the president (or the pope), to crash a Hollywood party and mingle with the stars, to wave like a fool in front of the television cameras for the *Today* show. Oh, for that fifteen seconds of fame.

Well, Job was the greatest! "This man was the greatest of all the people of the east" (1:3) — until misfortune befell him! It is useless to try and quantify tragedy or grade degrees of suffering. Job's suffering is simply presented as a great fall, from most enviable to most pitiable. Now, we are all familiar with falls that are deserved, as when Enron officials go to jail or public officials get caught taking bribes. We also know that falls can be invited, as when we tempt fate. Other falls come inevitably from natural forces, as when the bloom fades from the flower. Robert Frost expressed this inevitability in his poem "Provide, Provide." "Too many fall from great and good / For you to doubt the likelihood."[1]

Job's fall is presented as arbitrary, brought about by a strange testing, suggested by the tempter and then permitted by the almighty.

The fall is so great that we are left sitting in stunned silence, struggling for words. But still, Job worshiped! "Naked I came from my mother's womb, and naked shall I return there; the Lord gave, the Lord has taken away; blessed be the name of the Lord" (1:21).

Last week, we saw the shift from story to argument, from the passive sufferer to the combative hero, from piety to protest. Job's world suddenly makes no sense; the law of retribution does not work; there is no justice! Job wants answers. He wants his day in court. He wants to take God on, face-to-face. He will defend himself and then see what God has to say. Sometimes he is presented as determined but still respectful; other times, he is defiant and seems to overstep the bounds of propriety. Either way, he is relentless!

Then, suddenly, in this text, God speaks — out of the whirlwind. The storm is a common mode of revelation in the ancient Near East and it is meant to invoke terror! "Who is this that darkens counsel by words without knowledge?" (v. 2). It takes a secular age like ours to be blasé about the voice of God — to think of an audience with God as some unambiguously good thing. Once God becomes a kindly old grandfather, you get pious politicians pronouncing God's truth and arrogant evangelists assuring us that they talk regularly to God.

Job suggests that when God speaks, you had better run for cover. Job had demanded answers, God comes with questions. "Gird up your loins like a man, I will question you!" (v. 3). With a kind of repetitive excess, the questions come with machine-gun rapidity. Where were you when? Can you? Do you know? Who but me has? In chapters 38 and 39 (seventy verses — we burdened you with only fourteen in our text), we are regaled with a poetic description of God's works, covering creation, the earth, the heavens, the natural world, the animal world, even the mythical or the primordial. God hammers away at the fact that Job is just an infinitesimal part of an awesome creation.

The sum of it is, "Shall a faultfinder contend with the Almighty? Any one who argues with God must respond" (40:2). Job is stunned. The "once great" Job answers, "See, I am of small account; what shall I answer you? I lay my hand on my mouth" (40:4). Then, as if to put the final nails in the coffin, God goes on for two more chapters! These chapters center on the great primeval creatures, Behemoth and Leviathan. They count iron as straw and bronze as rotten wood (41:27). Creatures without fear, they have no equal. They are symbolic of those edges of life that are a part of the created world and yet are chaotic and beyond our control. In an age that tames the wilderness, inoculates against disease, seeks to clone for perfection, and flies to the moon, it is hard to find an analogy (the Loch Ness monster?). Our monsters are microcosmic ... the fear that comes with a virus that won't be tamed, a potential plague that has no answers or the AIDS pandemic. Or, it may be simply the dread of death. God says of all monsters, "But I made them just as I made you!"

Does Job get an answer? To the questions that plagues us, the questions of justice, of fairness, of proper retribution, the answer is probably, "No." The chaotic may be contained, but it is not fully eliminated. Behemoth and Leviathan still lurk out there. Though we spend a lot of our energy denying, or controlling, the tragic in life, children still drown, spouses succumb to cancer, friends are hit by drunk drivers. Whether on the grand scale of the tsunami or in the anonymous death of an indigent, there is little clarity. We may be impressed by God's performance, but not satisfied.

So did Job get an answer? In a different sense, yes he did. God did not leave Job alone in his agony. For a time, Job's challenge is met with a deafening silence. But, finally, God does respond. Like other great heroes of the faith, Abraham, Moses, and Elijah, Job goes face-to-face with God and lives to tell about it. God goes from the hidden God (*deus absconditus*) to the revealed God (*deus revelatus*).

But the God revealed in the whirlwind is still ambiguous. Yes, the order of creation is made clear and proper places are established — God is God and Job is Job! But is it enough? The natural world and our role in it may be clarified, but is the moral universe restored? The story, or folktale, makes an attempt at that. We note that in the end, Job gets it all back and more — his dignity, family, friends, and double his possessions. Of course, there is a certain naiveté to that end of the folk story, as though such things as family can be replaced, or such suffering forgotten. In MacLeish's play, *JB*, Nickles says, "Job won't take it! Job won't touch it! Job will fling it in God's face with half his guts to make it spatter!"[2] While such a response is understandable, we must acknowledge the human ability to persevere, as, for example, in Rwanda.

Just as after tragedy, with God's help one must learn to live again, to deal with memories, and go on with the story, so must Job. In fact, he becomes an intermediary, a priest, again. Just as he had made sacrifices for his children before his tragedy, now he must sacrifice on behalf of his comforters, who did not speak God's truth. So Job prays for them, and the Lord accepts Job's prayer (42:7-9).

Of course, we pray that our sufferings can be redeemed and that new beginnings can be made. Still, we know that it is never that simple! We may learn from a God who dwells in unapproachable majesty and reminds us of our place, and it is certainly helpful to know that behind the chaos is a God in control, but we are still left with that troublesome character of a God who banters with the tempter and permits his servant to be battered.

As we move to the New Testament lessons, we can move away from ambiguity, not to answers, but to paradox. Hebrews tells us that, in Jesus, we have a *great* high priest (4:14) who, like Job, makes sacrifices for us. In what sense is he great?

Hebrews says that Christ did not glorify himself, but was appointed by God to this task (5:5). So we look for the tasks God has for us. For Jesus, the task included sharing our humanity, as we learned last Sunday, tested in every way as we are, yet without sinning. Then we hear today, "In the days of his flesh, Jesus offered up prayers and supplications, with loud cries and tears, to the one who was able to save him from death" (5:7). Jesus shares that human agony that we know so well through the story of Job and our own stories.

Then it says, "and he *was heard* because of his reverent submission." Once again, if we think about it, it becomes more complicated. We know that he was *not* heard, if hearing means deliverance from the agony of death. So it must mean that God had a different plan, that God hears in a different way. There is no dramatic turn around as in Job, no doubling of abundance to make up for the loss, but rather a paradoxical plot. "Although he was a Son, he learned obedience through what he suffered" (5:8). His suffering was not an aberration, but a part of his perfection. This is God's way, salvation hidden in suffering, hope hidden in despair, life hidden in death.

In the gospel for today (Mark 10:35-45), this is what the disciples did not understand. They wanted the best seats in the house, but what they got was the cup of suffering. They wanted to be on the right and left, but what they got was the baptism unto death. This is God's way. "You know that among the Gentiles those whom they recognize as their rulers lord it over them, and their *great ones* [note that word again] are tyrants over them, but it is not so among you; but whoever wishes to become *great* among you must be your servant, and whoever wishes to be first among you must be slave of all. For the Son of Man came not to be served but to serve, and to give his life a ransom for many" (Mark 10:42-45 emphasis mine).

Jesus gives a counter-vision to the ethos of his day and of ours. Mark knew, from his encounter with Rome, that for an empire, the values are force, intimidation, and a network of patronage. For the kingdom of God, the values are suffering, submission, and servanthood.

But there is more to the story. Hebrews says of our priest, "And having been made perfect, he became the source of eternal salvation *for all* who obey him" (5:9). Our story has universal scope. All are invited to be a part of Christ's salvation.

Only when we reach the end of the story, can we see the full meaning; only through the cross and empty tomb are things fully redeemed. The God who speaks from the whirlwind is also the God who hangs on a cross for us. The God who created the universe, Leviathan and all, is the God who has redeemed and will restore it. The God who was hidden in deep darkness will be revealed to us in glory. Amen.

1. Robert Frost, *Selected Poems of Robert Frost* (New York: Holt, Rinehart and Winston, 1963), p. 201.

2. Archibald MacLeish, *JB* (Boston: Houghton Mifflin, 1956), p. 147.

Proper 25
Pentecost 23
Ordinary Time 30
Job 42:1-6, 10-17

All Is Restored?

Our text brings us to the climax of the book of Job. Last week, the denouement began in chapter 38, with the ominous voice of God speaking to Job out of the whirlwind: "Who is this that darkens counsel by words without knowledge? Gird up your loins like a man, I will question you, and you shall declare to me" (Job 38:2-3). Then, for two chapters, God thunders at Job, hammering away at his ignorance, his insignificance, his mere creatureliness. The sum of it is, "Shall a faultfinder contend with the Almighty? Anyone who argues with God must respond" (Job 40:2).

Job responds first by simply admitting his speechlessness. "See, I am of small account; what shall I answer you? I lay my hand on my mouth. I have spoken once, and I will not answer; twice, but will proceed no further" (Job 40:4-5). This is followed by two more chapters of divine rhetoric. By the time we are done with God's second speech, Job has been reminded of God's creation of the heavens and the earth, the whole natural world, the animal world, and even the mythical or primordial world, as symbolized by Behemoth and Leviathan! Once more Job responds, but this time with some substance.

The key to Job's response is given in terms of sight — or, in this case, we might say *insight*. We are familiar with the symbol of sight as used in the folk hymn, "Amazing Grace" — "I once was lost, but now am found; was blind, but now I see." Job contrasts his previous condition with his present sight by the adversative, "but." "But now my eye sees you" (v. 5b). How does Job characterize his previous condition?

First, he acknowledges that he was arguing out of ignorance. He quotes a line of God's (Job 42:3a), "Who is this that hides counsel without knowledge?" (see 38:2). Then he admits, "Therefore I have uttered what I did not understand, things too wonderful for me, which I did not know." This is simply an admission of ignorance.

Job begins his next point with another reference to God's speech. He quotes, "Hear, and I will speak; I will question you, and you declare to me" (v. 4). The second part of the sentence reflects 38:3b and 40:7b, but the first part seems to be a free parallel to the second, anticipating it and preparing for a contrast between hearing and seeing. God says, "Hear, and I will speak" just so Job can respond, "I had heard of you by the hearing of the ear, but now my eye sees you" (v. 5).

This could be a way of saying that hearing God is an inadequate form of knowledge compared to actually seeing God. So, we say, "seeing is believing." But it is more likely to be consequential. Having listened, as God had demanded, so now he can say he actually sees. We are all familiar with Job's plea for a "redeemer" and for a time when, in his own flesh, he should *see* God, "whom I shall see on my side, and my eyes shall behold, and not another" (Job 19:27). Finally, Job gets to see!

Certainly Job's claim of "having seen God" suggests a powerful encounter with God. To "see" God is rare in Israelite tradition (see Exodus 24:9-11) and to use that verb to describe his insight makes us take note. The result of this seeing is introduced by "therefore," after which we get "I despise myself, and repent in dust and ashes" (Job 42:6).

The verse is shocking and flies directly in the face of much of the human potential movement, which calls on us to "be all that you can be!" Despising oneself is the kind of groveling that no humanist can abide. So, in Archibald MacLeish's play, *JB*, the character Nickles characterizes Job's response:

> *Plays it the way a sheep would play it —*
> *Pious, contemptible, goddam sheep*
> *Without the spunk to spit on Christmas!*[1]

But the NRSV translation conceals some of the ambiguity that exists in the grammar of this sentence. The editors of the NRSV (Oxford Annotated Edition)[2] point out that the word "despise" normally requires an object, but none is present. It has to be supplied from the context. What is it that Job despises? Himself? His attitude or behavior? His arguments? And what does it mean to repent "in dust and ashes," since the phrase can refer simply to the human condition ("all we are is dust in the wind") or to human degradation (Job 30:19; Sirach 40:3).

It is certainly possible to see in this verse a strong rebuke of Job's previous audacity, contemporary humanism not withstanding. After all, acknowledging one's creatureliness and submitting to God's will, even without satisfactory answers for our rational demands, is not necessarily a betrayal of the human. Indeed, it could be understood as the first step toward becoming fully human. If God is truly to be God and we God's creatures, then it may be that we find ourselves only by losing ourselves.

At the same time, the verse could refer, not so much to a difference in essence between creator and creature as to a difference in understanding of the cosmos. Job may have been insisting on an interpretation of tragedy (dust and ashes), which would make sense within a neat and orderly moral universe. In that case, perhaps his reply could be paraphrased. "I retract my argument demanding justification. I recognize that within the universe there will always be Behemoth, causing destruction beyond human control (40:15 ff). There will always be Leviathan, thrashing about wreaking havoc (ch. 41). I repent (change my mind) of/about dust and ashes; i.e., there are no easy answers to the complicated human condition. I must trust that you are in control, but it is not easy to see."[3]

But, if the struggle is how to preserve God's divinity (God is, after all, God) while at the same time not losing God's justice or goodness, then it is hard to see how the second half of the text helps us out of this dilemma. Is it really enough to say that God is ultimately in charge of Leviathan, but has chosen, for now, only to set boundaries on the monster? That is the question that the first part of the text leaves us with.

When we turn to the second part of the text, we get a conclusion to the prose narrative, which set the stage for the book in the first two chapters. This conclusion may be as troubling as the other. Whereas the poetic section is full of complicated arguments befitting the complexities of the situation, the narrative itself seems to operate on a much simpler plane. God, in due time, will sustain and reward the pious.

In this concluding section of the narrative, we are told that everything in Job's life is restored and more. "And the Lord restored the fortunes of Job when he had prayed for his friends; and the Lord gave Job twice as much as he had before" (Job 42:10). Job's brothers and sisters and "all who had known him before" shared bread with him, comforting him and even giving him money and gold rings for a new start. "The Lord blessed the latter days of Job more than his beginning; and he had fourteen thousand sheep, six thousand camels, a thousand yoke of oxen, and a thousand donkeys. He also had seven sons and three daughters" (Job 42:12-13). This restored life was an exceedingly long one — 114 years — in which he got to see four generations of progeny!

While this latter section has the superficial sense of bringing a happy ending to the folktale — they lived happily ever after — it does not stand up well to the scrutiny of the poetic chapters in the middle. Even if we were to suspend our disbelief about such a reversal of fortune, we would find it somewhat hard to see how a new family can replace the old. Even more so, can such an ending really bring satisfaction in the light of all the complicated questions raised by Job and his comforters?

Did the compilers of the lectionary fail us by putting these two texts together? Although they create the opportunity for a great deal of musing about the human condition, and although one can use them to debate the nature and character of God, is there any gospel to be found? Where is the good news?

One way to go at it would to be to look at the verses in the narrative which are omitted by the lectionary.

> *After the Lord had spoken these words to Job, the Lord said to Eliphaz the Temanite: "My wrath is kindled*

against you and against your two friends; for you have not spoken of me what is right, as my servant Job has. Now therefore take seven bulls and seven rams, and go to my servant Job, and offer up for yourselves a burnt offering; and my servant Job shall pray for you, for I will accept his prayer not to deal with you according to your folly; for you have not spoken of me what is right, as my servant Job has done." So Eliphaz the Temanite and Bildad the Shuhite and Zophar the Naamathite went and did what the Lord had told them; and the Lord accepted Job's prayer. And the Lord restored the fortunes of Job when he had prayed for his friends.

— Job 42:7-10

According to this text, Job is portrayed as a righteous one, pleasing to God, who has spoken rightly about God. That, of course, does not correspond to the combative Job that we have seen in the poetic section, but to the docile Job of the folktale. In this conclusion to the folktale, Job is assigned the task of a priest who is able to restore the comforters in God's sight by praying for them and making sacrifice. Even though God is angry with them ("my wrath is kindled" — v. 7), God provides for their restoration through the priestly function of Job. This God is not aloof or detached, but is concerned about providing priests for the sake of reconciliation.

This same concern for salvation through a priestly function can be found in the second lesson for today, Hebrews 7:23-28. The letter presents Christ as our great high priest, appointed by God and able to sympathize with our weakness. "For it was fitting that we should have such a high priest, holy, blameless, undefiled, separated from sinners, and exalted above the heavens" (Hebrews 7:26).

Hebrews takes pains to show that the priesthood that Christ exercises is far superior to the Levitical priesthood. In this lesson, the first point of superiority is longevity. "Furthermore, the former priests were many in number, because they were prevented by death from continuing in office; but he holds his priesthood permanently, because he continues forever" (Hebrews 7:23-24). This means that he is eternally available as our intercessor. "Consequently he is able for all time to save those who approach God through him, since he always lives to make intercession for them" (Hebrews 7:25).

The second point of comparison is the "once-for-all" nature of his sacrifice. "Unlike the other high priests, he has no need to offer sacrifices day after day, first for his own sins, and then for those of the people; this he did once for all when he offered himself" (Hebrews 7:27).

In addition to these Christological insights from Hebrews, we can also make a point of contact with the Jesus of the gospel lesson for today, the healing of blind Bartimaeus (Mark 10:46-52). The miracle story comes as the conclusion to the third passion prediction unit which Mark sets up (10:32-45). First Jesus predicts his passion (10:31-34), then James and John show their misunderstanding by seeking greatness (10:35-40), followed by Jesus' reference to true greatness as servanthood (10:41-45). It is after this section, with its call for *insight*, that we get the story of Bartimaeus receiving his sight from Jesus, accompanied by the words, "Go; your faith has made you well" (10:52).

Just as Job was brought to sight by God's revelation ("but now my eye sees you" — 42:5b), and just as Bartimaeus regained his sight "immediately," so we are called to a new vision of God, one that goes beyond the realization of the great gulf between creator and creature. It is a vision of a God who, despite the fact that we are "dust and ashes," made provision for our salvation through our great high priest, who offered himself, once for all, for our sins. Like Bartimaeus, we too cry out, "Jesus, have mercy on me." To us, Jesus says, "Go; your faith has made you well." Like Bartimaeus, then, let us "follow him on the way." Amen.

---

1. Archibald MacLeish, *JB* (Boston: Houghton Mifflin, 1956), p. 136.

2. *The New Oxford Annotated Bible* (New York: Oxford University Press, 1991), p. 672.

3. This is essentially the argument of Carol A. Newsome in *The New Interpreter's Bible*, Vol. IV (Nashville: Abingdon Press, 1996), pp. 628-629.

Reformation Day
Jeremiah 31:31-34

God Begins Anew

In some ways the Old Testament lesson today (Jeremiah 31:31-34) may seem rather strange for Reformation Sunday. It speaks of law more than gospel and it is futuristic rather than realized. Still, it does speak of the sure saving will of God! It is that will which will result in a new covenant to go with the new act of salvation about to be accomplished by the Lord, namely the return from exile. That saving will of God is phrased beautifully in verse 34, "for I will forgive their iniquity and remember their sin no more." When we trust in that promise, we will know the freedom so essential to the Reformation.

That great freedom is spoken of in the gospel lesson for Reformation Sunday (John 8:31-36) as follows, "Then Jesus said to the Jews who had believed in him, 'If you continue in my word, you are truly my disciples; and you will know the truth, and the truth will make you free.' " Jesus says, "the truth will *make you* free." That assumes you are not now free, but need to be *made* free. Then, true to Johannine technique, the hearers misunderstand Jesus and initiate a dialogue. Jesus is talking about spiritual bondage, while they hear him referring to historical bondage. "We are descendants of Abraham and have never been slaves to anyone. What do you mean by saying, 'You will be made free'?"

The irony is that, even if you interpret freedom in a historical sense, they are not telling the truth. Israel's history contains a *number* of examples of forced bondage. So, for example, when Jeremiah wrote his oracles, they were directed to an Israel that was in bondage to Babylonia. Not only were they in physical bondage, it is clear that Jeremiah saw the people in spiritual bondage, also. Jeremiah said, "The heart is devious above all else; it is perverse — who can understand it?" (17:9). In other words, we are prisoners of our own opposition to God. In our walk through life, we always go astray; we cannot direct our own steps (10:23). Jeremiah asks, "Can Ethiopians change their skin or leopards their spots?" (13:23).

This same human perversity is addressed by Paul in the second lesson for today, Romans 3:19-28. Paul says "For there is no distinction, since all have sinned and fall short of the glory of God" (Romans 3:22b-23). This is the same bondage referred to by Jesus when he says, "Truly, truly I say to you, everyone who commits sin is a slave to sin" (John 8:34). We all fail God and neighbor, we bow down to idols, and we share in the brokenness of existence. Whether we live in pride or in guilt, in denial or in indifference, we are in bondage. So "every mouth may be silenced, and the whole world be held accountable to God" (Romans 8:19b). But Jesus says, "The truth will make you free." We are free when we acknowledge our bondage and receive God's freedom as a gift. "Then what becomes of boasting? It is excluded!" (Romans 8:27a).

The answer to bondage is found, not in hapless human boasting, but in the sure saving will of God. We turn to the first lesson, Jeremiah 31:31-34, to learn more about that saving will. It begins with a common formula reflecting that hope in God's salvation: "The days are surely coming, says the Lord." We may be unfaithful to the covenant, but God is not. *Surely* these coming days will be marked by the action of God! The Lord says, "I will make a new covenant with you" (29:11; 24:6-7; 32:39; 33:26). Note that it is purely objective; it is given without reason or explanation. I will do it! It comes out of the resolve that God has for the relation with Israel.

God defines the covenant first by contrast. "It will not be like the covenant I made with their ancestors" — referring to the exodus, when Israel was brought out of Egypt. "... a covenant that they broke," God notes, "though I was their husband" (v. 32). The word Jeremiah chooses for "husband" is Ba'al, which is also "Lord." Of course, it has sexist overtones, but it makes one think of all the other lords, or husbands (the Baals as they were called), which were part of the neighboring cults. Then we are reminded how often Israel played the unfaithful partner "on every high hill and under every green tree" (Jeremiah 2:20).

It is because of this radical infidelity, this tremendous rupture of relationship, that God says, "I will make a new covenant." This is the only time in the Old Testament that the adjective "new" modifies covenant. Elsewhere the Bible speaks of a new heart or a new spirit (Ezekiel 36:26); or of new things that God will do (Isaiah 42:9), but when the covenant is spoken of, it is usually a matter of "remembering." But here the estrangement is so dreadful, the apostasy so irreparable, that there must be a new covenant — but God has the capacity to begin anew.

It says that God will make a covenant with Israel, "after those days," for example, after God has made the first step by bringing Israel back from the Babylonian bondage. How, then, is the covenant described? "I will put my law within them, and I will write it on their hearts."

The commandments will no longer be an external rule that invites hostility. No longer can the law be co-opted by a perverse human will (the law always kills). Instead, it will be internalized, a natural function of a new identity, as natural as breathing. That solidarity between Yahweh and Israel is addressed with a restatement of the covenantal formula: "... and I will be their God, and they shall be my people."

With such a transformation of the people, there will be full knowledge of God. "No longer shall they teach one another, or say to each other, 'Know the Lord,' for they shall all know me, from the least of them to the greatest, says the Lord" (v. 34).

To know God is a multifaceted matter. What would it mean to know God? Having referred to Yahweh as husband to Israel, there is of course that dimension of knowing that suggests deep marital intimacy. It also means to know the story, to be in touch with the tradition, to be faithful in the life of worship — to the liturgy. Finally, it is clear that for Israel, to know Yahweh meant to do justice and righteousness. "Is not this to know me? says the Lord. To judge the cause of the poor and needy!" (22:16 cf).

This knowledge of Yahweh, this closeness to the Lord, is not for a select group of religious, but for all Israel. We have heard that the covenant is for both the north and the south, for Israel and Judah; here, we hear that they shall all know me, from the least to the greatest.

It can be for all because it is not dependent on any human qualifications. It is an objective grace! God has decided and God will do it. God must break the cycle of sin and punishment, which had become endemic. No matter how loud the cry for punishment, no matter how attractive the lure of law may seem as a solution, no matter how convinced we may be that we are secure in our own righteousness, God does not go that way. God breaks the cycle of sin and punishment, not by increasing the penalty, not by showing strength, but by showing mercy. "For I will forgive their iniquity, and remember their sin no more."

As Christians, we believe that God has broken this cycle in the cross of Jesus Christ. This is, above all, the new thing God is doing in the world. Not some cheap grace, promoting forgiveness without penitence, baptism without discipline, communion without confession. This is a costly grace, for it cost God the life of the Son.[1] This is a theology of the cross in which God is not a spectator above the fray, but incarnate deeply within it.

Sin and death are not dealt with by denial, optimism, or positive thinking, but by a life and death struggle that ends on a cross. God did not become some sort of ideal person, but the person we do not want to be: broken, outcast, and accursed. The cross is God in Christ being dehumanized, abandoned, and crucified for us. This is not some denial of the awful reality of our existence, but an embracing of it. The Son suffers the dying, the Father suffers the death of the Son — and all for us.

So this is how we know God. "God is not greater than he is in this humiliation. God is not more glorious than he is in this self-surrender. God is not more powerful than he is in this helplessness. God is not more divine than he is in this humanity."[2] It is the truth of this cross that *sets us free*. As Jesus says, "If you continue in my word, you are truly my disciples; and you will know the truth, and the truth will set you free" (John 8:31b-32).

We are set free from sin and death, from the vicious circles of our existence. If we know God is in the darkness, we do not need to be in the spotlight. If we know God is in the depths, we do not need to step on others to climb higher. If we know God has broken the back of death, we do not need to save our skins through detachment, denial, or violence. We do not need to be afraid of that which is different, the other, the alien, the stranger. Instead, we follow the example of God's love for us in Christ. God loves what is sinful, bad, foolish, weak, and hateful, in order to make it beautiful, good, wise, and righteous. "Therefore sinners are attractive because they are loved; they are not loved because they are attractive."[3] Amen.

---

1. Dietrich Bonhoeffer from *Dietrich Bonhoeffer, Discipleship* (Minneapolis: Fortress Press, 2001), pp. 44-45. This has been paraphrased.

2. Jürgen Moltmann, *The Crucified God* (New York: Harper and Row, 1974), p. 205.

3. Martin Luther, *Heidelberg Disputation*, vol. 31 of *Luther's Works*, ed. Harold Grimm (Philadelphia: Muhlenberg Press, 1957), p. 57.

All Saints
Isaiah 25:6-9

Death Is Swallowed Up Forever

All Saints is a time to celebrate the victory over death we share with all the saints and our risen Lord. Still, we must never think that victory is an easy one. Death is an overwhelming power that interrupts our communion with God and with one another. It is the destroyer of all that is true and good. Israel had known that power at work in her own communal disaster, the destruction of Jerusalem. Those kings anointed to be shepherds of Israel fleeced the sheep, and those appointed to care for the welfare of the lowly sought their own glory instead. Those who were supposed to be true to Yahweh played the harlot. The judgment of God was the military destruction of Jerusalem and the Babylonian captivity.

Still, death held sway, for the Babylonian captors were arrogant and ruthless, becoming the very epitome of a destructive dynasty in the eyes of the prophet. In the beginning of our chapter, the prophet anticipates the end to all such dynastic death dealers. The prophet praises the Lord and says, "For you have made the city a heap, the fortified city a ruin; the palace of aliens is a city no more, it will never be rebuilt" (Isaiah 25:2).

The death of the symbolic city is not to suggest that we are given instead some romantic view of rural isolation or independence. The rise of urban life was meant to be for the good of the whole. It was meant to beat back the darkness and gain control. People built cities, put walls around them, and moved into their protecting shadow to keep themselves safe from marauders, human or otherwise. The countryside is not very romantic when there is no security! The city provided stability, control, and safety —

and a sheriff, or an army. It also encouraged creativity, the growth of culture, and a sense of unity.

However, it was possible for the city to be co-opted. The city can become, like Babylon, the epitome of wealth, arrogance, power, and exploitation. Then the prophet says, God will judge the imperial city and it will become a heap, a ruin, a disaster. Like the burned-out portions of Beirut or Baghdad, it will be reduced to rubble.

Then comes the promise of a different city, a New Jerusalem. The promise begins, "On this mountain...." The mountain is the temple mount, Zion city of our God, the heart of Judah. It is Jerusalem, built as a city bound firmly together, to which the tribes of the Lord go up. It is Jerusalem the golden, with milk and honey blessed. *That* Jerusalem will be restored!

After the restoration, the next move is to feasting, to a banquet. "On this mountain the Lord of hosts will make for all peoples a feast of rich food" (25:6). A sumptuous banquet is used as a symbol of what God plans for us. The description, of course, is time bound — a feast of well-aged wines, of rich food filled with marrow ("Yuck," the kids say), of well-aged wines strained clear. Of course, you have to translate it into your own desirable form of cuisine (my entree is lobster) — though I doubt if fast food will qualify!

This banquet should not be seen as an escape, as self-indulgence, or a place to be seen, the way we often pervert our mealtimes. It is not a fund-raiser where the wealthy gather and pay big money to protect what they have. Rather, it is to be seen as relief from the ultimate acquisitiveness of the city, as nourishment for the whole person, as a Eucharist to God. It is a banquet of justice, peace, and community. It is not restricted. Not just Israel, but the nations are invited. It says, "The Lord will make for *all peoples* a feast." All peoples, all nations, all faces — clearly the prophet is striving for an inclusive invitation.

Then that image is broadened. In addition to this wonderful feast, "And he will destroy on this mountain the shroud that is cast over all peoples, the sheet that is spread over all nations; he will swallow up death forever" (v. 7).

Death is overcome. Death, which snatches away loved ones, which frightens us with its arbitrariness, which gloats over its finality, which leaves us cold and empty. Death, which circumscribes life, which negates well-being, which limits our community with one another and with God. Isaiah promises that God will swallow up this death, like a great sea creature consuming a bait fish, or like a tiger effortlessly disposing of its prey. The Bible is fond of the image of Leviathan, the great monster of chaos, the very symbol of death, devouring all it meets. Here, the tables are turned! Here God swallows up death forever. The image is picked up by Paul (1 Corinthians 15:54), when he says, "Death is swallowed up in victory."

When death has been swallowed up, the Lord God will wipe away the tears from all faces. It is a comforting image that gets reaffirmed by the Seer in the second lesson, Revelation 21:1-6a: "See, the home of God is among mortals. He will dwell with them; they will be his peoples, and God himself will be with them; he will wipe every tear from their eyes." Then there will be no cause for sadness, no sense of loss, and no occasion for mourning.

"For this we have waited," Isaiah says; and again, "This is the Lord for whom we have waited" (25:9). All of this happens on *that day*, which is a coming day. Judah saw a return from exile and a restoration of Jerusalem. But still, there were those who rejected the inclusive offer, who clung to dynasty, who chose arrogance.

The church, then, hoped for another intervention and the fulfillment of that hope in Jesus. The point of the gospel story today (John 11:32-44), the raising of Lazarus, is that God was at work in Jesus Christ in order to destroy death and bring life and immortality to light. God invades the territory of death to snatch Lazarus back, to show where the real power lies. But not without honesty!

Jesus says of Lazarus, "Unbind him, and let him go." The body of Lazarus had been wrapped in linen strips liberally laced with spices, according to Jewish custom. Even spices could not contain the corruption, which Martha recognizes in her warning to Jesus: "He has been dead already for four days; by now he stinks!" That is the reality Jesus faced — the reality we all face. That is the bondage and power of death. But Jesus says, "Unbind him, and let him go."

That is our hope, but we know it only in faith. For Lazarus must still die; and Jesus also. The story tells us that, from that day on, the authorities were determined to kill Jesus. The point is, if you promote true life in this world, you will surely stir up the forces of death. The Jesus who trembled at Lazarus' grave will tremble in his own garden of death. He will lie lost and silent in his own tomb, cut off from the land of the living. So still we wait.

The cross is his victory and the tomb is empty. "He is not here, he is risen," the angel will say. God has said, "Yes" to the cross and, "No" to death. The cry with which Jesus calls Lazarus out of the grave is only an echo of the call that called to life Jesus, the firstfruit, and will call us forth also. For the trumpet will sound and the dead will be raised and we shall be saved.

In the meantime, we live in hope. It is a hope expressed in endlessly beautiful and challenging visions in the book of the Revelation of John. The first image is cosmic. "I saw a new heaven and a new earth" — a restoration of creation, a return to paradise, a starting over. "And the sea was no more." The sea had always been a place for practicing devastation and exploitation. Rome had used it to dominate trading, to subjugate peoples, to support its legions. So it symbolized chaos, the home of the sea monsters, Leviathan of the deep. But now, the sea is no more!

Instead of the sea, we have the river of life flowing from the throne of God. Water nourishing the tree of life, whose leaves work for the healing of the nations. This is the water that corresponds to baptism. It is our access to the new life in Christ. It is in this new life in Christ that we rejoice through our baptism. Baptism snatches us from the chaotic waters, washes us clean, and incorporates us into Christ. The shroud is snatched away, death is swallowed up forever, and we are set free. Though for now our faces may be stained with the hard tears of grief, we believe that they will be finally wiped away forever.

In churches where the cemetery is out back, it was often the custom that they would take the water after baptism and pour it on the next gravesite as a sign that God has overcome death. Not having such a cemetery in the back, our baptismal water is poured out on the ground. But as with all water, it will go back to its task of nourishing God's creation with new life.

Then, the next image in the Apocalypse is urban, just as in Isaiah. "I saw the holy city, the new Jerusalem, coming down out of heaven from God"; not the product of human efforts, for all is gift. Just when you might think you would get a glowing picture in architectural terms, it switches metaphors and becomes marital. "Prepared as a bride adorned for her husband." Jerusalem is the bride, the people of God, and is adorned gorgeously, waiting for the bridegroom to escort her to the wedding banquet, that feast of rich foods, of well-aged wines, that Eucharist of thanksgiving. It will be the feast of a community that lives entirely with God and draws its life from God.

That is the God who then speaks from the throne. "I heard a loud voice from the throne saying: See, the home of God is among mortals" (Revelation 21:3). No longer does God reign as the Holy One in unapproachable distance; rather, this God is very near. God will dwell with them and they will be God's people. Then, in the image used in Isaiah, "God will wipe every tear from their eyes."

Because death is no more, so mourning and crying and pain will be no more; for the first things have passed away. God is in charge and makes all things new. It is then sealed with a promise, the promise of one who has conquered death: "Write this, for these words are trustworthy and true." Then he said to me, "It is done! I am the Alpha and the Omega, the beginning and the end" (vv. 5c-6). Amen.

Proper 26
Pentecost 24
Ordinary Time 31
Ruth 1:1-18

Your God Shall Be My God

Like the short story that gave structure to the book of Job, so the book of Ruth is considered to be a finely honed literary piece, often called a novella. It is meant to exhibit exemplary behavior. Just as Job proved faithful through good fortune and ill, so the characters in the book of Ruth are equally laudatory.

The story starts with an Israelite family in the time of the judges. (This historical setting becomes the reason that Ruth was put right after the book of Judges in the Septuagint.) This family consists of Elimelech, his wife Naomi, and their two sons, Mahlon and Chilion. There is a famine in Judah, but they hear that there is bread in Moab, so they seek refuge there. While there, Elimelech dies, but the sons marry Moabite women, Ruth and Orpah. Both marriages apparently remain childless and, after ten years, both the sons of Elimelech die, leaving the three widows, Naomi, Ruth, and Orpah, alone with no support.

The theme, so far, is one of emptiness and barrenness — empty bread baskets, empty wombs. There was no social safety net in those days. The assumption was that everyone would marry, that they would have some sons, and that the old people would be supported by their sons. Of course, it did not always work out that way. Women often survived their husbands and, if there were no sons to care for her, such a widow became a symbol of the destitute and powerless, along with orphans.

When Naomi hears that the famine in Judah has eased — "that the Lord had considered his people and given them food" (1:6b) — she decides she will be better off at home than in a land where she is a foreigner. Her two daughters-in-law, Orpah and Ruth, start to go with her. But Naomi said to each of the women, "Go back each of you to your mother's house." Assuming that they will find husbands and remarry, she says, "May the Lord deal kindly with you, as you have dealt with the dead and with me. The Lord grant that you may find security, each of you in the house of your husband." Naomi realizes that her daughters-in-law will be aliens in Judah, while in Moab they can be at home.

At first, Orpah and Ruth resist. "No," they say, "we will return with you to your people." Naomi tries to persuade them. "Why will you go with me? Do I still have sons in my womb that they may become your husbands?" This reflects the expectation in Jewish law that a surviving brother would marry a deceased brother's wife! What are the chances of Naomi remarrying and having more sons to carry out this duty? She goes on, "Even if I thought there was hope for me, even if I should have a husband tonight and bear sons, would you then wait until they were grown?" The situation seems totally hopeless.

Orpah is persuaded and leaves, but Ruth persists. She is given those memorable lines, "Do not press me to leave you or to turn back from following you! Where you go, I will go; where you lodge, I will lodge; your people shall be my people, and your God my God. Where you die, I will die — there will I be buried" (1:16-17a). Ruth is persistent in her faithfulness, despite the persuasive arguments of Naomi. She even takes a vow, saying, "May the Lord do thus and so to me, and more as well, if even death parts me from you!" (Ruth 1:17). Then Naomi relents.

These words reflect a commitment not only to a mother-in-law, Naomi, but also to a God, Yahweh, and to a people, Israel. Thus the story is celebrating not only Ruth's duty and the responsibility she feels to Naomi, but also her commitment to a whole tradition.

A generation ago, however, these words of faithfulness were put into a wedding song and turned in such a way that they became words spoken by the bride to the groom, promising obedience and faithfulness. "Whither thou goest, I will go; and whither thou lodgest, I will lodge. Thy people shall be my people, my love."

Now, there is nothing wrong with pledging faithfulness. After all, each couple has hard decisions to make — where they will live, whom they will worship, and how these decisions are to be made. Faithfulness can only help in such a situation. That wedding song sounded like a vow made just by the woman, like a one-way street, with no promises by the groom. That would be difficult to justify today.

We have to beware of taking a text out of context and twisting the tradition to fit our interests or needs. But, even when we do consider the context, we realize that the history of a tradition, or the stages it has gone through, may allow various possible interpretations. So, for example, Ruth, a Moabite woman, is portrayed so graciously that some suggest it is meant to counter the narrow particularism that characterized Israel after the return from exile (see Ezra and Nehemiah). Or, because at the conclusion of the story we are told that Ruth bore a child named Obed, who was to become the grandfather of David (4:17), the story may have served to flesh out the genealogy of David.

Our interpretation today, however, is constrained by the fact that, in our text, we are given only the opening part of the drama. Out text lacks the complexities that the developing plot will entail. It puts all its stress on the commitment Ruth makes to Naomi and her tradition. "Do not press me to leave you or to turn back from following you! Where you go, I will go; where you lodge, I will lodge; your people shall be my people, and your God my God. Where you die, I will die — there will I be buried" (Ruth 1:16b-17a). It is that commitment that we are left to work with.

Giving up one's tradition, family, and gods for the sake of another would have been seen as a large loss in a traditional society marked by strong communal commitments. In our day, however, seldom is a person's tradition taken that seriously. The opposite tends to be true. We live in an age where there is growing biblical illiteracy and a lack of familiarity with our western, Christian traditions. We may stress tolerance of the traditions of others, while we ourselves seldom seriously practice our own.

We have to assume that, from the standpoint of the first readers of this book, what Ruth did was considered very laudable and a testimony to the high caliber of the Israelite religion. Israel, after all, was very particularistic. They were a people who understood themselves to be chosen and blessed; therefore, this story shows the type of piety and commitment that should be emulated by all who came in contact with that faith.

We know from the gospel for today (Mark 12:28-34) that the heart of that tradition was what we know as the *Shema*, the Hebrew word for "hear" in the imperative. The story says that a scribe asked Jesus to name the commandment which is first of all. Jesus went right to Deuteronomy 6:4-5. Jesus answered, "The first is, 'Hear, O Israel: the Lord our God, the Lord is one; you shall love the Lord your God with all your heart, and with all your soul, and with all your mind, and with all your strength' " (Mark 12:29-30). To that Jesus adds, as was customary, "You shall love your neighbor as yourself" (Mark 12:31; see also Leviticus 19:18).

How serious these commands were for the tradition one can see by the obligations placed upon the observant Jew. "Keep these words that I am commanding you today in your heart. Recite them to your children and talk about them when you are at home and when you are away, when you lie down and when you rise" (Deuteronomy 6:6-7). Thus, every morning and evening the pious, observant Jew recited the *Shema*.

Moses commanded, "Bind them as a sign on your hand, fix them as an emblem on your forehead, and write them on the doorposts of your house and on your gates" (Deuteronomy 6:8-9). Since these words were taken both seriously and literally, little leather boxes were made into which were inserted pieces of paper with the texts written on them. These boxes were attached to leather thongs, so they could, indeed, be bound to hand and forehead when praying. In addition, the words were put into little metal cylinders to be attached to the doorpost. Such a *mezuzah* is frequently seen at the door of Jewish households.

Such symbolic actions are reminders that commitment to the God of Israel was to be at the heart of existence — in the home, with the family, beginning each day, ending each day, going in and out of the house — all of life was to be so ordered.

An ideal representative of such faithfulness was a rabbi of the first century, Rabbi Akiba, who was martyred by the Romans. When they took him out to kill him, it was the time of the day to say the *Shema*. As they were tearing the living flesh off his bones with hooks of iron, he began to recite this sacred creed. His disciples were astonished and said, "Master, even here?" He replied, "Now I understand what it means, to love God with all thy soul." Then he held out the last words, "the Lord is one," until he died.[1]

It is such a pious, faithful commitment to a tradition that Ruth illustrates also when she decides to follow her mother-in-law back to Judah. How are we to apply such an idealistic story?

Part of the beauty of our salvation is its universality — it is *for all*; but only in a complex and paradoxical way. For, as much as we desire a God who is universal, it is in the nature of God's work to be particular. God makes choices. God chose Israel; God did not choose Egypt, Assyria, or Phoenicia! God is very particular on behalf of Israel. God promises to come with recompense against those oppressing Israel — to right the wrong, to order chaos, to bring hope to you, O Israel. This is the particular! God is particular for the sake of the universal. God chose Israel for the sake of the nations. Just so, God works through Jesus, a particular person in time and place, for the salvation of the whole world.

Our culture is far removed from such a concern for the whole. Society glorifies individualism while community withers. Social clubs, political parties, workers guilds, and even families are in decline. When the church conforms to this trend, it becomes just one more venue for a pleasant experience or a spiritual escape. "I guess I am a Christian," we say, "but I am not a fanatic about it!" That usually means, if you stopped going to church, no one would notice or care. The church is just a random collection of people who happen to make the same choice that Sunday. Not much is expected of you.

The church is not a voluntary organization, which needs to mimic the world in order to get and keep members. It is the body of Christ and there is nothing "individual" about it. In the body, we are members one of another. When you bring your children to baptism, you give them to the church. You give them away to Christ and to the body of Christ — so the church shares responsibility for them. The church must be honest with them. The church will say to them, "We don't live by fad and fancy, for we are a different people." This is our story, not that; this is our standard, not that.

Jesus comes to give us a story we can live and die by. That is what we celebrate today — the story of the gospel! You can't teach doubt and disbelief to children. What they want is stories. Here we have a better story than the stories of the world — the story of the culture (who wants to be an American Idol?), the story of the market (what will be the best seller this Christmas?), the story of the media (who has pulled ahead in the presidential horse race?).

There is no story nearly as good as the story of God's love for us in Jesus Christ. God's victory over sin and death in the cross of Christ is the one story that really matters. It is a story to which, like Ruth, we can pledge our all. Amen.

---

1. David R. Cartlidge and David L. Dungan, *Documents for the Study of the Gospels* (Philadelphia: Fortress Press, 1980), p. 185.

Proper 27
Pentecost 25
Ordinary Time 32
Ruth 3:1-5; 4:13-17

From Emptiness To Fullness

Today, we learn from two women. The first is the woman we met last week, Ruth. Her story takes up a whole book of the Bible. We hear her speak, listen in on her deliberations, and follow her story. The second woman is nameless and speechless. She appears in only one short vignette in Mark and functions as an object lesson that Jesus uses in the gospel narrative. We are to learn from what she does. They are rather different stories, but they have two things in common: They are both about widows and they are both about values.

The story of Ruth requires a quick review. Naomi and her two daughters-in-law, Ruth and Orpah, find themselves widowed and childless. When Naomi hears that the famine in Judah has eased, she decides she will be better off there than in Moab. She encourages her daughters-in-law to stay in their homeland of Moab and start anew. Orpah is finally persuaded, but Ruth is not. Ruth is given those memorable lines, "Do not press me to leave you or to turn back from following you! Where you go, I will go; where you lodge, I will lodge; your people shall be my people, and your God my God. Where you die, I will die — there will I be buried" (Ruth 1:16, 17a). With that, Naomi relents.

When they get to Judah, to the town of Bethlehem, Naomi recognizes the bitterness of their situation. She says, "I went away full, but the Lord has brought me back empty" (Ruth 1:21). In the face of this emptiness, Ruth sets out to keep the two of them alive by gleaning in the fields behind the reapers. It was a custom during harvest not to be so miserly as to gather up every bit of grain, but to let that which is missed lie there for the poor to pick up (not unlike the Canadian Geese that clean up the grain in the fields). In the course of her gleaning, a wealthy farmer named Boaz notices her and deals kindly with her, making sure that she is protected and gets sent home with plenty of grain.

At that time, Naomi apparently remembers that her dead husband, Elimelech, happened to have a relative, that same Boaz who had been kind to Ruth. She also realizes that she should try to find security for Ruth, who has been so faithful. So she has a plan for Ruth. "See, our kinsman Boaz will be winnowing barley tonight at the threshing floor. Now wash and anoint yourself, and put on your best clothes (be attractive or desirable), and go down to the threshing floor" (3:2b-3 cf). Now here comes the important point. Don't make yourself known to the man while he is preoccupied with work, tired, and dirty. But wait until he has finished eating and drinking. "When he lies down, observe the place where he lies; then, go and uncover his feet and lie down; and he will tell you what to do" (v. 4).

Now all of this may appear quite rough around the edges, a bit crude, and certainly seductive! But we need to remember that Naomi knew there was a certain family obligation here — Boaz could be "next-of-kin," as the NRSV translates it, or the "one with the right to redeem," which is the alternative translation given in the margin. This designates the kinsman who was expected to marry the wife of a deceased member of the family, a kind of kinsman/redeemer.

In addition, there was a certain lack or emptiness in both their lives — Boaz being a bachelor and Ruth a childless widow. What Naomi was doing was playing the go between, the matchmaker (think of the matchmaker in *Fiddler On The Roof*). What is important is the response of Boaz when he awoke to what was obviously a pleasant surprise.

First, he wants clarification. "Who are you?" She answered, "I am Ruth, your servant; spread the cloak of your servant, for you are next-of-kin [kinsman/redeemer]" (v. 9). Boaz sees her action as a sign of her loyalty to Naomi and to the tradition. He calls her a worthy woman for not seeking simply a rich young man, then he promises to see how he can faithfully fulfill his role as next-of-kin.

Before he can go further, Boaz must clear up what seems to be some confusion about what his rights and duties were compared to another, unnamed kinsman/redeemer. The situation is explained to this unnamed rival. He can claim the field that had belonged to Elimelech but now belongs to his widow, Naomi; but, in order to claim the field, he must take Ruth as his wife also (4:1-5). At this, the [rival] next-of-kin says, "I cannot redeem it for myself without damaging my own inheritance. Take my right of redemption yourself, for I cannot redeem it" (Ruth 4:6).

With that cleared up, our text continues the story: So Boaz took Ruth and she became his wife. "When they came together, the Lord made her conceive, and she bore a son. Then the women said to Naomi, 'Blessed be the Lord, who has not left you this day without next-of-kin; and may his name be renowned in Israel! He shall be to you a restorer of life and a nourisher of your old age; for your daughter-in-law who loves you, who is more to you than seven sons, has borne him' " (4:13-15).

So we see how the story has moved from barrenness to birth, from famine to feasting, from emptiness to fullness. All of this is attributed to the goodness of the Lord. Ruth has entrusted herself to the Lord and has not been disappointed. It sounds a bit like Job, doesn't it, where he gets it all back in the end? "And they lived happily ever after!" We know there is much truth to the story; it would not have lasted this long if there were not. Still, as with Job, we need to contextualize it, or complicate it, in order to avoid a shallow treatment. We can do that by looking at the gospel for today, the story of the widow's mite (Mark 12:38-44).

The story of the widow is set in the context of a judgment on material greed and preoccupation with self. There are those, like certain scribes of Jesus' day, who demand respect, walk around in long robes, and take the best seats at banquets. They even devour widows' houses, then say long prayers for appearance. Today, we dress by the dictates of fashion, buy private boxes at stadiums, ride in limousines, let the market devour widows' pensions, and use religion as a veneer for our evil. Jesus says, "They will have the greater condemnation."

Then Jesus sits down opposite the temple treasury and watches people throw in their coins. The receptacle was made of brass and shaped like a horn, so when you threw your coins in, they would make a sound as they rolled in. Many rich people put in large sums (you can imagine the racket); then a poor widow came and put in two small coins (mites), worth only a penny. Jesus makes the point, "Truly I tell you, this poor widow has put in more than all those who are contributing to the treasury. For all of them have contributed out of their abundance; but she, out of her poverty, has put in everything she had, all she had to live on" (Mark 12:43-44).

Most of us know what abundance is. We have disposable income, money not needed for necessities, which we dispense with easily. How affluent we are is obvious from our language. Watch how the word "luxury" has become a key selling point: luxury condominiums; the luxury hotel, with all the amenities; the car with all the add-ons. Then there are the private storage bins for all we have that won't fit in our homes. So we know what it is to give out of our abundance, but she gave out of her poverty!

What are we to make of this poor widow, with no obvious means of support, who gives out of her emptiness? Empty womb, empty pockets — but she puts in everything she had, all she had to live on. It challenges us to consider the very meaning of life. At the same time, her story also complicates our consideration, for we realize that, despite her sacrificial offering, she remains just a poor widow. There is no sudden reversal; the temple treasury does not suddenly pour wealth in her lap as though she had hit the jackpot. There is no kinsman/redeemer waiting in the wings — except for the Lord himself.

Jesus has already shown the light of truth on our world. He teaches us the true meaning of fullness and emptiness. Those who promote themselves, devour widows' houses, and gild it all with the pretense of piety — they will receive the greater condemnation. They are dry and empty. But Psalm 146, our psalm for today, gives words to our values. We have a God:

> *... who executes justice for the oppressed; who gives food to the hungry. The Lord sets the prisoners free; the Lord opens the eyes of the blind. The Lord lifts up those who are bowed down; the Lord loves the righteous. The Lord watches over the strangers; he upholds the orphan and the widow, but the way of the wicked he brings to ruin.* — Psalm 146:7-9

It is to this Lord that we are invited to turn, first of all in our guilt and complicity, for we have been willing participants in this world of false values. At the same time, we turn to the Lord also in our helplessness. The second lesson for today, from the letter to the Hebrews (9:24-28), points us to Christ, who is our true kinsman/redeemer. It says that Christ presents himself to God "on our behalf" (v. 24). Unlike the high priest, who had to make sacrifice year after year with blood not his own, Christ has appeared once for all at the end of the age (this is the decisive move) to remove sin by the sacrifice of himself. For you, for me, for all!

Then, the application is made one more time. "And just as it is appointed for mortals to die once, and after that the judgment (our lives are not without consequence), so Christ, having been offered once to bear the sins of many, will appear a second time, not to deal with sin, but to save those who are eagerly waiting for him" (Hebrews 9:27-28).

That is our hope — to be redeemed and set free — to live with trust in God and in God's promise. So, we sing with the psalmist,

> *Happy are those whose help is the God of Jacob, whose hope is in the Lord their God, who made heaven and earth, the sea, and all that is in them; who keeps faith for ever.* — Psalm 146:5-6

> *The Lord will reign for ever, your God, O Zion, for all generations. Praise the Lord!* — Psalm 146:10

Amen.

Proper 28
Pentecost 26
Ordinary Time 33
1 Samuel 1:4-20

Do Not Forget Your Servant

How to have law and order without tyranny? That is the question. Israel began as a rather loosely connected tribal confederacy. The Israelite tribes were led by charismatic leaders, or judges, under the divine direction of Yahweh. They were supposed to be knit together in one harmonious unit. They would avoid the tyranny, which was the result of being governed by a king. Instead, they would have Yahweh alone as their king. It sounded good, and certainly the book of the Judges reflects moments of such peaceful unity, but reality was often quite different.

Israel was a very marginal community, economically weak, living under constant threat from the Philistines and getting mired in all sorts of tribal violence, brutality, and moral chaos. The situation is summed up at the end of the book of Judges: "In those days there was no king in Israel; all the people did what was right in their own eyes" (21:25).

We start where we have been before, with human inadequacy, with desperate need, moral failure, or, as it is often symbolized, with barrenness. Last week it was Naomi and Ruth. But the motif is common in the scriptures: We can remember Sarah, who had to wait for Isaac; Rachel, who had to wait for Joseph; Elizabeth waiting for John the Baptist. Facing infertility puts us in a hard place — to relinquish control and look to God. We are asked to believe that, in the midst of barren hopelessness, we can still know fruitful waiting and God's ultimate gift.

The issue is presented today through the story of the birth of Samuel. There is the Israelite Elkanah, with his two wives, Hannah and Peninnah. Elkanah loved Hannah, but because she did not conceive, Elkanah had taken a second wife, Peninnah, who bore many sons and daughters.

Not only was Peninnah prolific, it says she was also irritating, always provoking poor Hannah over the issue of progeny. Hannah wept and would not eat, so Elkanah, as a solicitous husband, tries to comfort her. It is hard to say if he is endearing or just self-important: "Why do you weep? ... Am I not more to you than ten sons?" (1 Samuel 1:8).

It was their custom to go regularly to the temple at Shiloh, which was the sacred place for the tribal confederacy. They would offer sacrifice there, then share the leftovers from the sacrifice, as was customary. Hannah was too distressed to eat, but wept bitterly and prayed to the Lord, making a vow: "O Lord of hosts, if only you will look on the misery of your servant, and remember me, and not forget your servant, but will give to your servant a male child, then I will set him before you as a nazirite until the day of his death. He shall drink neither wine nor intoxicants, and no razor shall touch his head" (1:11). This is a rather detailed way of saying he will be a dedicated priest to the Lord!

Hannah goes on weeping and praying silently. Eli the priest is sitting there, watching her. Eli is old, and his faculties aren't that good. He sees Hanna's lips moving, but hears nothing, so he misinterprets what he sees. He scolds Hannah: "How long will you make a drunken spectacle of yourself? Put away your wine!" Hannah respectfully corrects him. "I am not a good for nothing [daughter of Belial], like you think. I am a woman deeply troubled and I have been pouring out my soul before the Lord." Recognizing that she is a faithful woman, Eli blesses her saying, "Go in peace; the God of Israel grant the petition you have made to him" (1:17).

Since this affirmation comes from the high priest in the story, Hannah and the story assumes that it is a done deal. Like Mary, Hannah does not doubt "that there would be a fulfillment of what was spoken to her by the Lord" (Luke 1:45).

The family goes home and Hannah conceives and bears a son. She names him Samuel, for she said, "I have asked him of the

Lord." This is the popular etymology in the text, tying it in with the story. Samuel is "he who is asked," *shaul. El* is God. So, one could say, he is "Shauled of God." With this play on words, there is the suggestion that this child, Samuel, will lead to the first king, Saul, who will, indeed be anointed by Samuel. So we are at that complicated point where, although the tradition had dismissed the idea of a king, now Israel is moving toward one.

We are given the birth of Samuel, which proves to be the start of a sequence of great leaders in Israel: Samuel, then Saul, then David, then Solomon. These are kings with great ambition: to liberate and gather the tribes, to protect and defend them, and to make legitimate the existence of Israel. The climax of all of this was, of course, the eschatological hope for a new David, the great king who would come to make all things right. Here, of course, is where the church saw in the coming of Jesus the birth of a great king, a descendant of David, who would set us free.

In summary, then, the story begins in barrenness — a closed door, no hint of a future, no hope at all. But God is in charge and is never doubted in the narrative. Hannah prays in trust, "Remember me. Do not forget your servant." Yahweh is trustworthy and remembers! Hannah is faithful and gives thanks, offering her son to the Lord. Israel's life is made anew through the power and fidelity of God, which is evoked by lowly Hannah. The life and future of the whole community is renewed and Israel will have its mighty David.

However, Israel will be inordinately impressed with the power and pomp of the Davidic kingdom. Saul, David, and Solomon would come to have failings and sins probably equal to their gifts and virtues, with the result that many in Israel, especially the prophets, would question the value of the empire. The prophet Micah would preview Jesus' judgment by saying, "Zion shall be plowed as a field; Jerusalem shall become a heap of ruins, and the mountain of the house a wooded height" (Micah 3:12).

It is in the gospel for today (Mark 13:1-8) that Jesus also gets to denounce the empire. According to Mark, this is the only time the disciples make the trip to the big city of Jerusalem. When they see the second temple, which King Herod had constructed as quite a showpiece, they gawk like some Galilean hayseeds: "Look, Teacher, what large stones and what large buildings!" (v. 1).

Jesus dampens their excitement: "Do you see these great buildings? Not one stone will be left here upon another; all will be thrown down" (v. 2). It is true not only of temples, but also of palaces; of priests and princes; of heroes and stars — all will be thrown down. In the midst of such impermanence, we seek stability; in the midst of chaos, we seek order; in the mist of insecurity, we seek certitude.

The disciples sought such certitude. They were impressed with the empire, at least with its manifestation in great stones and great buildings. Jesus remarks on the impermanence of it all. The gospel lesson is part of what we call Mark's little apocalypse. It talks of judgment, but unlike the popular abuse of this language, it is cautious in its vision. It says, do not be alarmed. The end is still to come. This is only the beginning of the birth pangs. It is about God's ultimate judgment over all human pretence.

Empire, with all its pretence and brutality, lacks permanence. Nation will rise against nation, and kingdom against kingdom. All will be thrown down in the end. In the midst of this human failure, the gospel calls us to trust in a God who is faithful to God's promises.

Our second lesson today, Hebrews 10:11-25, locates the fulfillment of that promise in the Christ. It says that, having sacrificed himself for us, Christ has sat down at the right hand of God, and since then, is waiting until his enemies will be made a footstool for his feet. This is a different sort of empire we await. It is the power of the lamb, the one who is trustworthy.

So, like Hannah, we present ourselves before the Lord. In the words of the psalm for today we pray:

> *Protect me, O God, for in you I take refuge. I say to the Lord, "You are my Lord; I have no good apart from you." ... The Lord is my chosen portion and my cup; you hold my lot ... I bless the Lord who gives me counsel; in the night also my heart instructs me. I keep the*

> *Lord always before me; because he is at my right hand, I shall not be moved. Therefore my heart is glad, and my soul rejoices; my body also rests secure. For you do not give me up to Sheol, or let your faithful one see the Pit. You show me the path of life. In your presence there is fullness of joy; in your right hand are pleasures for evermore.* — Psalm 16:2, 5, 7-11

Amen.

Christ The King
Proper 29
2 Samuel 23:1-7

Are You A King?

Are you the king of the Jews? We are familiar with that question, which is asked of Jesus in the passion story. Everyone in those days knew what a king was! We are not talking here about best sport, or Miss Congeniality — we are talking kings! When Alexander the Great was the greatest king of the then-known world, he decided to conquer all of Asia Minor. Darius, the King of Persia, the only other ruler that could claim super-power status, sued for peace, saying to Alexander: "Let's you and me just divide up Asia together." To which Alexander replied, "Just as the earth can stand only one sun, so the world can have only one ruler!" Alexander promptly crushed Darius.

That is a king! As we learned last week, Israel had come to know kingship through the ministry of Samuel, who was called to anoint Saul as king, who was then succeeded by King David and his great dynasty. The lesson we have this morning is a glorification of that great Davidic dynasty. It comes at the end of the two books of Samuel, telling the story of David's kingship. It forms a bookend with the song of Hannah in 1 Samuel 2:1-10, which comes at the beginning of the story. It is lyrical and celebratory. We read, "The Lord! His adversaries shall be shattered; the Most High will thunder in heaven. The Lord will judge the ends of the earth; he will give strength to his king" (v. 10).

The king that Israel rejoiced in was David and our lesson purports to be his last words. There is no particular modesty in the description of the author: "The oracle of David, son of Jesse, the oracle of the man whom God exalted, the anointed of the God of Jacob, the favorite of the Strong One of Israel!" (v. 1).

What do we understand about kingship through this oracle? David says, in typical poetic repetition, "The spirit of the Lord speaks through me; his word is upon my tongue. The God of Israel has spoken, the Rock of Israel has said to me" (vv. 2-3). God inspired David, so his rule is not to be seen as a tenuous, historical construction, nor as a historical accident, nor as a calculated personal power grab. It is God's intent, an appointment from God through the Spirit.

Not only has David received God's call, but also his permanent commitment, his covenant. "For he has made with me an everlasting covenant, ordered in all things and secure" (v. 5). The eternal covenant (*berith 'olam*) with David is an important theological concept in the Old Testament. It was said of David, "He shall build a house for my name, and I will establish the throne of his kingdom forever" (2 Samuel 7:13). Then it says although David may have to be disciplined at times, "I will not take my steadfast love from him. Your house and your kingdom shall be made sure forever before me; your throne shall be established forever" (2 Samuel 7:15-16).

If David has God on his side, we can assume that the enemies of the king do not have a chance. They are portrayed as a pile of extremely sharp and ugly thorns, so harsh and evil that you need to push them into the furnace with implements. "But the godless are all like thorns that are thrown away; for they cannot be picked up with the hand; to touch them one uses an iron bar or the shaft of a spear. And they are entirely consumed in fire on the spot" (23:6-7).

The king can count not only on Yahweh's defense, but on Yahweh's blessing. David asks, "Will he not cause to prosper all my help and my desire?" (v. 5c). What might it look like for the king to prosper? David paints a beautiful picture of what such a blessed king could be compared to. He "is like the light of morning, like the sun rising on a cloudless morning, gleaming from the rain on the grassy land" (v. 4). It is a summery portrait, all brightness and light.

What is it about the reign of the king that such poetic language should be used? Who is like the light of the morning? Here comes the core of the argument! "One who rules over people *justly*, ruling in the fear of God" (v. 3b). This is the kind of rule that Israel hoped for and the type of kingship that Israel idealized. One who rules in the fear of God, driven by the values of God, concerned for the widow and orphan, the marginalized and oppressed. One who rules over people justly, which is to say, one who is concerned with the public's well-being, not just with the power and privilege of a few. One who is concerned with a fair distribution of goods, access, and power.

So, like two bookends, we have, at the beginning and end of the books of Samuel, an idealized picture of kingship under David. In between, however, are the actual stories of David and his rule. There we have the hard, ambiguous reality. We have stories of personal moral failure, like David and Bathsheba. We also have stories that are typical of an empire and its royal aggrandizement: stories of ambition, exploitation, self-indulgence, intrigue, vengeance.

So in the exercise of power, David lived not only with the gift of the Spirit and the covenant, but also under the law and the judgment of Yahweh. When David calls down judgment on godless thorns, as fuel for the fire (vv. 6-7), then David calls down judgment on himself. So we have stories of judgment and grace, of blessing and curse, of despair and hope. Whenever Yahweh would get to the point of disowning David, as it were, or divorcing himself from the kingdom, Yahweh always pulls back, remembers the covenant, forgives, and restores.

But the historical realities were harsh and the hope for the Davidic rule became more distant, more poetic, but no less hopeful. The intensity increased, even while the likelihood became dimmer. The promise remained along with this high, royal theology. The early church took this Davidic portrait and used it for its Christological affirmations

> *Lift up your heads, O gates! and be lifted up, O ancient doors! that the King of glory may come in. Who is the*

> *King of glory? The Lord, strong and mighty, the Lord, mighty in battle. Lift up your heads, O gates! and be lifted up, O ancient doors! that the King of glory may come in. Who is this King of glory? The Lord of hosts, he is the King of glory.* — Psalm 24:7-10

Jesus is the one raised to power, whose rule is just, and who bears God's abiding commitment.

How was the church to deal with the ambiguity built into kingship? In the gospel for today, John 18:33-37, Pilate asks Jesus, "Are you the king of the Jews?" Jesus answers, "My kingdom is not from this world, my kingdom is not from here." The fact that the rule of Jesus differs from Pilate's is evident from the gospel's visual presentation. Jesus is a king with a crown, but it is a crown of thorns! Jesus goes on to say: "For this I was born, and for this I came into the world, to testify to the truth." It was that truth, God's love for the whole world, God's unceasing commitment to the covenant, that neither church nor state could accept. Pilate's answer was, "What is truth?"

In the face of Pilate's cynical doubting, the church has confessed that death could not hold the crucified king. He is now our risen Lord. The second lesson, at the beginning of the Apocalypse, grants the faithful a blessing from Christ, the king.

> *Grace to you and peace from him who is and who was and who is to come, and from the seven spirits who are before his throne, and from Jesus Christ, the faithful witness, the firstborn of the dead, and the ruler of the kings of the earth. To him who loves us and freed us from our sins by his blood, and made us to be a kingdom, priests serving his God and Father, to him be glory and dominion forever and ever. Amen.*
>
> — Revelation 1:4b-6

So we are back to the language of kingdom, but in a chastened and purified mode.

In this world, we still must deal with ambiguity and live in hope. Another Christological image the church utilized was the coming of the Son of Man in glory, an image from Daniel 7:13-14. "I saw one like a son of man coming, on the clouds of heaven. When he reached the Ancient One and was presented before him, he received dominion, glory, and kingship, nations and peoples of every language serve him." It is against the background of this text that the Apocalypse says, "Look! He is coming with the clouds; and every eye will see him!" The tense is future, a promise to be trusted; but for now we wait.

Who is the king? What is truth? We must answer those questions in trust and in hope. We know we have been baptized into the body of this risen Christ. Baptism is the tomb in which we die with Christ, but also the womb from which we are reborn in the Spirit. We now live by the promise of baptism: We have been sealed by the Spirit and marked with the cross of Christ forever. If we have been marked with the cross, we know we will finally wear the crown in glory.

For now, we seek to live out the covenant God made with us in baptism, proclaiming the gospel of Christ in word and deed, following the example of our Lord Jesus Christ by compassionate living and working for the goals of peace and justice. We do all this, trusting in our Lord God who says to us this morning, "I am the Alpha and the Omega, says the Lord God, who is and who was and who is to come, the Almighty" (Revelation 1:8). Amen.

Thanksgiving Day
Joel 2:21-27

When Grace Dances

The church has been given some fine texts for Thanksgiving but, like all texts, they require a context. So, for example, in the gospel for today (Matthew 6:25-33), Jesus cautions against worry. "Therefore I tell you, do not worry about your life, what you will eat or what you will drink, or about your body, what you will wear." This is not the same as wondering, *Shall I have the lobster or the beef Wellington?* or worrying, *Which of these outfits goes best with my new shoes?* Clearly, this text does not assume the extreme affluence we enjoy today. How do we, affluent Americans, hear these texts that come to us from a very different context.

Let us start with the first lesson, which comes from the book of Joel. We are most familiar with it because it is read every Ash Wednesday as a call to repentance. Joel describes a terrible devastation caused by a swarm of locusts. Before them, the land is like the Garden of Eden, but after them a desolate wilderness. Nothing escapes them (1:3). Joel interprets the locusts as God's judgment on a wicked and unfaithful people, so he calls them to repentance. Wake up, wail, lament. "Sanctify a fast, call a solemn assembly. Gather the elders and all the inhabitants of the land to the house of the Lord your God; and cry out to the Lord" (Joel 1:14). "Between the vestibule and the altar let the priests, the ministers of the Lord, weep. Let them say, 'Spare your people, O Lord, and do not make your heritage a mockery, a byword among the nations. Why should it be said among the peoples, "Where is their God?" ' " (Joel 2:17).

It is only at this point, after Israel had been duly repentant, in sackcloth and ashes, that the prophet describes Yahweh's relenting, a change of heart. In the verses just before our text, the shift is described. "Then the Lord became jealous for his land, and had pity on his people" (Joel 2:18).

In response to his people the Lord said: "I am sending you grain, wine, and oil, and you will be satisfied; and I will no more make you a mockery among the nations" (Joel 2:19). "Do not fear, O soil; be glad and rejoice, for the Lord has done *great things*" (v. 21 emphasis mine). This is a play on the pride of the enemy, who, in their arrogance, thought they had done *great things*. But it is the Lord who does great things.

Then three aspects of creation are called upon to rejoice (2:21-23). First the land or the soil — be glad and rejoice! Then the animals of the field, they are to live in a richly bearing land — green pastures, fruit trees and vines giving their full yield. Then, finally, the people — O children of Zion, be glad and rejoice, for he gives you the early and late rains, so the harvest will be plentiful.

All of this is to balance God's earlier judgment. The Lord says, "I will repay you for the years that the swarming locust has eaten, the hopper, the destroyer, and the cutter, my great army, which I sent against you" (2:25). When the situation has changed, we note first that a response is expected. "You shall eat in plenty and be satisfied, and praise the name of the Lord your God" (v. 26). They are reminded who they are to praise and why. "I, the Lord, am your God and there is no other" (v. 27). This is a common recognition formula — the God who is in their midst is the true God. In addition, twice the promise is repeated, "And my people shall never again be put to shame" (vv. 26-27).

So God's heart is quickened and God's promise renewed because the people have come to confess their sin, acknowledge their dependency, and live only for the Lord.

In the gospel (Matthew 6:25-33), the context is not a broken people who are being restored by the Lord, as in Joel. Instead, the context seems to be the anxiety that is brought on by the radicality of the gospel. We know that there was a significant core of early Christians who understood the core of the gospel to be a call to radical discipleship, to forsake all and follow Jesus. This is certainly reflected in the calls of the twelve — they left their nets to follow — and also in the challenge of Jesus: Whoever has left mother, father, brothers, sisters, and fields for my name's sake will receive a hundredfold.

So there developed in the church an itinerant set of wandering preachers who needed to be supported in their journeying by the more settled church. But Matthew saw this tradition, though rooted in those itinerant radicals, as having a more general application. For the settled community also, or perhaps *especially* for the settled community, the dangers of mammon and the destructive values of the world need to be warned against. "For it is the Gentiles who strive after these things," Jesus says. "And, indeed, your heavenly Father knows you need all these things" (6:32). This reflects the faith of the praying community, whose heavenly Father knows what they need even before they ask. Such faith, then, calls us, not to some passive waiting, but to an active practice of God's righteousness. "But strive first for the kingdom of God and his righteousness, and all these things will be given to you as well" (v. 33).

So the context is that of a community beginning to lose some of the radical edge of its discipleship and being called back to the trust and values of their master. Is not life more than food and the body more than clothing?

The same image of a church in danger of settling in can be found in the second lesson (1 Timothy 2:1-7), where a young church decides to promote stability and peace as it makes its way in the midst of the Roman empire. Gone is the violent conflict between world and church in the book of Revelation, between loyalty to the empire or loyalty to Christ. Gone is the tension that Paul saw between this world and God's world, and the many misunderstandings, beatings, and imprisonments that he suffered. What we have is the hope that the empire might see the loyalty of the church and be hospitable to it: "First of all, then, I urge that supplications, prayers, intercessions, and thanksgivings be made for everyone, for kings and all who are in high positions, so that we may lead a quiet and peaceable life in all godliness and dignity" (1 Timothy 2:1-2).

We said we have wonderful texts, which talk in hopeful and grateful ways about God's blessings and hope for harmony with all. At the same time, the context of these texts will not let us be comfortable with our abundance. Certainly the church has struggled through the years with the radical challenge of the gospel, reflected in the early disciples forsaking all, or the author of the Apocalypse naming Rome as the anti-Christ. We have preferred, with 1 Timothy, to make our peace with empire and seek to live the life of the virtuous good citizen.

The empire has not been hospitable to God or to the world. We have to admit that we benefit from an affluence that is not fairly distributed; or we consume vast resources in a way that is not sustainable. Thus, we find ourselves back with Joel before God's judgment. Only, this time, we ourselves are the hopper, the destroyer, and the cutter, a great army devouring everything in its path. The vine withers, the fig tree droops, the seed shrivels, the grain fails, the animals groan. How can the land be glad and rejoice? How can the animals of the field not be afraid? How can the children of Zion rejoice in the normalcy of the early and late rains?

So how do we interpret Joel when we are both the threatened ones and the enemy at the same time? We, the powerful and the privileged, with our ruthless exploitation of the earth, are responsible for the mortal danger that the cosmos finds itself in. At the same time, we will be the victims, or certainly our progeny. The call of Ash Wednesday is appropriate every day. Blow the trumpet, declare a fast, call an assembly. Repent, turn to the Lord, strive for God's rule and God's righteousness.

There is judgment in these texts. Nowhere do the people of God get to avoid the hard turn we must make from empire to God's kingdom, from self-righteousness to servanthood. We need to hear these hard challenges: "Is not life more than food and the body more than clothing?" (Matthew 6:25). There is never despair. Instead, there is trust: "indeed, your heavenly father knows you need these things" (Matthew 6:32).

Finally, after the people relinquish their control and return to the Lord, there is promise: "You shall eat in plenty and be satisfied, and praise the name of the Lord your God, who has dealt wondrously with you. And my people shall never again be put to shame" (Joel 2:27).

The last thing in the world I want is to scold on Thanksgiving, but I also want to be faithful. God would not want us to disdain these blessings. W. H. Auden has wrote: "... about catastrophe or how to behave in one what do I know, except what everyone knows — if there when Grace dances, I should dance."[1] At the same time, we need to heed the collect for Thanksgiving: "Almighty God our Father, your generous goodness comes to us new every day. By the work of your Spirit, lead us to acknowledge your goodness, give thanks for your benefits, and serve you in willing obedience."[2] Amen.

---

1. W. H. Auden, "Whitsunday in Kirchstetten" in *Collected Poems*, ed. Edward Mendelsohn (New York: Vintage Books, 1976), p. 745.

2. *Lutheran Book of Worship* (Minneapolis: Augsburg Publishing House, 1978), p. 40.

Lectionary Preaching After Pentecost

The following index will aid the user of this book in matching the correct Sunday with the appropriate text during Pentecost. All texts in this book are from the series for the first readings, Revised Common Lectionary. (Note that the ELCA division of Lutheranism is now following the Revised Common Lectionary.) The Lutheran designations indicate days comparable to Sundays on which Revised Common Lectionary Propers or Ordinary Time designations are used.

(Fixed dates do not pertain to Lutheran Lectionary)

Fixed Date Lectionaries *Revised Common (including ELCA) and Roman Catholic*	**Lutheran Lectionary** *Lutheran*
The Day Of Pentecost	The Day Of Pentecost
The Holy Trinity	The Holy Trinity
May 29-June 4 — Proper 4, Ordinary Time 9	Pentecost 2
June 5-11 — Proper 5, Ordinary Time 10	Pentecost 3
June 12-18 — Proper 6, Ordinary Time 11	Pentecost 4
June 19-25 — Proper 7, Ordinary Time 12	Pentecost 5
June 26-July 2 — Proper 8, Ordinary Time 13	Pentecost 6
July 3-9 — Proper 9, Ordinary Time 14	Pentecost 7
July 10-16 — Proper 10, Ordinary Time 15	Pentecost 8
July 17-23 — Proper 11, Ordinary Time 16	Pentecost 9
July 24-30 — Proper 12, Ordinary Time 17	Pentecost 10
July 31-Aug. 6 — Proper 13, Ordinary Time 18	Pentecost 11
Aug. 7-13 — Proper 14, Ordinary Time 19	Pentecost 12
Aug. 14-20 — Proper 15, Ordinary Time 20	Pentecost 13
Aug. 21-27 — Proper 16, Ordinary Time 21	Pentecost 14
Aug. 28-Sept. 3 — Proper 17, Ordinary Time 22	Pentecost 15
Sept. 4-10 — Proper 18, Ordinary Time 23	Pentecost 16
Sept. 11-17 — Proper 19, Ordinary Time 24	Pentecost 17
Sept. 18-24 — Proper 20, Ordinary Time 25	Pentecost 18

Sept. 25-Oct. 1 — Proper 21, Ordinary Time 26	Pentecost 19
Oct. 2-8 — Proper 22, Ordinary Time 27	Pentecost 20
Oct. 9-15 — Proper 23, Ordinary Time 28	Pentecost 21
Oct. 16-22 — Proper 24, Ordinary Time 29	Pentecost 22
Oct. 23-29 — Proper 25, Ordinary Time 30	Pentecost 23
Oct. 30-Nov. 5 — Proper 26, Ordinary Time 31	Pentecost 24
Nov. 6-12 — Proper 27, Ordinary Time 32	Pentecost 25
Nov. 13-19 — Proper 28, Ordinary Time 33	Pentecost 26
	Pentecost 27
Nov. 20-26 — Christ The King	Christ The King

Reformation Day (or last Sunday in October) is October 31 (Revised Common, Lutheran)

All Saints (or first Sunday in November) is November 1 (Revised Common, Lutheran, Roman Catholic)

US/Canadian Lectionary Comparison

The following index shows the correlation between the Sundays and special days of the church year as they are titled or labeled in the Revised Common Lectionary published by the Consultation On Common Texts and used in the United States (the reference used for this book) and the Sundays and special days of the church year as they are titled or labeled in the Revised Common Lectionary used in Canada.

Revised Common Lectionary	**Canadian Revised Common Lectionary**
Advent 1	Advent 1
Advent 2	Advent 2
Advent 3	Advent 3
Advent 4	Advent 4
Christmas Eve	Christmas Eve
The Nativity Of Our Lord/ Christmas Day	The Nativity Of Our Lord
Christmas 1	Christmas 1
January 1/New Year's Day	January 1/The Name Of Jesus
Christmas 2	Christmas 2
The Epiphany Of Our Lord	The Epiphany Of Our Lord
The Baptism Of Our Lord/ Epiphany 1	The Baptism Of Our Lord/ Proper 1
Epiphany 2/Ordinary Time 2	Epiphany 2/Proper 2
Epiphany 3/Ordinary Time 3	Epiphany 3/Proper 3
Epiphany 4/Ordinary Time 4	Epiphany 4/Proper 4
Epiphany 5/Ordinary Time 5	Epiphany 5/Proper 5
Epiphany 6/Ordinary Time 6	Epiphany 6/Proper 6
Epiphany 7/Ordinary Time 7	Epiphany 7/Proper 7
Epiphany 8/Ordinary Time 8	Epiphany 8/Proper 8
The Transfiguration Of Our Lord/ Last Sunday After Epiphany	The Transfiguration Of Our Lord/ Last Sunday After Epiphany
Ash Wednesday	Ash Wednesday
Lent 1	Lent 1
Lent 2	Lent 2
Lent 3	Lent 3
Lent 4	Lent 4
Lent 5	Lent 5
Passion/Palm Sunday	Passion/Palm Sunday
Maundy Thursday	Holy/Maundy Thursday
Good Friday	Good Friday

Easter Day	The Resurrection Of Our Lord
Easter 2	Easter 2
Easter 3	Easter 3
Easter 4	Easter 4
Easter 5	Easter 5
Easter 6	Easter 6
The Ascension Of Our Lord	The Ascension Of Our Lord
Easter 7	Easter 7
The Day Of Pentecost	The Day Of Pentecost
The Holy Trinity	The Holy Trinity
Proper 4/Pentecost 2/O T 9*	Proper 9
Proper 5/Pent 3/O T 10	Proper 10
Proper 6/Pent 4/O T 11	Proper 11
Proper 7/Pent 5/O T 12	Proper 12
Proper 8/Pent 6/O T 13	Proper 13
Proper 9/Pent 7/O T 14	Proper 14
Proper 10/Pent 8/O T 15	Proper 15
Proper 11/Pent 9/O T 16	Proper 16
Proper 12/Pent 10/O T 17	Proper 17
Proper 13/Pent 11/O T 18	Proper 18
Proper 14/Pent 12/O T 19	Proper 19
Proper 15/Pent 13/O T 20	Proper 20
Proper 16/Pent 14/O T 21	Proper 21
Proper 17/Pent 15/O T 22	Proper 22
Proper 18/Pent 16/O T 23	Proper 23
Proper 19/Pent 17/O T 24	Proper 24
Proper 20/Pent 18/O T 25	Proper 25
Proper 21/Pent 19/O T 26	Proper 26
Proper 22/Pent 20/O T 27	Proper 27
Proper 23/Pent 21/O T 28	Proper 28
Proper 24/Pent 22/O T 29	Proper 29
Proper 25/Pent 23/O T 30	Proper 30
Proper 26/Pent 24/O T 31	Proper 31
Proper 27/Pent 25/O T 32	Proper 32
Proper 28/Pent 26/O T 33	Proper 33
Christ The King (Proper 29/O T 34)	Proper 34/Christ The King/ Reign Of Christ
Reformation Day (October 31)	Reformation Day (October 31)
All Saints (November 1 or 1st Sunday in November)	All Saints' Day (November 1)
Thanksgiving Day (4th Thursday of November)	Thanksgiving Day (2nd Monday of October)

*O T = Ordinary Time

About The Authors

Richard Gribble, CSC is an associate professor of religious studies at Stonehill College in North Easton, Massachusetts. He is the author of 25 books, including a three-volume series on *The Parables of Jesus* (CSS), as well as more than 200 articles and reviews. A Catholic priest and member of the Congregation of Holy Cross, Father Gribble is a graduate of the United States Naval Academy who served on nuclear submarines prior to entering the priesthood. Gribble holds a Ph.D. from The Catholic University of America, and he has also earned degrees from the University of Southern California and the Jesuit School of Theology at Berkeley.

Ken Lentz presently serves as a transition pastor for congregations in the Evangelical Lutheran Church in America's Grand Canyon Synod. During nearly four decades in ministry, he has been the pastor of churches in Florida, California, Michigan, and Ohio; served for six months as the pastor of a 1,000-year-old parish in Buxtehude, Germany; and taught at Pacific Lutheran Theological Seminary. Lentz holds degrees from Capital University, Trinity Lutheran Seminary, and the University of Heidelberg, Germany, where he earned a Th.D. in church history.

William J. Carl III is the president of Pittsburgh Theological Seminary. Prior to his current position, Carl served for 22 years as the senior pastor of the 1,700-member First Presbyterian Church in Dallas, Texas. He has also taught at Union Theological Seminary in Virginia, and lectured at dozens of divinity schools and conferences both in the US and abroad. Carl is the author of six books, including *The Lord's Prayer for Today* (Westminster John Knox). He is a graduate of the University of Tulsa, Louisville Presbyterian Theological Seminary, and the University of Pittsburgh (Ph.D.).

Donna E. Schaper has had a varied career as a writer, pastor, denominational executive, college chaplain, and community organizer. She is currently the senior minister of historic Judson Memorial Church in New York City. Schaper is the author of more than two dozen books, including *Living Well While Doing Good* (Seabury), *Mature Grief: When a Parent Dies* (Cowley), and *The Art of Spiritual Rock Gardening* (Paulist Press), and her articles and meditations frequently appear in a variety of national publications. She is a graduate of Gettysburg College, Gettysburg Seminary, and the University of Chicago. To learn more, visit her website at www.donnaschaper.org.

Robert A. Hausman is the pastor of Lutheran Church of the Resurrection (ELCA) in St. Paul, Minnesota. In addition to parish ministry, Hausman has served as a campus pastor, a college and seminary professor, a book editor, and a public relations specialist. He holds a Ph.D. from the University of Chicago. Hausman is the author of *The Days Are Surely Coming!* (CSS).

www.ingramcontent.com/pod-product-compliance
Lightning Source LLC
LaVergne TN
LVHW020520100826
845148LV00010B/1293

* 9 7 8 0 7 8 8 0 2 5 4 2 6 *